THE MAN FARTHEST DOWN

BLACK CLASSICS OF SOCIAL SCIENCE

Wilbur H. Watson, series editor

This series of classics focuses on major contributions by Black social scientists to understanding human behavior, history, and social change. A basic goal of the series is the reprinting of important theoretical and empirical works now out of print, and which address issues relevant to contemporary social science and policy. In addition to titles originally written as slave protest pamphlets but never widely circulated, this series offers works by twentieth-century figures who have influenced social scientific thought. In the selection of both titles and writers of introductory essays, we attempt to draw attention to points of convergence and divergence among Black American, African, and West-Indian social scientists, ranging from general to specific issues.

THE MAN FARTHEST DOWN

A Record of Observation and Study in Europe

BOOKER T. WASHINGTON

With the collaboration of
ROBERT E. PARK

With a New Introduction by
St. Clair Drake

Routledge
Taylor & Francis Group
LONDON AND NEW YORK

First published 1984 by Transaction Publishers

Published 2017 by Routledge
2 Park Square, Milton Park, Abingdon, Oxon OX14 4RN
711 Third Avenue, New York, NY 10017, USA

Routledge is an imprint of the Taylor & Francis Group, an informa business

Library of Congress Catalog Number: 82-19593

Library of Congress Cataloging in Publication Data

Washington, Booker T., 1856-1915.
The man farthest down.

Reprint. Originally published: Garden City, N.Y.: Doubleday, Page, 1912.
1. Labor and laboring classes—Europe. 2. Poor-Europe. I. Park, Robert Ezra, 1864-1944. II. Title.
HD8376.W37 1983 305.5′69′094 82-19593
ISBN 0-87855-933-7 (pbk.)

ISBN 13: 978-0-87855-933-6 (pbk)

Introduction To the Transaction Edition

St. Clair Drake

I

The editors of Transaction are to be commended for making available this important "record of observation and study in Europe" written during 1910 and 1911 by Booker T. Washington, as the title page informs us, "with the collaboration of Robert E. Park." At that time the Tuskegee educator was one of the two best-known Afro-Americans in the world, the other being the pugilist Jack Johnson. His collaborator, a practicing journalist with a Ph.D. in philosophy from Heidelberg, had not yet become a college professor and America's most influential sociologist. His career at the University of Chicago would begin two years after *The Man Farthest Down* appeared. For five years before its publication Robert Ezra Park had been serving as amanuensis and assistant in the writing of books and articles to Booker T. Washington. The "Sage of Tuskegee" was a gifted orator and his Atlanta Compromise Speech of 1895 has the kind of simplicity and sincerity that gives it a place in American history alongside the Gettysburg Address. But for articles that required extensive research or professional polish, he like other very busy public men, used the services of aides whose skills were literary rather than oratorical. Park was such a person, and he became a companion and adviser as well. Others who sustained this special relation were Afro-Americans—among them Washington's secretary, Emmett J. Scott; the distinguished journalist, T. Thomas Fortune; and the sociologist who established the Tuskegee research bureau, Monroe Work.

When Washington decided that he wanted to go overseas in 1910 to observe what conversations with Park and his own observation of immigrants to the United States, as well as his reading, had led him to believe was "the man farthest down"—down farther than a Mississippi sharecropper—Park went to England and Europe to prepare the way. Later, he traveled with Washington for six weeks in the British Isles, France, Italy, Poland, Denmark, and the Austro-Hungarian Empire. As a "race leader," Booker T. Washington viewed the floods of European immigrants as a threat to the economic future of Black Americans who were less than fifty years out of slavery. He wanted to know more about what induced Europeans to immigrate to the United States in the past and the conditions that might lead to further immigration in the future. He expected to use the same data about immigrants' homelands to impress descendants of Southern slaves with how much better off they were than farmers, miners, and urban slum dwellers in Europe and Great Britain.

Park's account of the origin of the project and of Washington's concept of the "the man farthest down" takes the only tenable position in any argument about comparative misery—an equivocal one. The excerpt below is from a lengthy statement by Park about the trip that Winifred Raushenbush presents in her biography of the sociologist:

> One of the most interesting things I did during my connection with Tuskegee was to take a trip across Europe with Booker Washington. He had a plan to take a look at the laborers in Europe. He had an impression that, in spite of all the disadvantages that the Negro laborer lived under in America, his condition was not much worse than that of the laborer in Europe. *In one way he was right about that; in another he was wrong.* In Europe the status of any class is pretty well

> defined in custom and in law, and he is protected in that status. The Negro's position as defined in law nowhere corresponds to his actual status as defined in custom, and custom is everywhere different.
>
> I was eager to show Dr. Washington the condition of the European peasant as I had come to know it through my studies. . . . The result was that, in the late summer of 1910, we sailed for Europe. . . . It was, as I look back upon it, a most remarkable journey[1] (italics added).

It *was* a remarkable journey and the book conveys the spirit of some of the intellectual excitement the two men experienced. Park's retrospective comment did not mention, however, the almost boyish enthusiasm Washington displayed as he searched for "the man farthest down," nor his views on why some Europeans were formidable competitors vis à vis Afro-Americans after they emigrated to the United States. Washington, speaking for the team, had to admit: "We never found the man farthest down." Even when he thought they might have found a case, Washington considered the people back home in the South to be better off: "The Negro is not the man farthest down. The condition of the coloured farmer in the most backward parts of the Southern States in America, even where he has the least education and the least encouragement, is incomparably better than the condition and opportunities of the agricultural population in Sicily."[2] He was fascinated with the markets, the system of land tenure, superstitious beliefs, the process of making wine, the details of how the lottery was played, the horrors of work in the sulphur mines, and the plight of working children in the land from whence so many Italian migrants came to America. Some of the most interesting pages of description in the book are in the five chapters devoted to Sicily, and they also reveal significant facets of Washington's personality.

The trip offered an opportunity for Park and Washington to take each other's measure in a milieu not saturated with color prejudice and full of legal and customary barriers to free and easy association. The 46-year-old son of a moderately well-to-do Midwestern White businessman and the 54-year-old Southern educator whose mother was a Black slave and whose White father never recognized his existence, had both overcome whatever mild prejudices of class and race had constituted an initial barrier between them. Nevertheless, Raushenbush reports a tale told by Park that suggests some insecurities surrounding differences in color and status that five years of working together had not completely dissipated. Once while they were in Eastern Europe there was a shortage of accommodations and Park and Washington had to share a room. On getting up the next morning Washington remarked that he had not liked sleeping with "a great big White man," and Park replied that he had not liked sleeping with "a great big Black man" either.[3] In this case, they were able to create a joking relationship for relaxing tensions, some of which may have been built up and suppressed during the previous years of collaboration that involved a self-made Black man, highly successful, but still dependent upon a more highly trained White man. Washington paid Park a compliment by initiating a discussion of race and status in this bantering fashion. Washington, thereby, made Park a member of his "in" group. Indeed, it looks very much as if Washington was indulging in the practice of "sounding," one form of "ritual insult" Labov has described as characteristic of some contemporary Afro-American communities.[4] It is an old custom. In any event, America's "biggest" "big Black man" and Park, all masks stripped away, confronted each other this one time as equals, far away from the racist context to which they must return. Whether such episodes occurred on other occasions during the trip we do not know.

The two men had met originally because of a common interest in doing something for the welfare of Africans through the Congo Reform Association of which Park was secretary from 1903 to 1905. Washington was a vice-president. Raushenbush quotes Park as saying of that first meeting that the Tuskegee principal had no *real* interest in Africa.[5] This was a misunderstanding of Washington's telling Park that if he would write an article against the Congo atrocities, he would sign it. The truth seems to be that both men had a deep interest in Africa. Washington told Park in 1908, when they were preparing the manuscript for *The Story of the Negro,* that when he was a student at Hampton he had a strong desire "to go out some day to Africa as a missionary," and that although he gave up his "ambition of going to Africa," he never lost sight of trying to do something to aid the continent of his ancestors (more accurately *some* of them, since his father was White).[6] Park always insisted that he had no sentimental interest in Negroes or in any kind of "uplift"; that both the job with the Congo Reform Association and with Tuskegee were just that—jobs, taken at crucial moments when he needed them and providing welcome learning situations too. This hard-boiled stance belies the loyalty and even zeal with which he carried out his tasks in both positions, the encouragement he gave to a number of Black aspiring sociologists after he left Tuskegee, and his decision to work closely with the Urban League after it was founded in 1911, as well as his acceptance of a post at Fisk University after he retired from Chicago. His protégé, Charles S. Johnson, a well-known sociologist who had become president of Fisk and invited Park to take a post at that institution, said of his mentor:

> If anyone ever made the verbal mistake of calling him a "race benefactor" or humanitarian, or friend of the Negro, Dr. Park would be likely to let loose an impatient torrent of an old reporter's private and uncensored vocabulary of disgust. Vigorous, sturdy, commanding in appearance, and often, on the surface, brusque in manner, he detested sentimentality and unctuous professions of sympathy for the Negroes. Yet he was at heart as gentle as a mother.[7] [Incidentally, Park's father was a Civil War veteran who had fought on the Union side.]

Whatever their commitments to the cause of Black people, no matter how sincere and dedicated they were, both men not only worked for a "cause" like their academic and missionary counterparts, but also fulfilled their intellectual and emotional needs and sought to advance their careers by doing so. Unlike others who worked for "racial advancement," they did not line their own pockets above and beyond the needs for sustaining the lifestyle expected of people of their status.

During 1905, Park was toying with the idea of relinquishing his post with the Congo Reform Association and going to South Africa to observe an industrial school for Bantu youth. He wanted to test a hypothesis he had about the development of "primitive peoples in the modern world." He told Washington of his plans, and the educator, who was proud of his school in Alabama, persuaded him to come to Tuskegee for a look before taking off for South Africa. Park came. That first visit to Tuskegee changed Park's life completely. It put him in the mood to accept an invitation from Booker T. Washington to join the staff of the institution and remain affiliated with it as a full-time aide to Washington for seven years.[8] *The Man Farthest Down* documents one especially meaningful episode in the Park-Washington relationship.

II

The trip Park and Washington took to Britain and Europe in 1910 was not the Black educator's first. The Northern philanthropists who supported Tuskegee had sent him and Mrs. Washington on such a journey in 1900 partly for relaxation after a strenuous period of fund raising and partly to expose some influential people in Britain to Frederick Douglass's successor as "the spokesman for the Negroes in America." The Washingtons enjoyed participating briefly in the way of life of their upper-class British hosts and hostesses who lived on country estates. Washington returned with great respect for many aspects of British culture and character. He found much to criticize in France, however, and felt that some of what he considered the character deficiencies there were the same as those attributed to Negroes. It was his judgment in the end that "I do not believe that the average Frenchman is ahead of the average Negro." Washington devoted a chapter to this experience abroad in *Up from Slavery*, and Professor Louis R. Harlan, in *Booker T. Washington: The Making of a Black Leader, 1856-1901*, assesses the importance of the 1900 trip in Washington's development:

> The significance of Washington's travel in the Old World was not so much in his public addresses or the people he met, for he said what he had always said. The journey broadened his outlook somewhat, made him more of a man of the world, and enhanced his image as the leading black spokesman not only in America but abroad. Most important, however, he returned home with his old protean energy, "strong as a young man to run a race." In a variety of activi-

> ties in the next two years he brought his career to a peak.[9]

The trip in the company of Park, made ten years later, came after Washington had reached that peak. His reaction to England and Europe then is that of the mature leader who has been playing an important role in the politics of the national Republican machine while building up what Dr. DuBois criticized as "The Tuskegee Machine."

Soon after Washington returned from his first trip abroad he completed the writing of an autobiography at the insistence of Northern friends and advisers. They wanted it to aid in fund raising. The simple direct narrative turned out to have international human appeal. *Up from Slavery* was off the press within two years after Washington returned from Europe and was soon translated into French and Spanish, to be followed by editions in German, Norwegian, Swedish, Danish, Dutch, Finnish, and Russian. Later translations came in Arabic, Hindi, Malaysian, Chinese, Japanese, and Zulu, as well as a Braille edition in 1903. No one ever questioned the authenticity of the document, although Harlan speaks of a New England journalist, Max B. Thrasher, as the ghostwriter chosen by Washington to help him produce the book. (A similar relationship between Alex Haley and Malcolm X.

has not led anyone to question the authenticity of the *Autobiography*.) In fact Harlan's description of the Thrasher-Washington interaction reveals a much more decisive authorial role than the pejorative term *ghostwriter* suggests: "Sometime in the summer of 1900 Washington began to dictate autobiographical notes to Thrasher, on trains or between trains, as they traveled together. *Washington then wrote a draft of the autobiography from Thrasher's notes and let Thrasher check the manuscript . . . and he kept an unusually tight rein on his ghost writer*" (italics added). On one occasion Thrasher wrote an apologetic letter in answer to a note of reprimand: "I have not left out anything that you wrote except that one brief paragraph of perhaps a dozen lines in the first copy which you told me yourself you had decided to omit."[10] Washington developed a procedure in writing a book that allowed him to keep control of the operation. Thrasher—Washington's confidential secretary—Emmett Scott, and others, sometimes ghosted a magazine article, a statement to the press, the first draft of a speech, or a reply to a letter; but Washington insisted that *Up from Slavery* be his, in style and idiom as well as content.

When Thrasher died in 1903, Washington tried to persuade the outstanding young Afro-American scholar W. E. B. DuBois to come to Tuskegee to do much of Thrasher's work as well as to conduct a research center. In his posthumous *Autobiography*, DuBois recounts the story of two personal conferences with Washington about the matter and the failure of the negotiations. He was suspicious about Washington's intentions despite his promise, as DuBois put it, "not to reduce me to the level of a ghost writer." When a number of Northern philanthropists urged him to move his already successful research center from Atlanta University to Tuskegee, DuBois became convinced that this was a conspiracy to enlist his support for Washington's conservative accommodationist stance with regard to pressure for full civil and political rights. He not only refused the post but also included an article criticizing the political aspect of Washington's leadership in *Souls of Black Folk*, the book of essays he published that same year.[11] In any event, the position demanded a man with a passion for anonymity and this DuBois certainly did not have.

DuBois does not indulge in any "what might have been" reflections on these 1903 negotiations with Booker T. Washington, but does state that his career and Afro-American history, too, might have been very different if an 1893 telegram from Booker T. had reached him earlier than it did. He had just received a Ph.D. from Harvard and needed a job. Washington offered him a position teaching mathematics, but he had already jumped at an offer from Wilberforce University while waiting for a reply to the letter he had written Booker T. Washington.[12] Ten years later, in 1903, when DuBois refused another offer, Washington tendered the position to Robert Ezra Park, a White man. He had recently returned from Germany where he had studied for his doctorate and was serving as a teaching assistant in the philosophy department at Harvard while editing the Sunday edition of a Boston newspaper and performing his duties as secretary of the Congo Reform Association.[13]

In accepting the offer of the post in 1905 that DuBois had refused in 1903, the 39-year-old White man wrote to Emmett Scott, Black secretary to Tuskegee's Black principal: "I distrust my ability to perform any great original task in this world, but I believe that I can do good work as a lieutenant and have no other ambition except that of doing the best that lies in me under the direction of a first class man."[14] There is no reason to believe that this is mock modesty compounded with flattery or ambition disguised as obesquiousness. Park had that sense of insecurity and self-doubt to be expected of a man his age and social class who was still "trying to find himself." In an autobiographical note Park states that he was impressed with Booker T. Washington from the time of the first discussion he had with him. His letter of resignation in 1912 gives a plausible reason for leaving: "After thinking the matter all over I have determined to leave Tuskegee. My reason for doing so is my desire to spend the next few years, while they are growing up, in closer contact with my children."[15] He did not mention his other reason, to seek a new career as a professor at the University of Chicago with sociologist W. I. Thomas. He continued:

> I want to say, now that I am leaving here, that I have never been so happy in my life as I have since I became associated with you in this work. Some of the best friends I have in the world are at Tuskegee. I feel and shall always feel that I belong, in a sort of way, to the Negro race and shall continue to share, through good and evil, all its joys and sorrows. I want to help you in the future as in the past in any way that I can and would gladly remain if I could persuade my family to come South to live. I am very grateful to you for the privilege of knowing you as intimately as I have. I feel that I am a better man for having been here.[16]

It is understandable why Park did not "level" with Washington about the attractions of teaching at Chicago, and attributed it all to his desire to be a better family man. The question remains as to whether the rest of the letter is mere routine politeness. Park's biographer has found some unpublished notes Park wrote, presumably for his own eyes, in which he compares Washington and DuBois. He reveals respect and admiration for both, but does not praise one above the other. He compares Washington to Andrew Carnegie and Benjamin Franklin, noting: "Self-made man. Vigorous common sense." As he sees it "Washington represented the masses of freed men . . . is cooperative despite divergences and differences, not however, minimizing the conflict of interest where it exists."[17] There is very little *affect* in any comments about Washington in the excerpts from Park's papers available to the public.

Raushenbush refers to Park as Washington's secretary but no systematic picture is available in print of what all his duties were. In letters and autobiographical notes Park speaks of extensive traveling throughout the South with Washington, and it can be assumed that they had frequent conversations about a wide range of regional, national, and international affairs. Sociologist W. I. Thomas discovered that some of the magazine articles attributed to Washington had been written by Park, but his duties also involved intensive research and other types of writing. Professor Harlan and his associates have a tendency to use the term *ghostwriting* to describe all of Park's written work at Tuskegee that involved collaboration with Washington. The term has some justification in the case of *The Story of the Negro,* published in 1909, where "grateful mention" is made in the Preface to Park and to Black sociologist Monroe Work. Part 1 of that book integrates a great deal of historical and anthropological data about Africa, and part 2 is a compendium of Afro-American history. Preparing the basic document required a type of training Washington did not have, although the final product includes considerable first-person comment. *The Man Farthest Down* is a very different kind of book.

Park did not ask for more than mention in the preface of his role in the production of *The Story of the Negro* where his input is so evident. The report of the 1910 trip, however, was an entirely different matter from his point of view, and what it meant to him was revealed in a comment he made in retrospect:

> We made this journey in the incredibly short time of six weeks and, strange as it may seem, I learned more that was interesting and profitable there than I ever did in the same period before or since. I learned, perhaps more than Dr. Washington did, for I was well prepared by my previous studies and my four years in Europe, for what we were to see. Out of observations on that journey we made the book called *The Man*

> *Farthest Down.* This title was taken from a phrase that Ray Stannard Baker in his volume *Following the Color Line* had applied to the Negro.[18]

The volume was presented to the public with Booker T. Washington listed on the title page as author and a credit line in much smaller type: "With the collaboration of Robert E. Park." This form of allocating credit seems to have been a compromise between the wish of Park and the will of Washington. Raushenbush has published a portion of a letter from Park to Washington dated April 26, 1911 where, in answering Washington's query as to how they should handle credit for authorship, he said: "It seems to me the best thing to do would be to put my name on the book as a joint author. In case that is done a statement could be made in the preface or in the introduction as to what my part in the book was. . . . In that way it can not be said that you hired an outsider to write the book as I fear they are likely to say otherwise."[19]

Park wanted the preface to emphasize the close working relationship that he and Washington had sustained over a period of five years before embarking on the trip. Washington did not accept the joint authorship suggestion but did devote five pages in the first chapter to a full explanation of the way in which the two men collected the data, discussed it daily as they traveled about, and wrote it up. Washington went so far as to say that "a large part of what I saw and learned about Europe is due directly to the assistance of Doctor Park," and that "it should be remembered that although this book is written throughout in the first person it contains the observations of two different individuals." Washington noted that during their travels, "*as soon as we reached a large city I got hold of a stenographer and dictated as fully as I was able, the story of what we had seen and learned.*" Meanwhile Park would collect books, papers, letters, statistics, and other such documentation. Washington is frank about what happened next: "With these documents Doctor Park then set to work to straighten out and complete the matter that I had dictated, filling in and adding to what I had written. The chapters which follow are the result." This was not ghostwriting but true collaboration. However, since Washington had dictated the backbone of the work in the first person, it would have been inappropriate to speak of the men as coauthors. Unlike *The Story of the Negro,* this is Washington's book, not somebody else's.[20]

A close study of the text will reveal that Washington learned a great deal from Park on this trip, but there was little that Park could learn from him on this occasion as compared with their travels together in the South. Looking back on his seven years at Tuskegee, Park wrote: "Booker Washington gave me an opportunity such as no one else ever had, I am sure, to get acquainted with the actual and intimate life of the Negro in the South."[21] That opportunity opened the door to an academic career at the University of Chicago, the first course he ever taught there being on "The Negro." Washington and Tuskegee provided Park with the content for illustrating the categories of formal sociology that he adapted from those of his teacher, Simmel, and provided the first empirical data for elaborating his famous "race relations cycle." He should have understood why Booker T. Washington was not disposed to write a book about their trip in which he, a relatively unknown White man, would be listed as a coauthor.

Park was temperamentally a moderate and a gradualist with regard to Black-American advancement, but he expressed his admiration for the militant DuBois in his private notes. He saw conflict as necessary and natural, whatever his own predilections and those of Washington were. He saw a role for both Washington and DuBois. In referring to some action taken by Washington in 1906, soon after the race riots in Atlanta, he wrote: "Washington was a man of courage; he was no white man's nigger."[22] However, had Park's name appeared as the coauthor of this book, he would certainly have been accused of being one, not only by the Afro-American "Young Turks," but also by his Southern White supporters. Coauthorship with a relatively unknown White journalist would not have advanced the cause of Tuskegee, Washington, or "The Race" in 1912, when the radicals associated with DuBois and Trotter, on one hand, and Southerners on the other, were watching Washington's every move. The latter group included racists who were publishing books with titles such as *The Negro a Beast* as well as "moderates" who held up Washington to substantiate their argument that "*some* negras *do* have brains."

Park, with all his insight into American race relations did not seem to sense the possibility of damage to Washington's image if their names appeared as equals on the title page. But he like Washington had an emotional investment in this book. After five years with only a few bylines, Park, a newspaperman, must have been a bit anxious to have something in print in his own name of which his family and friends and former professors could be proud. And living away from his family he had been giving thought to eventually terminating the Tuskegee connection and seeking employment where they could join him.

A book based on his work with Washington would be an asset: even if only as coauthor. Yet it is difficult to see how he could have visualized this particular book as one that would have enhanced his career unless the whole first person authorial stance was abandoned. And he should have had enough "feel" for Washington's reactions to know that he was not in the mood for that kind of book.

Whatever literary merit *The Man Farthest Down* has is similar to that found in Washington's autobiography, *Up from Slavery*—a simple, almost naive approach to a complex world, impressing the reader as ingenuous and sincere. But this volume is significant, also, because it is a revealing and refreshing personal statement by a public figure who was most often seen playing a social role, not as an individual reacting spontaneously and directly. Park lost nothing by letting Washington "call the shots" in assigning credit for producing the book. Rather he gained by it. His peers in the academy could not blame him for whatever lack of sophistication in thought and style it displays. He gained, too, because as it stands, the book exemplifies his own "greatness" as an editor. Raushenbush states that Park once made a generalization about editing the work of his wife Clara and that of Booker T. Washington, saying that he could "make Clara sound more like Clara and Washington more like Washington than either could sound alone."[23] It was that kind of unobtrusive collaboration in the writing phase of their joint project that gives this book its historic significance.

Park helped make this Washington's book—in tone, idiomatic expression, and even in retention of repeated clichés heavy editing might have eliminated or obtrusive "collaboration" could not have allowed. The final product is also a tribute to Washington's stubborn insistence that it was *his* book and that while a paragraph or two of ghostwriting here and there might be tolerable, he permitted no tampering with his mode of thought and writing style, nor his musing, philosophizing, and generalizing. The following observations are bits of pure Washington optimism untempered by Parkian objectivity or tentativeness:

> There is hardly any one thing in which the people of Europe are more concerned than in the progress and future of the man farthest down.[24]

> The future of the world farthest down is bright because those above realize that they are a burden dragging them down.[25]

> The world looks, on the whole, more interesting, more hopeful, and more filled with God's providence when you are at the bottom looking up than when you are at the top looking down.[26]

Nor did Park's editorial pen strike such obvious bits of deadpan "playing dumb" directed at Southern conservatives as Washington's conclusion after an animated discussion of rural labor strikes in Hungary and Italy: "The possibility that farm hands might be organized into labour unions, and make use of this form of organization in order to compel landowners to raise wages, had never occurred to me."[27] In general, however, Washington did not keep up his guard.

That Booker T. Washington decided to tell the American public how he felt as he talked with British suffragettes and Austrian socialist leaders; observed strikes and pondered over the use of that weapon by agricultural laborers; observed and approved of Danish cooperatives and folk schools, and even refrained from denouncing socialism as his mentor, General Armstrong of Hampton, had explicitly taught him to do, seems to indicate an unconscious rebellion against having his personality totally circumscribed by either Southern pressures or the thinking of the capitalist philanthropists who supported his efforts financially. Raushenbush feels that a fundamental change took place in Booker T. Washington during the trip:

> This 1910 tour was important to Washington's intellectual development. Although he was a

> patriot, believing or wishing to believe that everything in the United States was better than in Europe, he noted that the European lowest classes were exerting pressure on their governments to make changes and that the governments were not wholly unresponsive to it. . . . Some of Washington's biographers have observed that he took a stronger position on black civil rights during the latter part of his life than he had taken in the 1890s. This undoubtedly had more than one cause, but the amount of instruction in European history that Park gave Washington on their European tour combined with Washington's own powers of observation, probably contributed. If so, it may have been Park's most important service for Washington during the seven years they were together.[28]

We must await publication of volume 10 of *The Booker T. Washington Papers* for any possible documentary corroboration of this estimate of Park's impact during the trip. Of the profound direct impact of the trip itself there is no doubt. The less inhibited discussion of controversial matters in *The Man Farthest Down* and what Rauschenbush called the "stronger position on black civil rights" that came later, were due to a more complex nexus of influences than the experience of traveling six weeks abroad with Park in 1910. An upsurge of violence in American race relations had led to the founding of the NAACP just before the two men left for England, and to the sharpening of attacks on Washington by Black radicals. August Meier points out that Washington's political power as a patronage dispenser began to weaken after the 1908 presidential election and that Theodore Roosevelt's shift to being a progressive leader rather than a Republican president left Washington bereft of a powerful ally.[29] A physical assault made upon him in 1911 cannot be dismissed as the kind of traumatizing event that would lead to a questioning of what all his years of an extreme accommodationist stance had been worth.[30] However, the book is a significant weathervane pointing toward the ideological direction Washington would take during the next four years leading up to his death.

The Man Farthest Down reveals Booker T. Washington as a person with a sensitive, open, inquiring mind, eager to gain knowledge and insights and willing to revise old points of view and correct some stereotypes. It reveals an accommodationist "race leader" with his mask slightly lifted, so that the person behind it can be appreciated. If the reader enters into the spirit of Washington's quest, this book can be enjoyed even while smiling an occasional knowing smile.

III

Despite Park's role as mentor on the trip and his guiding hand during production of the book, *The Man Farthest Down* shows some intellectual weaknesses related to the fact that he had not yet taken on the role of sociologist. He would eventually become widely known for his theory of race relations that hypothesized a cycle when two or more races come into contact, beginning with competition and conflict, proceeding on to a state of societal accommodation that would eventually lead to cultural assimilation.[31] The process of biological miscegenation accompanied these sociocultural processes and influenced the rate of movement toward assimilation. When he and Washington were on the trip in Europe, Park not only did not have this theory to offer his traveling companion as a paradigm to assist in interpretation, he had not yet arrived at a clear conception of what entity he wanted to use the term *race* to designate.

Park, like most publicists and many scholars of the period, was employing a loose definition of race that included ethnic groups, nations, and "peoples" as well as groups defined by cephalic index, skin color, hair type, and other anatomical traits. Yet it was the Black/White question, not the immigrant problem, that sent them on their quest: "the man farthest down" for whom Washington searched in Europe was "White"; the man at the bottom in America with whom he would compare him was "Black." Yet America's "Negroes" ranged in color from white through a variety of shades of brown to near black. But it is not this anomaly but another that is relevant here. One of Washington's conclusions revealed that he was not using the term race in a strictly physical anthropological sense. He wrote: "*Racial* hatred works in much the same way whether it exists among people of the same colour but different speech, or among people of different colour and the same speech"[32] (italics added). He was thinking of the Jews and what he called "the many races of the Austrian Empire," and searching for a concept that would bring the Black experience and European "minority" problems within the same frame of reference.

The use of the term *race* to refer to groups defined by characteristics other than physical went out of vogue during the thirties and forties when Franz Boas's concepts in anthropology were dominant in the social sciences. Later the term *social race* was coined to apply to linguistic or cultural groups that people persisted in reacting to racially, or that were thought of as inheriting distinctive mental, psychological, and emotional traits through the genes. By this time anthropologist Ashley Montagu was suggesting that the term *race* be abandoned in favor of *ethnic group*. Since the mid-1970s *ethnicity* has replaced *race relations* as a focus of American research in intergroup relations. (Some Black critics point out that this orientation deemphasizes the most vicious kind of discrimination in society, that based on skin color and degree of Negroidness, and view its popularity with suspicion.) Both Park and Washington had an interest in the consequences of color discrimination as their basic theme, with ethnicity a subsidiary concern. Their tendency to use the term *racial* to cover groups defined by culture and nationality as well as physical traits is disconcerting to modern ears, yet the book's concern with comparative dimensions of ethnicity gives it contemporary social science relevance despite this fact.

In the concluding chapter, Washington states candidly: "I have been so busy with the task immediately in front of me that I have never had the time to think out my experiences and formulate my ideas in general terms."[33] This did not inhibit him from making many generalizations in the book that are based on superficial knowledge of history, economics, and sociology. He equated feudal serfdom with slavery in America, writing that "it was the same system, in a very large degree, as that which existed in the Southern states before the war, with the exception that the serfs in Europe were white, while the slaves in the Southern state were black."[34] He was constantly looking for Jewish influences in public life and in the marketplace because, as he explained, he had "a special and peculiar interest in the history and progress of the Jewish race" with which his own people identified in episodes involving the Exodus.[35] He revealed some conceptions that came close to anti-Semitic stereotyping when he tried to generalize from a few observations and interviews, as well as from bits of history gleaned from Park regarding the role of Jews in London, Denmark, Germany, Poland, and parts of the Austro-Hungarian Empire. He observed at one point that "some individuals and some people like the Jews, for example, will know how to make their disadvantages their opportunities and so get the best of the rest of the world, no matter how things are arranged."[36] Park's views on ethnopsychology expressed in an article in 1918 may have found earlier expression in this interpretation of Jewish behavior with a characteristic Washingtonian twist added.[37]

Frequent generalizations about the consequences of urbanization contain an overlay of Washington's moralizing about the virtues of rural life added to Park's nonnormative observations about the process. Whatever theoretical assumptions, formulations, or sociological concepts appear in the book represent Park's input (such as a number of observations about the sociological effects on a worldwide scale of urbanization, or some correct generalizations about feudalism, anarchism, or socialism). But unscholarly lack of precision abounds. Park and Washington were studying disadvantaged groups within hierarchical social formations, but terms such as class and caste, serf and slave, are used in the book with little concern for terminological precision. For instance reference is made to a "long-standing *feud*" between the Polish peasants and nobility that ignores the fact of it being a class struggle (Park had a pronounced blind spot regarding Marxian sociological concepts and terminology), and then the same discussion speaks of "a sentiment of caste which separates the two classes of the Polish people."[38] Nevertheless the empirical data on Poland, however inadequate its conceptualization, is interesting, vivid, and well-written, and reveals the authors at their investigative best—resourceful and even adventurous—in their pursuit of the elusive "man farthest down."

Lack of terminological rigor and conceptual clarity should not be surprising. Park's Ph.D. was in philosophy. He took only one course in sociology as a student. He worked eleven years as a newspaperman. He did not begin to clarify his own concepts for use in sociological research until after 1912 when W.I. Thomas persuaded him to come to the University of Chicago from Tuskegee. Park then spent three years retooling himself for an academic career in a department of sociology (he was first placed in the Divinity School at Chicago!). He did so by intensive reading and constant discussion with W.I. Thomas who did have a doctorate in sociology. He soon began to relate race relations to general sociological theory. While preparing a course on "The Negro" to be taught at the University of Chicago, Park published an article on "Racial Assimilation in Secondary Groups,"[39] where he contrasted voluntary ethnic segregation in Europe with the "interests" and "caste sentiment" that kept the races apart in the United States. In both situations Park discerned a struggle of subordinate groups against dominant "races" (although not always overt or violent) accompanied by the growth of "a sort of racial consciousness" within the subordinate group. As he reflected on the observations made when he and Washington toured Europe and compared the situations there with that of Afro-Americans, he formulated a "scientific" generalization that some Black leaders had been espousing as an ideology for over fifty years: that black Americans were evolving into a "nation," as were numerous ethnic groups in Europe. He defined nationality as "a racial group which has attained self consciousness, no matter whether it has, at the same time, gained political independence or not."[40] Other ideas about ethnicity and race implicit in *The Man Farthest Down* found explicit expression in 1918 in an article by Park entitled "Education in Its Relation to the Conflict and Fusion of Cultures."

Park, like the Afro-American leaders DuBois and Kelly Miller (and presumably Booker T. Washington also), was imbued with what George M. Fredrickson in *The Black Image in the White Mind* calls "romantic racialism," an intellectual inheritance from Herder. Park tried to give it a social science grounding and wrote: "The Negro is, by natural disposition, neither an intellectual nor an idealist, like the Jew, nor a brooding introspective like the East Indian; nor a pioneer and frontiersman, like the Anglo-Saxon. He is primarily an artist, loving life for its own sake. His *metier* is expression rather than action. He is, so to speak, the lady among the races."[41] During the thirties and forties most of Park's students and many Afro-Americans who might have accepted this as a rough and ready, albeit stereotyped description of an empirical situation in the Western world during the last three or four hundred years, were not prepared to accept Park's explanation of the differences: "The temperament of the Negro, as I conceive it, consists in a few elementary but distinctive characteristics, *determined by physical organizations and transmitted biologically* . . . this racial temperament has selected out of the mass of cultural materials to which it has had access, such technical, mechanical, and intellectual devices as met its needs at a particular period of its existence" (italics added).[42]

Park felt that "racial characteristics manifest themselves in an extraordinary way in large homogeneous gatherings." Like other racial romanticists, he denied that differences in temperament carried with them any necessary differences in ability to learn as expressed by I.Q. or otherwise. Park felt that they had political implications, that "where individuals of the same race and hence the same temperament are associated, the temperamental interests will tend to reinforce one another. . . . In this way racial qualities become the basis for nationalties"[43] and eventually a political society founded on racial inheritance.

Park must have felt that people like Booker T. Washington had certain special characteristics that his successor at Tuskegee, Robert Russa Moten, who claimed to be "unmixed" did not have, for he wrote that when miscegenation occurred there was "a breaking up of the complex of the biologically inherited qualities which constitute the temperament of the race." As miscegenation proceeded within the group the process would bring about "changes in the mores, traditions and eventually in the institutions of the community." This would modify the external forms only slightly but was "likely to change profoundly the content and the meaning."[44] Park seemed to be saying the same thing as the Southern antimiscegenationists, but he did not seem to fear the consequences.

Soon after completion of *The Man Farthest Down,* Park began to devote a great deal of time to the organization of what turned out to be the very successful International Conference on the Negro that convened on April 19, 1912 at Tuskegee. The Raushenbush biography of Park is in error, however, when it states that the conference was "entirely Park's idea," and that "Washington, though never much interested in Africa, was prepared to help Park do what he wanted to do."[45] It does not detract from Park's organizational efforts or the keynote address he delivered at the conference to set the record straight by noting that Washington had conferred briefly with the group of intellectuals in London who organized a Pan-African Congress in 1900 and that he sent a technical assistance mission to Togoland that year, or that six years later Tuskegee dispatched a similar team to the Sudan. Washington corresponded with these people from Tuskegee who were trying to help Africans become successful cotton growers and certainly showed no lack of interest in their work. His private secretary, Emmet J. Scott, was on a mission to Liberia in 1911 while Park was setting up the conference for 1912, and Washington himself would have been more actively involved in Liberian Affairs had the Department of State not advised him to concentrate on the home front during a critical period in race relations.

Four days after the conference was over, W.I. Thomas from the University of Chicago addressed a letter to Park with the salutation "My dear brother in Christ" (the import of the religious greeting is not clear), saying "I am amazed to find how ignorant I was before I met you and how wise I seem to be now . . . I think something is going to result from a comparison of the Negro and the peasant."[46] A few weeks later he wrote again from the University of Chicago: "I think you had better come here and teach eventually but would not rob the negro of you just yet."[47] In the fall of 1913 Park delivered a lecture at Chicago on "Racial Assimilation in Reference to the Negro." The next year he gave a course in the Department of Sociology on the same subject. By then he had resigned from Tuskegee where, as an associate of Booker T. Washington for seven years, he had received a solid postdoctoral education.

IV

The two years before the Park-Washington trip to Europe and the two years after their return constitute a critical period in race relations in the United States. In 1908 a lynching took place in Springfield, Illinois, the shrine city of Abraham Lincoln, that so shocked the White liberals and socialists in the North that they formed an alliance with some of the young radical Blacks to organize the National Association for the Advancement of Colored People (NAACP). That organization was incorporated during the year of the search for "the man farthest down." While the NAACP did not directly attack Washington that year, its leading Black member, W. E. B. DuBois, and a group of Black militants did, warning the British public to pay no heed to anything Washington might have to say about how much improvement had taken place in the status of Afro-Americans since the Civil War, that they were still disfranchised, segregated, and sometimes lynched.

Two books by a White Baptist minister that depicted the Black man as a brute were highly popular in the South on the eve of the Washington-Park trip—Thomas Dixon's *The Leopard's Spots* and *The Clansman*—but while Park and Washington were abroad a Southern liberal churchman, Benjamin R. Riley, published *The White Man's Burden*, a book that tried to reinforce the pro-Washington line, commenting that "the dominant characteristic of the Negro is that of submission and tractableness" and that "left to himself, the Negro raises no tumults, incites no strikes . . . and where others would cherish malice and hatred, he returns a quiet good humor."[48] A respected medical journal, on the other hand, gave sanction to widespread folk beliefs manipulated by reactionary demagogues when it published an article saying that "the attacks on defenseless white women are evidence of racial instincts that are about as amenable to ethical culture as is the inherent odor of the race . . . the African's birthright is 'sexual madness and excess.' "[49] These defenders of White supremacy ignored the socially sanctioned demand for sexual favors from Black women that Southern White males claimed as *their* birthright. Prurience, guilt, and fear as well as suppressed sentiments of affection and love had characterized Southern White male attitudes toward women of the opposite race for over 250 years and the "mixed-blood" progeny proliferated. Mulattoes were then defined as "a social problem," products of "mongrelization," prone to be unstable and obstreperous, but also, when properly socialized, able to supply constructive leadership to the less intelligent unmixed Negroes. Washington was the prime example of a "good" mulatto; DuBois of a "bad" one.

Park had a social scientist's interest in the mulatto as a marginal man and as an agent in the process of cultural assimilation. In 1912 when W. I. Thomas and Park were first beginning to plan joint research on race relations, the former wrote an enthusiastic letter stating that "we are evidently going to have a good deal of fun out of this thing. . . . I will come on to Boston just as you say, I think as early as June 8th, and we can beat about the town and see the mulattos."[50] Such matters could not be "fun" to Washington.

The Tuskegee principal was sensitive to the phenomenon of miscegenation too, but his concern with its political ramifications was not in terms of research. His own high prestige among Southern Whites rested in part on his constant reassurance that his leadership meant a future in which "race mixing," or "mongrelization" as they called it, would constantly diminish, and in which Blacks would all wish to remain "as separate as the fingers on the hand in all things purely social," which included all things sexual. And then, less than a year after the return from the search for "the man farthest down," a tragedy with a miscegenation angle occurred.

On March 19, 1911, after delivering an afternoon address at a church in New York, Washington returned to his hotel room around five o'clock. At about nine he took a subway to 59th Street and walked to 11½ West 63rd, where he had been informed by a telegram from Tuskegee that someone wished to see him. While fumbling with a doorbell in the hallway a White man rushed up to him, choked him, and began to beat him with his fists and a stick. The man alleged at his trial for assault that he had caught Washington peering under a windowshade and through a keyhole. A woman of questionable reputation testified that he had spoken to her in a "familiar fashion" in the hallway. Washington said he was looking for a specific person and must have entered the wrong building and rung the wrong bell. The jury acquitted the White man of the charge of assault. The acquittal added insult to injury. Blacks everywhere, regardless of ideology, were angry over this outcome. They believed Washington had been framed. The facts are still in dispute. For years, mention of this episode was taboo in writing about Washington, but Arna Bontemps in *100 Years of Negro Freedom* (1962) decided to discuss it in detail and evaluate its repercussion on Washington and the public.[51] About fifty years ago when visiting Tuskegee, I was told in hush-hush tones by old-timers that the student body sang spirituals and cried when Washington came home and stood before them in the chapel with his head swathed in bandages. Not since he had dined with Theodore Roosevelt at the White House in 1901, they said, had Washington's reputation sunk so low among White Southerners. Rumors spread that he had betrayed the Atlanta Compromise, that he was a miscegenationist in disguise. Not only was doubt thrown on his sincerity and his morals, but his own self-confidence seems to have been shaken. He died four years later. There were rumors in some quarters that he had lost the will to live.

Outlook, a magazine that frequently carried articles by Washington, was printing the chapters of *The Man Farthest Down* in installments at the time the attack on Washington occurred.[52] Meanwhile a bodyguard of cadets accompanied Washington everywhere on the campus at Tuskegee, because, as Arna Bontemps phrased it, "some folks at Tuskegee were not dismissing the gossip that local white people might turn on him with violence as a result of this talk about Washington and the white woman."[53] It was a real act of courage that *Outlook* and Washington did not withdraw the planned May 6th installment which was a chapter on women in Europe. After all, they were *White*. In his report on his first trip to Europe, despite a few comments, Washington may have deliberately avoided discussion of what Dixon in *The Clansman* refers to in almost sacred mystical terms—the White woman. Yet for reasons that Freudians and feminists can speculate about, Washington assigned high priority to the significance of findings about women in reporting on his 1910 European tour. He wrote: "In all my observations and study . . . I found that the facts which I have learned about the condition of women tended to set themselves off and assume a special importance in my mind."[54] Given the temper of the times and Washington's accommodationist leadership position, this was a somewhat daring and perhaps even foolhardy thing for Washington to say. But it was true and he not only had the courage to say it and scatter comments on the subject throughout the book, but also to devote a whole chapter to discussing women at work in Europe. Apparently Park and other aides did not bring any pressure on him to avoid the subject.

This empathy with Europe's women found concrete expression early in the trip when a London newspaper girl caught his eye. Her voice and manner, "timid, ingratiating, and a little insolent" appealed to him as being "something different" from that of other women in her social stratum as he observed them. He found that she was selling a suffragette paper, and through her he was directed to a sample of "the women insurgents" of England. He began to "enter into the spirit of their crusade" as he responded to "the bright and witty accounts of these young women." (They must have elicited some comparison with his own 27-year-old daughter Portia.) There was irony in his telling of this identification with these suffragettes, for as the symbol of "accommodation" he could not identify with any crusade for granting the franchise to his own people of either sex back home in the South. After commenting on his admiration for these militant women, Washington hastened to insert a typical caveat in the record: "I do not believe that voting alone will improve the condition of working women."[55]

Washington had made a few comments about European women when he and Mrs. Washington visited England and Europe in 1900. He met Queen Victoria and compared her with Susan B. Anthony who was in London for a conference, calling them both "remarkable" persons. He was sensitive to aesthetic matters, too, noting that the Duchess of Sutherland, who was unusually friendly to the Washingtons, was "said to be the most beautiful woman in England." He liked

Holland for the neatness of its farms, the efficiency of its agriculture, and especially for its fine Holsteins. Of its women he remarked: "I do not think I exaggerate when I say that in all Holland I did not see a single beautiful woman." A decade later, as he and Park moved about together, he noted that he saw several types of women (his descriptions of them are scattered through the book). He said he "saw none who looked so handsome, fresh and vigorous as these Polish peasant women."[56] (How interesting it would be if we could have had a record of his reaction if someone had told him that the patron saint of Poland was a *Black* Madonna.) Washington also spoke of "a heavy stolid type" of woman he saw in Europe that he obviously found less attractive, but made no other remarks about their bodies as he noted with admiration that they "did their work as rapidly and as easily as the men beside them."[57] One thing he could not abide was women in bare feet! In addition to the shoeless phenomenon that he found in many places, two other conditions among women shocked him. One was the prevalence of drunkenness in public among lower-class women in London; the other was the extent to which women were "engaged in rough and unskilled labor of every kind" on the continent—all types of hard agricultural work as well as digging ditches, pulling carts, shoveling and hauling coal, and working in quarries and brickyards. He scored a point for his major theme by insisting that "I had never seen Negro women doing the sort of work I saw the women of southern Europe doing."[58] Then comparing all the women he had seen with the men, he made the surprising generalization that "in Europe, the man farthest down is woman."[59]

Park once wrote a long description of some Negro women in rural Alabama in his notebook. He described the activities of a group of young women on a farm and mentioned casually that one was barefoot, but he did not discuss them in esthetic terms. Power, not beauty, was on his mind and he wrote: "A gigantic black woman, slim as an athlete and straight as an arrow, her black head cropped in a white turban did the cooking. A couple of young girls served the table. I have rarely seen anything human that impressed me more with a sense of power than this big, primitive, black woman."[60] Unfortunately, we do not have Park's reaction to the women of Europe to compare with Washington's.

Although it is obvious from this report that Washington had an eye for female beauty, there is nothing of either the pure esthete or the sexist voyeur in his attitude toward English and European women. Yet the simple esthetic judgments he made would not have been acceptable to White Southern males if he were talking about "their" women living in the United States. Of course, it was impossible for him as for any other Afro-American to have lived in the South without ever making esthetic appraisals of the White women who were a part of their environment. However, expressions of such evaluations were either repressed or expressed only among Black male friends. England and Europe may have functioned for Washington as a projective screen, as a massive TAT instrument, eliciting attitudes and feelings repressed by the Southern caste system within which he had been socialized. If so, the significant thing is not that Booker T. Washington experienced an emergence of subconsciously repressed material, but that he admitted it in the pages of his book. Perhaps such neo-Freudian explanations are not required to account for his decision to speak openly and frankly on an aspect of his trip that he found interesting and significant.

V

The Man Farthest Down is an important contribution to the growing body of literature that is providing us with the data for constructing a more accurate image of both Park and Washington. August Meier started the revisionist process in 1957 with an article in the *Journal of Southern History*, "Toward a Reinterpretation of Booker T. Washington," to be followed in 1963 by his definitive book, *Negro Thought in America, 1880-1915: the Age of Booker T. Washington.* Louis R. Harlan integrated a wealth of new data into *Booker T. Washington: the Making of a Black Leader, 1856-1901*, published in 1972 as the first volume of what will be the definitive Washington biography. One special study of Washington's relationship to African affairs was of great value in clearing up misconceptions due to some remarks made by Park about the Tuskegee principal's lack of concern for Africa. Publication of the first nine volumes of the Washington papers under Harlan's editorship brings additional evidence to shatter the stereotype of Booker T. Washington as an "Uncle Tom," unconcerned about such issues as abolishing segregation in public places or restoring Black voting rights in the South. The picture is emerging of an "accommodationist" leader who wore his mask well but who was also a shrewd clandestine tactician in trying to move toward some limited civil rights goals, and who opposed the crystallization of race relations into a caste system.

To most college-trained Americans of the interwar years, Robert Ezra Park was known as the leader of the Chicago School of sociology and as an expert in the field of race relations. Many Afro-Americans knew him also as the professor who was teacher and intellectual patron of the first two nationally known secular Black sociologists, E. Franklin Frazier and Charles S. Johnson (R. R. Wright and Edmund G. Haynes had received Ph.D.s in sociology much earlier but they were both preachers). His seminal ideas on ecology and his "social processes"—competition, conflict, accommodation, assimilation—were mentioned in virtually every sociology textbook. Park's close involvement with Booker T. Washington and Tuskegee was not widely known even among college-trained Blacks, and the details of his life before and after his career at Chicago remained the subject of rumor and gossip. In 1979 one of his students and colleagues, Winifred Raushenbush, took the first step toward letting the world know something of his career and inner life when she published *Robert E. Park: Biography of a Sociologist*, from which we have quoted occasionally in this introduction. Perhaps the most revealing statement in her book that is relevant to our concerns is a quotation from Park when he was looking back on the seven years he spent in association with Tuskegee before coming to Chicago: "Booker Washington gave me an opportunity such as no one else ever had, I am sure, to be acquainted with the actual and intimate life of the Negro in the South. . . . I became, for all intents and purposes, a Negro myself."[61] Perhaps he *did* in the sense of an anthropologist utilizing the participant-observation method, or a person seeing a situation from the point of view of the actor in a Weberian sense, or taking the role of the other in the Mead-Cooley way. We shall have to await a more sophisticated analysis of Park's letters and notebooks and of reports on interviews with those who knew him best, before accepting the view that Park's fascination with Blacks stemmed solely from a desire to study them, to use them as data for his intellectual ruminations. His preoccupation with Africa and the New World diaspora suggests that his interest ran far deeper than that. I have not always felt so, however. My first impression when I heard of Park's seven years at Tuskegee was that he considered it a laboratory and the Blacks as guinea pigs. Later, I viewed his ideas about ethnopsychology as a subtle (even if unintended) reinforcement of those who would confine Black people to certain specialized occupations, and resented the fact that he lent his prestige to a stereotype. With the passage of time I came to understand the complexities of his conception of Blacks, and to apply the principles of the sociology of knowledge to explaining him as I did to explaining myself.

I was born during the year that *The Man Farthest Down* was published. I was four when Booker T. Washington died in 1915. Until I entered Hampton in 1927 I was never among people, whether relatives, friends, or teachers, who extolled his educational or political philosophy. And this despite the fact that I attended a Booker T. Washington High School in Staunton, Virginia. Most of my acquaintances simply took it for granted that Booker T. Washington had been a "great Negro like Fredrick Douglass, Dr. DuBois, and Marcus Garvey" and let it go at that. Then, for four years, I experienced a highly concentrated exposure to the Armstrong-Washington philosophy of race relations and education as a student at Hampton. I was a student delegate in 1931, to Tuskegee's 50th Anniversary Celebration. The result of these experiences was to increase my respect for Booker T. Washington as an expert in raising money for his institution and to generate some personal commitment to the idea that one's education should be used for "service to the Race." But Hampton-Tuskegee conservatism didn't "take," and even before graduation I was attracted to the NAACP and W. E. B. DuBois for my political "line." Since I took no sociology courses at Hampton I never heard Park mentioned and I cannot recall reading anything at the time that Washington wrote other than *Up from Slavery.*

When I began graduate work in anthropology at the University of Chicago in 1937, I met a graduate student in sociology, Horace R. Cayton, who had taught one summer at Tuskegee and whose attitudes toward the Hampton-Tuskegee philosophy were similar to mine. We became close associates for the next five years in a research project on race relations in Chicago and the internal structure of the Black community in the city. Park had retired, but I heard him lecture on one occasion. Cayton knew Park very well. He had come to Chicago from the West Coast at Park's suggestion to work toward a doctorate in sociology, and had been associated with him at Fisk University during the previous year before my arrival in Chicago. I picked up a great deal of Parkiana from Cayton and his friends during the next four or five years. Much of it was apocryphal. Some of the stories concerned Park's relations with Washington as well as his attitude and behavior toward other Black people and various racial and ethnic groups throughout the world. There was a tendency among many Black graduate students to dismiss *The Man Farthest Down* as "the book that Park 'ghosted' for Booker T. to prove that being black down South wasn't so bad after all." I never bothered to read it.

In 1944 when Horace Cayton and I were preparing the front matter for our book, *Black Metropolis,* Cayton suggested that we dedicate the book to "the late Professor Robert E. Park of Tuskegee, the University of Chicago, and Fisk, American scholar and friend of the Negro people." Park had died the year before, and Cayton, who had known him well, felt he merited this tribute. I was not so sure at first. I knew that Park had taught at Fisk during the 1936-37 academic year. Many of Cayton's stories were not very reassuring and implied that Park was on the ultraconservative side with regard to economic matters and prone to make remarks in private that could be interpreted as anti-Semitic. I found his "lady of the races" designation of the Negro temperament as offensive as it was inaccurate, and Cayton believed that Park had never abandoned the views on ethnopsychology he had espoused in 1918. Yet Cayton emphasized that Park was vigorous in his assertions that there was no evidence to support the view that Africans or people of African descent had a cognitive deficit as compared with other people, however different they might be in temperament. Many older Black scholars, including DuBois, had held views similar to Park's, clinging to the belief in special "gifts" that Negroes inherited. But by the mid-thirties, even those who believed in the reality of "soul" or Negritude thought it was conserved and transmitted by the culture, not genes.

During the thirties, anthropologists with whom I was studying, including Park's own son-in-law Robert Redfield, were teaching me to be sceptical of any positive assertions about the inheritability of mental and emotional traits that could be accounted for alternatively in terms of culture and child-training practices. Nevertheless, as I reflected upon Park's choice to work with the Congo Reform Association, his closeness to Frazier and Johnson, his work with the Urban League, and his decision to spend his declining years with Johnson at Fisk, I let Cayton persuade me. It was obvious that he was not a "racist." I added a quote of Park's expressing his approval of anthropology and we let the dedication stand. I do not regret our decision.

After reading *The Man Farthest Down* in conjunction with the Raushenbush biography of Park, the Harlan and Mathews biographies, and several books bearing Washington's name, my knowledge and understanding of both men has increased. So has my respect for them. *The Man Farthest Down* is a tribute to Washington's latent intellectual abilities that had to be sacrificed in the interest of institution building and which were obscured by the necessity to wear the mask of an accommodationist leader in a racist society. The book is also an outstanding example of Park's superb, self-effacing editorial skill displayed during the period when he was still essentially a journalist and had not yet become an "expert" on race relations and one of America's most esteemed sociologists. What Mills called "the sociological imagination" is already evident to the discerning reader.

Both men found confirmation, as they journeyed through Europe, of their belief that education and community action of the Hampton-Tuskegee type could transform individuals and groups among those "farthest down" despite handicaps imposed by the "racial temperament" they were thought to inherit, and would even prepare them to participate in some social movements for the elimination of social injustices. There is an implicit recognition in the book that such education would have unintended political consequences although not necessarily of revolutionary intensity. The book was a challenge to the theories of biological determinism and social Darwinism so popular during the two decades prior to World War I.

NOTES

A description of the journey to Europe by Washington and Park is included in a chapter on "Transatlantic Perspective" in Basil Mathews, *Booker T. Washington: Educator and Interracial Interpreter* (Cambridge: Harvard University Press, 1948). He emphasizes Washington's "gift of single-minded concentration" and flashes of humor revealed in *The Man Farthest Down.* Mathews did not have access to the type of sources provided in the Winifred Raushenbush biography that make this present appraisal of the trip and the book possible. The most valuable new source will be the forthcoming volume 10 of *The Booker T. Washington Papers,* edited by Louis R. Harlan and Raymond W. Smock and published by the University of Illinois Press. The papers in volume 9 include the years 1906-08. For insight into Washington's concept of himself and his mission in life on the eve of the European trip, see his book published in 1911 by Doubleday, Page, *My Larger Education.* Washington's attitude toward the use of immigrant labor in the

South was made clear in his famous Atlanta Exposition Speech of 1895. Basil Mathews reprints it with comments on pp. 84-91 of his book referred to above. See also Everett C. Hughes et al., *The Collected Papers of Robert Ezra park*, vol. 1, *Race and Culture* (Glencoe, Ill.: Free Press, 1950). Familiarity with the American context within which the journey was made and the book produced can be secured from two chapters in George M. Fredrickson, *The Black Image in the White Mind: The Debate on Afro-American Character and Destiny, 1817-1914* (New York: Harper & Row, 1972), ch. 9, "The Negro as Beast: Southern Neogrophobia at the Turn of the Century," and ch. 10, "Accommodationist Racism and the Progressive Mentality."

1. Winifred Raushenbush, *Robert E. Park: Biography of a Sociologist,* with a foreword and epilogue by Everett C. Hughes (Durham, N.C.: Duke University Press, 1979), p. 52. This book is the only comprehensive biography of Park. Raushenbush was a research assistant to Park on two important studies he directed, one on Americanization of immigrants funded by the Carnegie Corporation, and the other a survey of race relations on the West Coast sponsored by the Institute of Social and Religious Research.
2. Booker T. Washington, *The Man Farthest Down: A Record of Observation and Study in Europe with the Collaboration of Robert E. Park*, (Gar-

den City, N.Y.: Doubleday, Page, 1911), p. 144.

3. Raushenbush, p. 55.
4. William Labov, "Rules for Ritual Insults," in Thomas Kochman (ed.), *Rappin and Stylin' Out* (Urbana: University of Illinois Press, 1972), esp. pp. 273–74.
5. Raushenbush, p. 39. For a well-documented account of Washington's concern with African affairs that found expression at least a decade before he met Park, see Louis R. Harlan, "Booker T. Washington and the White Man's Burden," *American Historical Review* 71 (January 1966): 441–67.
6. The quotations are from ch. 3, "The African at Home" (pp. 36, 37) in Washington's book, *The Story of the Negro,* published in 1909 by Doubleday, Page. Ch. 1, "First Notions of Africa," is an intimate account of his ambivalence toward African peoples and cultures. The next three chapters document his reassessment of African cultures as he read a number of books recommended by Park.
7. Raushenbush, p. 157.
8. Ibid., p. 39.
9. Louis R. Harlan, *Booker T. Washington: The Making of a Black Leader, 1856-1901* (New York: Oxford University Press, 1972), pp. 242–43.
10. The quotations concerning Thrasher are from ibid., pp. 246–47.
11. *The Autobiography of W. E. B. DuBois: A Soliloquy on Viewing My Life from the Last Decade of Its First Century* (New York: International Publishers, 1968), pp. 242–43.

12. Ibid., p. 185.
13. Raushenbush, p. 40.
14. Ibid., p. 40.
15. Ibid., p. 63.
16. Ibid.
17. Ibid., pp. 74–75.
18. Ibid., p. 53.
19. Ibid., p. 56.
20. Washington's account of his collaboration with Park, including the quotations in this paragraph, are from *The Man Farthest Down*, pp. 13–18. For an account based on all the existing documents see ch. 7, "Washington and Park Tour Europe," in Raushenbush, pp. 51–66.
21. Raushenbush, p. 49.
22. Ibid., p. 47.
23. Ibid., p. 18.
24. Ibid., p. 389.
25. Ibid.
26. Ibid.
27. Ibid., p. 91.
28. Ibid., pp. 55–56.
29. August Meier, *Negro Thought in America, 1880-1915: Racial Ideologies in the Age of Booker T. Washington* (Ann Arbor: University of Michigan Press), pp. 164–65.
30. Arna Bontemps, *100 Years of Negro Freedom* (New York: Dodd, Mead, 1962), pp. 214–17.
31. For a perceptive critical analysis see "The Race Relations Cycle of Robert E. Park," in Stanford M. Lyman, *The Black American in Sociological Thought* (New York: G.P. Putnam's Sons, 1972).
32. *The Man Farthest Down*, p. 378.
33. Ibid., p. 378.

34. Ibid., p. 383.
35. Ibid., p. 240.
36. Ibid., p. 382.
37. Robert E. Park, "Education in Its Relation to the Conflict and Fusion of Cultures" (1918), reprinted in Robert E. Park and Ernest W. Burgess, *Introduction to the Science of Sociology* (Chicago: University of Chicago Press, 1921), pp. 138–42.
38. *The Man Farthest Down*, pp. 74–75.
39. *Publications of the American Sociological Society* 8 (1913): 75–82.
40. Robert E. Park and Ernest W. Burgess, *Introduction to the Science of Sociology* (Chicago: University of Chicago Press, 1921), p. 633, in reprint of Robert E. Park, "Racial Assimilation in Secondary Groups," *Publications of the American Sociological Society* 8 (1913): 75–82.
41. Robert E. Park and Ernest W. Burgess, *Introduction to the Science of Sociology* (Chicago: University of Chicago Press, 1921), p. 139, from Robert E. Park, "Education in Its Relation to the Conflict and Fusion of Cultures," *Publications of the American Sociological Society* 13 (1918): 58–63.
42. Ibid., pp. 138–39.
43. Ibid., p. 141.
44. Ibid., pp. 141–42.
45. Raushenbush, p. 67. This biographer was not interested in a critical analysis of statements in Park's letters, diaries and memoranda. Another biographer states that Park had suggested an international conference to "sell" the idea of industrial education to colonial office officials and missionaries, but does not say this particular conference was "entirely Park's idea" or even that

he suggested it. See, Basil Mathews, *Booker T. Washington: Educator and Interracial Interpreter* (Cambridge: Harvard University Press, 1948), chapter on "Transatlantic Perspective." This book also documents the fact that Washington's interest in Africa predated his meeting with Park. On this point see also Booker T. Washington, *The Story of the Negro* (New York: Doubleday, Page and Co., 1909), Ch. III, "The African at Home," pp. 36 and 37. Harlan, op. cit., in n.5 does not mention Park as the originator of the idea for the 1912 conference.

46. Ibid., p. 68.
47. Ibid.
48. See George M. Fredrickson, *The Black Image in the White Mind: The Debate on Afro-American Character and Destiny,* 1817-1914 (New York: Harper & Row, 1972), pp. 280–81, 288–89.
49. Quoted in ibid., p. 279.
50. Raushenbush, p. 70.
51. Arna Bontemps, *100 Years of Negro Freedom* (New York: Dodd, Mead, 1962), pp. 214–17.
52. *Outlook* carried an account of the assault in vol. 97 (April 1, 1911).
53. Arna Bontemps, *100 Years of Negro Freedom,* pp. 214-17.
54. *The Man Farthest Down,* p. 298.
55. Ibid., pp. 296–97, 317.
56. Ibid., p. 315.
57. Ibid., p. 312.
58. Ibid., p. 308.
59. Ibid., p. 318.
60. Raushenbush, p. 45.
61. Ibid., pp. 49–50.

CONTENTS

CONTENTS

THE MAN FARTHEST DOWN

The Man Farthest Down

CHAPTER I

HUNTING THE MAN FARTHEST DOWN

ON THE 20th of August, 1910, I sailed from New York City for Liverpool, England. I had been given a leave of absence of two months from my work at Tuskegee, on condition that I would spend that time in some way that would give me recreation and rest.

Now I have found that about the only comfortable and satisfactory way for me to rest is to find some new kind of work or occupation. I determined therefore to carry out a plan I had long had in mind of making myself acquainted with the condition of the poorer and working classes in Europe, particularly in those regions from which an ever-increasing number of immigrants are coming to our country each year.

There have been a number of efforts made in recent years to divert a portion of this immigration to the Southern States, and these efforts have been the source of wide differences of opinion in the South. Some people have contended that in these immigrants the Southern people would eventually find a substitute for the Negro labourer and that in this direction a solution for the race problem would be found. In some parts of the South, in fact, the experiment of using immigrants from Europe to take the place of the Negro on the sugar plantations and in the cotton fields has been tried. Naturally I have been interested in these experiments and as a consequence in the peoples with whom the experiments have been tried.

The best way to get acquainted with an individual, or with a people, according to my experience, is to visit them at their work and in their homes, and in this way find out what is back of them.

So it was that I determined to make use of my stay in Europe to visit the people in their homes, to talk with them at their work, and to find out everything I could, not only in regard to their present situation, but also in regard to their future prospects, opportunities, hopes, and ambitions.

I was curious, for one thing, to learn why it was that so many of these European people were leaving the countries in which they were born and reared, in order to seek their fortunes in a new country and among strangers in a distant part of the world, and to this question I think I may say that I have found, in a general way, an answer. One general fact, at any rate, in regard to this matter of emigration, I may, perhaps, without attempting to go into details, mention here at the outset. It is this:

The majority of the people who reach this country as immigrants from Europe are, as one might expect, from the farming regions. They are farm labourers or tenant farmers. Now there exists, as I discovered, a very definite relation between the condition of agriculture and the agricultural peoples in Europe and the extent of emigration to this country. In other words, wherever in any part of Europe I found the condition of agriculture and the situation of the farm labourers at their worst, there I almost invariably found emigration at the highest. On the other hand, wherever I visited a part of the country where emigration had, in recent years, decreased, there I quite as invariably found that the situation of the man on the soil had improved.

What interested me still more was the fact that this improvement had been, to a very large extent, brought about through the influence of schools. Agricultural education has stimulated an intensive culture of the soil; this in turn has helped to multiply the number of small land owners and stimulate the organization of agriculture; the resulting prosperity has made itself felt not only in the country but in the cities. For example, I found that where the people were prosperous and contented in the country, there were fewer idle, discontented, starving and criminal people in the cities. It is just as true of the poorer and labouring classes in Europe as it is of the Negro in the South: that most of the problems that arise in the cities have their roots in the country.

Another matter in regard to which I hoped to get some first-hand information during my stay abroad was what I may call the European, as distinguished from the American, race problem. I knew that in the south of Europe a number of races of widely different origin and characteristics had been thrown together in close contact and in large numbers, and I suspected that in this whirlpool of contending races and classes I should find problems — race problems and educational problems — different, to be sure, but quite as complicated, difficult and interesting as in our own country.

While every race and every nation must solve its own problems in its own way, and for that reason it is not possible to make any very extended comparison between the race problems of Europe and of America, there is, at least, a certain advantage in knowing that other nations and other peoples have problems within their national life which are quite as difficult and perplexing as our own.

We sometimes think and speak of the conditions existing in our own country as if they were wholly exceptional and without parallel in other parts of the world. My stay in Europe has convinced me that we are not worse off in America in this respect than other peoples. Even if they had the choice, I do not believe, for instance, that the Southern people, black or white, would be willing to exchange their own troubles, such as they are, for those of any other nation or group of people in Europe or elsewhere.

There was another thing that made the trip I had outlined peculiarly attractive to me: I believed that I would find in some parts of Europe peoples who in respect to education, opportunity, and civilization generally were much nearer the level of the masses of the Negro people in the South than I was likely to find anywhere in America. I believed, also, that if I went far enough and deep enough I should find even in Europe great numbers of people who, in their homes, in their labour, and in their manner of living, were little, if any, in advance of the Negroes in the Southern States, and I wanted to study at first hand, as far as I was able, the methods which European nations were using to uplift the masses of the people who were at the bottom in the scale of civilization.

In view of the rather elaborate plan I have sketched, I am certain that some of my readers will wonder how I expected to be able, in the eight weeks to which my vacation was limited, to cover all the ground or get any definite or satisfactory notions in regard to the special matters which interested me in the places I proposed to visit. It seems to me, therefore, that I ought to say something, by way of explanation and introduction, as to just how this journey was made and in regard to the manner in which the impressions and facts which make up the remainder of this book were obtained.

In the first place, it should be remembered that I was looking in all the different countries I visited for one class of facts and seeking to make myself familiar with merely one phase of life. During the whole course of this journey, therefore, I kept myself religiously from the temptation that was constantly offered to look at anything, however important and interesting, that did not concern itself with the purpose of my journey.

In the second place, I found that, while there were great differences to be observed in the condition of the different peoples whom I visited, there were, also, many broad similarities. I found, for example, that what I learned in London was very useful and valuable to me, by way of comparison, in studying and observing what I wanted to see in Copenhagen and in Denmark. I found that the things I observed among the peasants of Italy were a great help to me when I reached Austria and was able to compare the conditions of the farming population in these two different countries. The result was that the farther I went and the more familiar I became with the general situation of the labouring classes, the more I gained in insight and understanding of all that I saw.

In fact I am convinced that if there is anything of special value in the studies and observations that I have set down in this book it will be found, not so much in the facts themselves, as in the attempt to bring them together into a single point of view.

One of the first things I learned in Europe was the difficulty of meeting the ordinary man and seeing and getting acquainted with the matters of everyday life. I soon discovered that the most difficult things to see are not the sights that every one goes to look at, but the commonplace things that no one sees. In order to carry out the plan I had in mind it was necessary for me to leave the ordinary beaten track of European travel and to plunge into regions which have not been charted and mapped, and where ordinary guides and guide-books are of little or no avail.

As a matter of fact, I found less difficulty in this respect in London than I did on the Continent, where it seemed to me that railways, guides, guide-books, and the friends I met on the way were in a conspiracy to compel me to see the things I did not want to see, and to prevent me from seeing all the things that I did want to see.

For example, I had registered a firm resolution, before I sailed from America, that if I could prevent it I would not enter a single palace, museum, gallery, or cathedral. I succeeded partly in living up to this resolution. When I reached Cracow in Poland, however, my fate overtook me. I had heard a great deal of the ancient salt mines of Wieliczka. I knew that in many places women were employed side by side with the men in loading and carrying out the products of the mines, and for this reason, and because I had myself at one time been a miner in America, I was very anxious to see how the work was carried on in Europe.

The salt mines are about ten miles from Cracow, and in order to reach them I found it necessary to take a carriage. At the entrance to the mines I was surprised to find a large number of sightseers waiting to go down in the shaft, and a dark suspicion crossed my mind that I had made a mistake. My worst suspicions were confirmed when, after descending some two or three hundred feet below the surface, I found myself suddenly ushered into an ancient underground chapel. The place was beautifully lighted and decorated with glistening figures which had been hewn from solid blocks of salt by the pious miners who had worked in these mines some three or four hundred years before.

From this chapel we again descended, through a dark, damp passageway, into still another and then another large, elaborately decorated and brilliantly lighted chapel. In one of these we ran upon a great crowd of several hundred people carrying lighted torches and accompanied by a brass band. They were peasants who were making an annual pilgrimage to the mine for the purpose of visiting the underground chapels, which have acquired a wide fame in the surrounding country.

For two or three hours we wandered on from

one large chamber to another, going deeper and deeper into the mine, but never coming, as near as I could see, any nearer to the miners. Finally it began to dawn upon me that so far from being in an actual salt mine, I was really in a sort of underground museum. There were chapels and monuments and crowds of people in holiday attire; there were lights and music and paper lanterns, but there was nothing that would in any way remind you of the actual daily life of the miners that I had come there to see; in fact, the only miners with whom I came in contact were those who acted as guides or played in the band. It was all very strange and very interesting, and there was, I learned, no possible means of escape.

From what I have already said I fear that some of my readers will feel, as a great many people whom I met abroad did, that in my journey across Europe I must have gained a very unfortunate and one-sided view of the countries and the peoples I visited. It will seem to them, perhaps, that I was looking for everything that was commonplace or bad in the countries I visited, and avoiding everything that was extraordinary or in any way worth looking at. My only excuse is that I was, in fact, not looking for the best, but for the worst; I was hunting for the man farthest down.

Most people who travel in Europe seem to me to be chiefly interested in two sorts of things: They want to see what is old, and they want to see what is dead. The regular routes of travel run through palaces, museums, art galleries, ancient ruins, monuments, churches, and graveyards.

I have never been greatly interested in the past, for the past is something that you cannot change. I like the new, the unfinished and the problematic. My experience is that the man who is interested in living things must seek them in the grime and dirt of everyday life. To be sure, the things one sees there are not always pleasant, but the people one meets are interesting, and if they are sometimes among the worst they are also frequently among the best people in the world. At any rate, wherever there is struggle and effort there is life.

I have referred to the way in which I tried and, to a reasonable extent, succeeded in confining my observations to a certain definite point of view. Aside from this I had certain other advantages upon this expedition in finding what I wanted to see and avoiding the things I did not want to see, without which I certainly could neither have covered the ground I did, nor have found my way to so many things that had for me special and peculiar interest. Some years ago I made the acquaintance, in Boston, of Dr. Robert E. Park, who has for some time past assisted me in my work at Tuskegee. At the time I first met him Doctor Park was interested in the movement to bring about a reform of the conditions then existing in the Congo Free State in Africa; in fact, he was at that time secretary of the Congo Reform Association, and it was through his efforts to interest me in that movement that I came to know him. He had a notion, as he explained to me, that the conditions of the natives in the Congo, as well as in other parts of Africa, could not be permanently improved only through a system of education, somewhat similar to that at Hampton and Tuskegee. The Congo Reform Association, as he explained, was engaged in a work of destruction, but what interested him chiefly was what should be done in the way of construction or reconstruction after the work of destruction was completed. We had frequent conversations upon the subject, and it was in this way that he finally became interested in the work that was being done for the Negro in the Southern States. Since that time he has spent the larger part of every year in the South, assisting me in my work at Tuskegee and using the opportunity thus offered to study what is called the Negro problem. The reason I make this statement here is because Doctor Park was not only my companion in all of my trip through Europe, but he also went to Europe some months in advance of me and thus had an opportunity to study the situation and make it possible for me to see more in a short space of time than I could otherwise have been able to do. In this and in other ways he has been largely responsible for what appears in this book.

For instance, it was Doctor Park who studied out the general plans and details of our trip. He acted, also, not merely as a companion but as a guide and interpreter. He assisted me also in getting hold of the documents and literature in the different countries we visited which enabled me to correct the impressions I had formed on the spot and to supplement them with the facts and statistics in regard to the conditions we had observed.

In several directions Doctor Park was peculiarly fitted for giving me this sort of assistance. In the first place, during the years he had been at Tuskegee he had become thoroughly acquainted with conditions in the Southern States and, in the course of the journey of observation and study on which he had accompanied me, we had become thoroughly acquainted with each other, so that he understood not only what I desired, but what it was important for me to see in Europe.

In the second place, shortly before I met him, Doctor Park had just returned from four years of study in Europe. He was familiar with much of the ground we intended to cover and at the same time spoke the language which was of greatest use in most of the countries we visited — namely, German.

Two people travelling together can, under any circumstances, see and learn a great deal more than one. When it comes to travelling in a new and unfamiliar country this is emphatically true. For this reason a large part of what I saw and learned about Europe is due directly to the assistance of Doctor Park. Our method of procedure was about as follows: When we reached a city or other part of the country which we wished to study we would usually start out together. I had a notebook in which I jotted down on the spot what I saw that interested me, and Doctor Park, who had had experience as a newspaper reporter, used his eyes and ears. Then in the course of our long stretches of railway travel we compared notes and comments and sifted, as thoroughly as we were able, the facts and observations we had been able to gather. Then as soon as we reached a large city I got hold of a stenographer and dictated, as fully as I was able, the story of what we had seen and learned. In doing this I used Doctor Park's observations, I suppose, quite as much as I did my own. In fact, I do not believe I am able to say now how much of what I have written is based upon my own personal observations and what is based upon those of Doctor Park. Thus, it should be remembered that although this book is written throughout in the first person it contains the observations of two different individuals.

In another direction Doctor Park has contributed to make this book what it is. While I was dictating my own account of our adventures he would usually spend the time hunting through the book stores and libraries for any books or information which would throw any light on the matter in which we were interested. The result was that we returned with nearly a trunkful of books, papers, and letters which we had obtained in different places and from different people we met. With these documents Doctor Park then set to work to straighten out and complete the matter that I had dictated, filling in and adding to what I had written. The chapters which follow are the result.

I set out from America, as I have said, to find the man farthest down. In a period of about six weeks I visited parts of England,

Scotland, Germany, Austria-Hungary, Italy, Sicily, Poland, and Denmark. I spent some time among the poorer classes of London and in several cities in Austria and Italy. I investigated, to a certain extent, the condition of the agricultural populations in Sicily, in Bohemia, Poland, and Denmark. I saw much that was sad and depressing, but I saw much, also, that was hopeful and inspiring. Bad as conditions are in some places, I do not think I visited any place where things are not better now than they were some years ago.

I found also that the connection between Europe and America is much closer and more intimate than I had imagined. I am sure that very few persons in this country realize the extent to which America has touched and influenced the masses of the people in Europe. I think it is safe to say that no single influence which is to-day tending to change and raise the condition of the working people in the agricultural regions of southern Europe is greater than the constant stream of emigration which is pouring out of Europe into America and back again into Europe. It should be remembered that not only do large numbers of these people emigrate to America, but many of these emigrants return and bring with them not only money to buy lands, but new ideas, higher ambitions, and a wider outlook on the world.

Everywhere that I went, even in the most distant parts of the country, where as yet the people have been almost untouched by the influences of modern civilization, I met men who spoke in broken English, but with genuine enthusiasm, of America. Once, when I had made a half-day's journey by rail and wagon into a distant village in Poland, in order to see something of life in a primitive farming village, I was enthusiastically welcomed at the country tavern by the proprietor and two or three other persons, all of whom had lived for some time in America and were able to speak a little English.

At another time, when I visited the sulphur mines in the mountains of central Sicily, I was surprised and delighted to encounter, deep down in one of these mines, several hundred feet below the surface, a man with whom I was able to speak familiarly about the coal mines of West Virginia, where each of us, at different times, had been employed in mine labour.

There seemed to be no part of Europe so distant or so remote that the legend of America had not penetrated to it; and the influence of America, of American ideas, is certainly making itself felt in a very definite way in the lowest strata of European civilization.

The thing that impressed me most, however, was the condition of the labouring women of Europe. I do not know the statistics, but if I am permitted to judge by what I saw I should say that three fourths of the work on the farms, and a considerable part of the heavy work in the cities of Europe, is performed by women. Not only that, but in the low life of great cities, like London, it seems to me that the women suffer more from the evil influences of slum life than the men. In short, if I may put it that way, the man farthest down in Europe is woman. Women have the narrowest outlook, do the hardest work, stand in greatest need of education, and are farthest removed from influences which are everywhere raising the level of life among the masses of the European people.

CHAPTER II

THE MAN AT THE BOTTOM IN LONDON

THE *Carmania*, the ship in which I had sailed, disembarked its passengers late Saturday at Fishguard, off the coast of Wales. The special train which sped us on to London reached the city early Sunday morning, August 28.

As I drove from the railway station in the gray of the early morning my attention was attracted by a strange, shapeless and disreputable figure which slunk out of the shadow of a building and moved slowly and dejectedly down the silent and empty street. In that quarter of the city, and in comparison with the solid respectability and comfort represented by the houses around him, the figure of this man seemed grotesquely wretched. In fact, he struck me as the most lonely object I had ever laid my eyes on. I watched him down the street as far as I could see. He turned neither to the left nor to the right, but moved slowly on, his head bent toward the ground, apparently looking for something he did not hope to find. In the course of my journey across Europe I saw much poverty, but I do not think I saw anything quite so hopeless and wretched.

I had not been long in London before I learned that this man was a type. It is said that there are ten thousand of these homeless and houseless men and women in East London alone. They are, however, not confined to any part of the city. They may be found in the fashionable West End, lounging on the benches of St. James's Park, as well as in the East End, where the masses of the labouring people live. The Salvation Army has erected shelters for them in many of the poorer parts of the city, where, for anything from two to eight cents, they may get a room for the night, and sometimes a piece of bread and a bowl of soup. Thousands of them are not able to compass the small sum necessary to obtain even this minimum of food and comfort. These are the outcasts and the rejected, the human waste of a great city. They represent the man at the bottom in London.

Later, in the course of my wanderings about the city, I met many of these hopeless and broken men. I saw them sitting, on sunshiny days, not only men but women also, crumpled up on benches or stretched out on the grass of the parks. I discovered them on rainy nights crouching in doorways or huddled away in dark corners where an arch or a wall protected them from the cold. I met them in the early morning hours, before the city was awake, creeping along the Strand and digging with their hands in the garbage-boxes; and again, late at night, on the Thames Embankment, where hundreds of them sleep — when the night watchman permits — on the benches or stretched out on the stone pavements. After a time I learned to distinguish the same type under the disguise of those street venders who stand on street corners and sell collar-buttons, matches, and other trifles, stretching out their hands in a pitiful sort of supplication to passers-by to buy their wares.

Whenever I found an opportunity to do so, I talked with some of these outcasts. Gradually, partly from themselves and partly from others, I learned something of their histories. I found that it was usually drink that had been the immediate cause of their downfall. But there were always other and deeper causes. Most of them, it seemed to me, had simply been borne down by the temptations and the fierce competition of life in a great city. There comes a time when trade is dull; men who had been accustomed to spend much money begin to spend less, and there is no work to be had. At these times it is "the less efficient, the less energetic, the less strong, the less young, the less regular, the less temperate, or the less docile" who are crowded out. In this way these men have lost their hold and sunk to the bottom.

I remember meeting one of these men late at night wandering along the Thames Embankment. In the course of my conversation with him I asked him, among other things, if he voted, and, if so, to what political party he belonged.

He looked at me in amazement, and then he said he had never voted in his life. It was his expression rather than his words that impressed me. This expression told me how out of touch he was with the world about him. He had, in fact, as I learned, no family, no home, friends, trade; he belonged to no society; he had, so far as I could learn, no views on life. In the very midst of this great city he was as solitary as a hermit.

A few weeks later, in a little village in Galicia, I asked the same question of a Polish peasant. "Oh, yes," he eagerly replied; "every one votes here now."

Sixty years ago most of the peasants in this village to which I have referred were serfs, and it was not until two years ago that the Government gave them all the right to vote. Nevertheless, at the present time the people in this village are represented by one of their own number in the Imperial Parliament at Vienna. I stopped on my way through the village at the little store kept by this man. I found two young girls tending the store, his daughters, but the representative himself was not at home.

I do not know why I should mention this circumstance here, except that I was impressed by the contrast in the reply of these two men, the one coming from a peasant in Poland and the other from an Englishman in London.

It is generally said that the Negro represents in America the man farthest down. In going to Europe I had in mind to compare the masses of the Negro people of the Southern States with the masses in Europe in something like the same stage of civilization. It would not be difficult to compare the Negro in the South with the Polish peasant, for example, because the masses of the Poles are, like the masses of the Negroes, an agricultural people.

I know no class among the Negroes in America, however, with whom I could compare the man at the bottom in England. Whatever one may say of the Negro in America, he is not, as a rule, a beggar. It is very rarely that any one sees a black hand stretched out for alms. One does see, to be sure, too many idle and loafing Negroes standing on the street corners and around the railway stations in the South, but the Negro is not, as a rule, a degenerate. If he is at the bottom in America, it is not because he has gone backward and sunk down, but because he has never risen.

Another thing in regard to the Negro: although he is frequently poor, he is never without hope and a certain joy in living. No hardship he has yet encountered, either in slavery or in freedom, has robbed the Negro of the desire to live. The race constantly grew and increased in slavery, and it has considerably more than doubled in freedom. There are some people among the members of my race who complain about the hardships which the Negro suffers, but none of them yet, so far as I know, has ever recommended "race suicide" as a solution of the race problem.

I mention this because I found just the contrary to be the case in England. I do not think that anything I saw or heard while I was in England gave me a more poignant impression of the hardships of the labouring man in England than the discovery that one of the most widely read weekly papers in England, under the caption of "The White Slaves of Morality," was making a public campaign in favour of reducing the size of the families among the working classes.

The articles I refer to, which were written by a woman, were a protest, on the one hand, against the clergy because they taught that it would be immoral for women to refuse to have children, and, on the other hand, against the physicians who withheld from these women the knowledge by which they might be able to limit the size of their families. These articles were followed from week to week by letters purporting to come from working men and women telling of the heartbreaking struggle they were making to support their children on the wages they were able to earn.

What made these articles the more startling was the fact that, at the very time when they were proposing to the English labourer what ex-President Roosevelt has defined as "race suicide," thousands of immigrants from the south of Europe were pouring into London every year to take the places left vacant by the recession of the native Anglo-Saxon.

On my previous visit to England I had been struck by what seemed to me the cold and formal character of the English newspapers. It seemed to me that they were wholly lacking in human interest. Upon my last visit my opinion in regard to the London newspapers was considerably altered. A careful study of the daily newspaper, I found, will repay any one who wants to get an insight into social conditions in England.

I had not been in London more than a day or two, for example, when my attention was attracted to the following item in one of the morning papers:

STARVING FAMILY

CORONER'S APPEAL TO THE PUBLIC FOR AID

Telling of a terrible case of starvation in the Stoke Newington Coroner's Court, Dr. Wynn Westcott, the coroner, asked the press to bring a deserving case before the notice of the charitable public.

He said that he had held an inquest upon a three-weeks-old baby which had died of starvation. Its father had had no regular work for three years, and only a little casual work in that time. There was so little money that the mother, Mrs. Attewell, of White Hart Street, Stoke Newington, was half starved too. She had only had a crust of bread to sustain her on the day her child died, although she had done nine and a half hours' washing to assist the home.

The home was perfectly clean, although practically destitute of furniture. It was a most deserving case.

After reading this item I began studying the papers more closely, and I was surprised at the frequency with which items of this kind occurred. I learned that the Local Government Board, which is represented in the English Cabinet by Mr. John Burns, has issued since 1871 an annual report, or return, as it is called, of the cases in which, upon formal investigation by a coroner's jury, it appears that the persons came to their death in London as a result of starvation. I obtained a copy of the return for 1908, in which are included the statistics on starvation not merely for London but for the rest of England and Wales.

The forms issued to coroners were explicit. They provided that the return should include only cases in which the jury found that death was brought about by starvation or privation due to destitution. Cases in which death was caused by cold, starvation, exposure, etc., unconnected with destitution, were not entered in this return. Of the one hundred and twenty-five cases of starvation reported, fifty-two occurred in London. In eleven cases death was described as due to starvation in conjunction with some other cause — that is to say, disease, drink, exposure, or self-neglect. In eighty of the one hundred and twenty-five cases no application was made for poor relief, or application was made only when the deceased had been in a dying condition.

A few days after I had succeeded in getting this report my attention was attracted one morning by the heading of a newspaper article: "How the Poor Die." The article was an account of the finding of the body of an unknown woman in a cellar in the basement of a house not very far from where I was stopping.

"It appears," the article said, "that during the earlier part of the morning a tenant of the building observed a woman sleeping in the cellar, but no particular notice was taken of this because of the fact that strangers frequently utilized the cellar for such purposes. Mr. Oliver, one of the occupants of the building, had occasion to go downstairs, and saw the woman. She was crouched in a corner and her head was lying back. The police were called in and the services of Doctor Barton were requisitioned. . . . Although the cause of death will not be known until a post-mortem examination of the body has been made, death, it is thought, was due to starvation. The woman was about six feet in height, between forty and fifty years of age, and was in a very emaciated condition and clad in very scanty attire."

Not infrequently, when in my public speeches I have made some reference to the condition of the Negro in the South, certain members of my own race in the North have objected because, they said, I did not paint conditions in the South black enough. During my stay in England I had the unusual experience of being criticised in the London newspapers for the same reason, this time by an American white man. At the very moment that this man attacked me because in my public interviews I emphasized the opportunities rather than the wrongs of the Negro in the South I had in my possession the document to which I have referred, which gives the official history of fifty-two persons, one for every week in the year, who had died in the city of London alone for want of food.

I have never denied that the Negro in the South frequently meets with wrong and injustice; but he does not starve. I do not think a single case was ever heard of, in the South, where a Negro died from want of food. In fact, unless because of sickness or some other reason he has been unable to work, it is comparatively rare to find a Negro in an almshouse.

It has not been my purpose in anything I have written to pass judgment upon the people or the conditions that I have found in the countries which I have visited. Criticism is an ungrateful task at best, and one for which I am not well fitted. Neither shall I attempt to offer any suggestions as to how conditions may be improved; in fact, I am convinced from what I learned that the people on the ground understand conditions much better than I possibly could, and in a later chapter I hope to tell something of the great work that has been done in

England and elsewhere to raise the level of life and comfort among the people who are at the bottom in the countries which I visited. What I am anxious to do here is to emphasize some of the advantages which it seems the members of my own race, and particularly those living in the Southern States, have at the present time. It is not difficult to discover the disadvantages under which the Negroes in the South labour. Every traveller who passes through the South sees the conditions existing, and frequently returns to write books about them. There is danger, however, that the opportunities to which I have referred will be overlooked or not fully appreciated by the members of my race until it is too late.

One direction in which the Negro in the South has an advantage is in the matter of labour. One of the most pitiful things I saw in London, Liverpool, and other English cities was the groups of idle men standing about on the street corners, especially around the bar-rooms, because they were not able to get work.

One day, as I was going along one of the main avenues of the city, I noticed an unusually large crowd standing in front of a street organ which was drawn up at the side of the pavement. Pausing to see what there was about this organ that attracted so much attention and interest,

I found that the man who owned this instrument was using it as a method of advertising his poverty.

All over the front of the organ were plastered papers and documents of various kinds. On one side there was a list of advertisements cut from the "Want" columns of the daily newspapers. Attached to this was a statement that these were some of the places that the man had visited the day before in search of work, which he was not able to find. On the other side of the organ were attached six or seven pawn tickets, with the statement that "these are some of the articles which my dear wife pawned to get food for our children." This was followed by a pitiful appeal for help. The pathetic thing about it was that the only persons who stopped to look at these exhibits besides myself were a group of hungry and disreputable-looking men who were evidently in just as great want as the man who ground the organ. I watched those men. After reading the signs they would look inquiringly at the other members of the group and then relapse into the same stolid silence which I had noticed so many times in the forlorn figures that filled the benches of the parks.

It seemed to me that they both pitied and admired the man who had conceived this novel way of advertising his misfortune. I have noticed these same people in other cases where it seemed to me they looked with something like envy upon a beggar who was blind or lame or had some other interesting misfortune which enabled him to win the sympathy of the public.

Of course the persons that I have attempted to describe do not represent the labouring classes. They represent the man at the bottom, who lives by begging or casual labour. It shows, nevertheless, how bitter is the struggle for existence among the labouring class higher up, that the class below, the class which lives in actual poverty, is so large and so much in evidence.

While I was in London I received letters from a great many persons of all classes and conditions. One of these was from a coloured man who was born and raised in the South and was anxious to get back home. I am tempted to quote some passages of his letter here, because they show how conditions impressed a coloured man from the South who got closer to them than I was able to. He had been living, he said, in London for fourteen months without work.

"I have tried to apply for work," he continued. "They said they want Englishmen. It seems to me that all Britain are against the Negro race. Some say, 'Go back to your own country,' knowing if I had the means I would fly to-morrow."

Perhaps I would do better to quote some passages from his letter verbatim. He says:

> I cannot get a passage; to be alone in London without any help or funds, like a pin in a haystack, nothing but sorrow and distress. Hearing Mr. B. T. Washington were in London I appeal to him in the name of God Almighty if he can possibly help me with a ticket to get across, because the lady that was kind enough to give me a shelter is without fund herself; being a Christian woman she gave me food for what she can afford. At night I have to sleep in a house with a widow which has two children which has to make her living by chopping wood, whom some day, does not earn enough to buy a loaf of bread for her children. The winter is coming on and I like to get home to shuck corn or to get to Maryland for a oyster draggin. It is a long time since I had watermelon, pig's feet and corn. Say, Mr. Washington, if you ever knew what a man in a hole is I guess I am in a hole and the cover over. I can see the pork chops and the corn bread and the hot biscuits calling me to come over and get some and many a time I have tried but failed. I can't reach them; the great Atlantic Ocean stop me and I remain
>
> Your Obedient Servant,——

This letter from which I have given a few extracts is but one of many which I received during my stay in London, not only from coloured but from white Americans who had come to England to better their condition or seek their fortune.

These letters served still further to impress me with the fact that the masses of my own people in the South do not fully appreciate the advantages which they have in living in a country where there is a constant demand for labour of all kinds and where even poor people do not starve.

If I were asked what I believed would be the greatest boon that could be conferred upon the English labourer, I should say that it would be for him to have the same opportunities for constant and steady work that the Negro now has in the South. If I were asked what would be the next greatest benefit that could be conferred upon the English labourer, I should say that it would be to have schools in which every class could learn to do some one thing well — to have, in other words, the benefit of the kind of industrial education that we are seeking, in some measure, to give to the Negro at the present time in the Southern States.

CHAPTER III

FROM PETTICOAT LANE TO SKIBO CASTLE

THE first thing about London that impressed me was its size; the second was the wide division between the different elements in the population.

London is not only the largest city in the world; it is also the city in which the segregation of the classes has gone farthest. The West End, for example, is the home of the King and the Court. Here are the Houses of Parliament, Westminster Abbey, the British Museum, most of the historical monuments, the art galleries, and nearly everything that is interesting, refined, and beautiful in the lives of seven millions of people who make up the inhabitants of the city.

If you take a cab at Trafalgar Square, however, and ride eastward down the Strand through Fleet Street, where all the principal newspapers of London are published, past the Bank of England, St. Paul's Cathedral, and the interesting sights and scenes of the older part of the city, you come, all of a sudden, into a very different region, the centre of which is the famous Whitechapel.

The difference between the East End and the West End of London is that East London has no monuments, no banks, no hotels, theatres, art galleries; no history—nothing that is interesting and attractive but its poverty and its problems. Everything else is drab and commonplace.

It is, however, a mistake, as I soon learned, to assume that East London is a slum. It is, in fact, a city by itself, and a very remarkable city, for it has, including what you may call its suburbs, East Ham and West Ham, a population of something over two millions, made up for the most part of hard-working, thrifty labouring people. It has its dark places, also, but I visited several parts of London during my stay in the city which were considerably worse in every respect than anything I saw in the East End.

Nevertheless, it is said that more than one hundred thousand of the people in this part of the city, in spite of all the efforts that have been made to help them, are living on the verge of starvation. So poor and so helpless are these people that it was, at one time, seriously proposed to separate them from the rest of the population and set them off in a city by themselves, where they could live and work entirely under the direction of the state. It was proposed to put this hundred thousand of the very poor under the direction and care of the state because they were not able to take care of themselves, and because it was declared that all the service which they rendered the community could be performed by the remaining portion of the population in their leisure moments, so that they were, in fact, not a help but a hindrance to the life of the city as a whole.

I got my first view of one of the characteristic sights of the East End life at Middlesex Street, or Petticoat Lane, as it was formerly called. Petticoat Lane is in the centre of the Jewish quarter, and on Sunday morning there is a famous market in this street. On both sides of the thoroughfare, running northward from Whitechapel Road until they lose themselves in some of the side streets, one sees a double line of pushcarts, upon which every imaginable sort of ware, from wedding rings to eels in jelly, is exposed for sale. On both sides of these carts and in the middle of the street a motley throng of bargain-hunters are pushing their way through the crowds, stopping to look over the curious wares in the carts or to listen to the shrill cries of some hawker selling painkiller or some other sort of magic cure-all.

Nearly all of the merchants are Jews, but the majority of their customers belong to the tribes of the Gentiles. Among others I noticed a class of professional customers. They were evidently artisans of some sort or other who had come to pick out from the goods exposed for sale a plane or a saw or some other sort of second-hand tool; there were others searching for useful bits of old iron, bolts, brass, springs, keys, and other things of that sort which they would be able to turn to some use in their trades.

I spent an hour or more wandering through this street and the neighbouring lane into which this petty pushcart traffic had overflowed. Second-hand clothing, second-hand household articles, the waste meats of the Saturday market, all kinds of wornout and cast-off articles which had been fished out of the junk heaps of the city or thrust out of the regular channels of trade, find here a ready market.

I think that the thing which impressed me most was not the poverty, which was evident enough, but the sombre tone of the crowd and the whole proceeding. It was not a happy crowd; there were no bright colours, and very little laughter. It was an ill-dressed crowd, made up of people who had long been accustomed to live, as it were, at second-hand and in close relations with the pawnbroker.

In the Southern States it would be hard to find a coloured man who did not make some change in his appearance on Sunday. The Negro labourer is never so poor that he forgets to put on a clean collar or a bright necktie or something out of the ordinary out of respect for the Sabbath. In the midst of this busy, pushing throng it was hard for me to remember that I was in England and that it was Sunday. Somehow or other I had got a very different notion of the English Sabbath.

Petticoat Lane is in the midst of the "sweating" district, where most of the cheap clothing in London is made. Through windows and open doors I could see the pale faces of the garment-makers bent over their work. There is much furniture made in this region, also, I understand. Looking down into some of the cellars as I passed, I saw men working at the lathes. Down at the end of the street was a bar-room, which was doing a rushing business. The law in London is, as I understand, that travellers may be served at a public bar on Sunday, but not others. To be a traveller, a bona-fide traveller, you must have come from a distance of at least three miles. There were a great many travellers in Petticoat Lane on the Sunday morning that I was there.

This same morning I visited Bethnal Green,

another and a quite different quarter of the East End. There are a number of these different quarters of the East End, like Stepney, Poplar, St. George's in the East, and so forth. Each of these has its peculiar type of population and its own peculiar conditions. Whitechapel is Jewish; St. George's in the East is Jewish at one end and Irish at the other, but Bethnal Green is English. For nearly half a mile along Bethnal Green Road I found another Sunday market in full swing, and it was, if anything, louder and more picturesque than the one in Petticoat Lane

It was about eleven o'clock in the morning; the housewives of Bethnal Green were out on the street hunting bargains in meat and vegetables for the Sunday dinner. One of the most interesting groups I passed was crowded about a pushcart where three sturdy old women, shouting at the top of their lungs, were reeling off bolt after bolt of cheap cotton cloth to a crowd of women gathered about their cart.

At another point a man was "knocking down" at auction cheap cuts of frozen beef from Australia at prices ranging from 4 to 8 cents a pound. Another was selling fish, another crockery, and a third tinware, and so through the whole list of household staples.

The market on Bethnal Green Road extends

across a street called Brick Lane and branches off again from that into other and narrower streets. In one of these there is a market exclusively for birds, and another for various sorts of fancy articles not of the first necessity. The interesting thing about all this traffic was that, although no one seemed to exercise any sort of control over it, somehow the different classes of trade had managed to organize themselves so that all the wares of one particular sort were displayed in one place and all the wares of another sort in another, everything in regular and systematic order. The streets were so busy and crowded that I wondered if there were any people left in that part of the town to attend the churches.

One of the marvels of London is the number of handsome and stately churches. One meets these beautiful edifices everywhere, not merely in the West End, where there is wealth sufficient to build and support them, but in the crowded streets of the business part of the city, where there are no longer any people to attend them. Even in the grimiest precincts of the East End, where all is dirt and squalor, one is likely to come unexpectedly upon one of these beautiful old churches, with its quiet churchyard and little space of green, recalling the time when the region, which is now crowded with endless rows of squalid city dwellings, was, perhaps, dotted with pleasant country villages. These churches are beautiful, but as far as I could see they were, for the most part, silent and empty. The masses of the people enjoy the green spaces outside, but do not as a rule, I fear, attend the services on the inside. They are too busy.

It is not because the churches are not making an effort to reach the people that the masses do not go to them. One has only to read the notices posted outside of any of the church buildings in regard to night schools, lectures, men's clubs and women's clubs, and many other organizations of various sorts, to know that there is much earnestness and effort on the part of the churches to reach down and help the people. The trouble seems to be that the people are not at the same time reaching up to the church. It is one of the results of the distance between the classes that rule and the classes that work. It is too far from Whitechapel to St. James's Park. What Mr. Kipling says, in another connection, seems to be true of London:

> "The East is East, and the West is West,
> And never these twain shall meet."

While on one side of Bethnal Green Road the hucksters were shouting and the crowd was busy dickering and chaffering for food and clothes, I noticed on the other side of the street a wayside preacher. I went over and listened to what he had to say, and then I noted the effect of his words upon his hearers. He had gathered about him perhaps a dozen persons, most of them, however, seeming to be his own adherents who had come out to the meeting merely to give him the benefit of their moral support. The great mass of the people who passed up and down the street did not pay the slightest attention to him. There was no doubt about the earnestness and sincerity of the man, but as I listened to what he had to say I could find in his words nothing that seemed to me to touch in any direct or definite way the lives of the people about him. In fact, I doubted whether the majority of them could really understand what he was talking about.

Somewhat later, in another part of the city, I had an opportunity to listen to another of these street preachers. In this case he was a young man, apparently fresh from college, and he was making a very genuine effort, as it seemed to me, to reach and influence in a practical way the people whom the lights of the torches and the music had attracted to the meeting. I observed that the people listened respectfully to what he had to say, and I have no doubt they were impressed, as I was, with his evident desire to help them. It was only too evident, however, that he was speaking another language than theirs; that, in fact, one might almost say he belonged to a different race of people. The gulf between them was too great.

After listening to this man I thought I could understand in a way that I had not understood before the great success which the Salvation Army at one time had among the masses of the people of East London. In its early days, at least, the Salvation Army was of the people; it picked its preachers from the streets; it appealed to the masses it was seeking to help for its support; in fact, it set the slums to work to save itself. The Salvation Army is not so popular in East London, I understand, as it used to be. One trouble with the Salvation Army, as with much of the effort that has been made to help the people of East London, is that the Salvation Army seeks to reach only those who are already down; it does not attempt to deal with the larger and deeper problem of saving those who have not yet fallen.

The problem of the man farthest down, whether he lives in America or in Europe, and whether he be black or white, is, in my opinion, not one of conversion merely, but of education as well. It is necessary, in other words, to inspire the masses in the lower strata of life with a disposition to live a sober, honest, and useful life, but it is necessary also to give them an opportunity and a preparation to live such a life after they have gained the disposition to do so.

The Negro in America, whatever his drawbacks in other directions, is not indifferent to religious influences. The Negro is not only naturally religious, but the religion he enjoys in America is his own in a sense that is not true, it seems to me, of much of the religious life and work among the people of East London.

The most powerful and influential organization among the Negroes in America to-day is the Negro church, and the Negroes support their own churches. They not only support the churches and the ministers, but they support also a large number of schools and colleges in which their children, and especially those who desire to be ministers, may get their education. These little theological seminaries are frequently poorly equipped and lacking in almost everything but good intentions; they are generally, however, as good as the people are able to make them. The Negro ministers in the backwoods districts of the South are frequently rude and ignorant and sometimes immoral, but they have this advantage, that they spring from and represent the people, and the religion which they preach is a religion which has grown up in response to the actual needs and feelings of the masses of the Negro people. In other words, the religion of the Negro in America is on a sound basis, because the Negro church has never got out of touch with the masses of the Negro people.

After leaving East London on my first Sunday in England, I drove about fifteen miles through the famous Epping Forest to Waltham Abbey, the country seat of Sir T. Fowell Buxton, a grandson of Sir T. Fowell Buxton, who succeeded Wilberforce as leader of the anti-slavery party in parliament, and who framed the bill that finally resulted in the emancipation of the slaves in the English West Indies.

There is certainly no more beautiful country to look upon than rural England. Flowering vines cover the humble cottage of the farm labourer as well as the luxurious country seats of the landowners, and lend a charm to everything the eye rests upon. I was all the more impressed with the blooming freshness of the country because I had come out of the stifling life of the crowded city. I learned, however, that rural England has for a long time past been steadily losing its population. From 1891 to 1900 it is said that the number of farm labourers in England decreased 20 per cent., and it has been estimated that the rural population of England and Wales has diminished something like 30 or 40 per cent. during the past century, at a time when the urban population has multiplied itself many times over.

There are, of course, many reasons for this decrease in the agricultural population. One is, that at the present time not more than 15 per cent. of the land in England is farmed by the people who own it. Thirty-eight thousand landowners hold four fifths of all the agricultural land in England.

A few days after my visit to Sir Fowell Buxton at Waltham Abbey I went into northern Scotland to visit Mr. Andrew Carnegie at Skibo Castle. While I was there I had opportunity to get some sort of acquaintance with farming conditions in that part of the world.

In Scotland the opportunities for the small farmer to obtain land are even less than they are in England. Some years ago, it is said, twenty-four persons in Scotland owned estates of more than 100,000 acres. The Duke of Sutherland owns a tract stretching, I was told, clear across Scotland from coast to coast.

In no country in the world is so small a portion

of the population engaged in agriculture as is true in England. For instance, 68 per cent. of the population of Hungary, 59 per cent. of the population of Italy, 48 per cent. of the population of Denmark, 37.5 per cent. of the population of the United States are engaged in agriculture. In England and in Wales in 1901 only 8 per cent. were engaged in agriculture.

Not only is it true that a larger proportion of the population of England than of other countries has removed from the country to the city, but in England, also, the distance between the man in the city and the man on the soil is greater than elsewhere. For example, in Italy the distinction between the agricultural labourer and the labourer in the city may be said hardly to exist; the man who, at one part of the year, finds work in the city, is very likely to be found at work at some other time of the year in the country.

In Germany also I noticed that a great many of the manufacturing plants were located in the country, where the factory labourer had an opportunity to cultivate a small patch of land. To the extent that he has been able to raise his own food, the factory hand in Germany has made himself independent of the manufacturers and the market.

In Hungary I was told that in harvest time

the public works were deserted and many of the factories were compelled to shut down, because every one went away to the country to work in the fields.

Now, the thing that interested me in observing the vast dislocation of the rural population of England, represented by this vast labouring community of East London, was the extent to which the English labourer, in moving from the country to the city, had lost his natural independence.

In losing his hold upon the soil the English labourer has made himself peculiarly dependent upon the organization of the society about him. He can, for instance, neither build his own home nor raise his own food. In the city he must pay a much larger rent than it would be necessary for him to pay in the country. He must work more steadily in order to live, and he has to depend upon some one else to give him the opportunity to work. In this respect, although the English labourer is probably better paid and better fed than any other labourer in Europe, he is less protected from the effects of competition. He is more likely to suffer from the lack of opportunity to work.

In the same way England as a whole is more dependent upon foreign countries for the sale of its manufactured products and the purchase of its food supply than is any other country in Europe. Thus it will be found that most of the great questions which are now agitating England, like most of the great questions which are agitating other countries in Europe, are more or less directly concerned with the matter of agriculture and the condition of the labourer on the land.

I said in the preceding chapter that one advantage that the Negro in the South had was the opportunity to work for the asking. The Negro in the South has opportunities in another direction that no other man in his position has, outside of America: he has the opportunity to get land. No one who has not visited Europe can understand what the opportunity to get land means to a race that has so recently gained its freedom.

No one who has not seen something of the hardships of the average workingman in a great city like London can understand the privilege that we in the Southern States have in living in the country districts, where there is independence and a living for every man, and where we have the opportunity to fix ourselves forever on the soil.

CHAPTER IV

FIRST IMPRESSION OF LIFE AND LABOUR ON THE CONTINENT

ONE clear, cold morning, about the first of September, I took a train at Bonar Bridge, in the north of Scotland, southward bound. There was a cold wind blowing, and Bonar Bridge is about the latitude, as I learned from looking at my atlas, of northern Labrador — farther north, in fact, than I had ever in my lifetime dreamed of going.

I spent the next four or five hours looking out of a car window across the bleak, brown moors, studying the flocks of sheep and the little thatch-roofed cottages clinging to the lonesome hill-sides.

Three days later I was in the beautiful mountain region below Dresden, on my way to Prague, the capital of Bohemia. In many ways conditions in the farming regions of Bohemia are quite as primitive as they are among the crofters of northern Scotland. There are, for example, a larger number of small farmers owning their own land in Bohemia than there are in Scotland, but the Scottish crofter, although he remains a tenant on a large estate, has, at the present time, a more secure position on the soil than the man who rents his land in Bohemia. In other respects the Scotch Highlanders, whose country I had just left, and the Czechs, whose country I was just entering, are, I should say, about as different as one could well imagine.

Among other things I noticed that the farming people in this part of the world do not live apart, scattered about in the open country, as they do in Scotland, and as is the case everywhere in America. On the contrary, the Bohemian farmers live huddled together in little villages, in the centre of the surrounding fields, from which they go out to their work in the morning and to which they return in the evening.

These different manners of settling on the soil are one of the marks by which the people in the north of Europe are distinguished from those in the south. The northern people settle in widely scattered homesteads, while the southern people invariably herd together in little villages, and each individual becomes, to a great extent, dependent upon the community and loses himself in the life about him. This accounts, in large measure, for the difference in character of the northern and southern people. In the north the people are more independent; in the south they are more social. The northern people have more initiative; they are natural pioneers. The southern people are more docile, and get on better under the restraints and restrictions of city life. It is said, also, that this explains why it is that the people who are now coming to America from the south of Europe, although most of them come from the land, do not go out into the country districts in America, but prefer to live in the cities, or, as seems to be the case with the Italians, colonize the suburbs of the great cities.

Another thing that interested me was the sight of women working on the land. I had not gone far on my way south from Berlin before my attention was attracted by the number of women in the fields. As I proceeded southward, the number of these women labourers steadily increased until they equalled and even outnumbered the men. One of these I had an opportunity to see close at hand; she was coarsely clad, barefoot, and carried a rake over her shoulder. I had seen pictures of something like that before, but never the real thing.

Outside of Italy I have rarely seen men going barefoot either in the country or in the city, but in southern Europe it seems to be the custom among the working women, and I took it as an indication of the lower position which women occupy among the people of southern Europe as compared with the position that they occupy in America. I saw many barefoot women later in the course of my journey, both in the field and elsewhere. I confess, however, I was surprised to meet in Vienna, Austria, as I did on several occasions while I was there, women walking barefoot on the pavements in one of the most fashionable streets of the city. One day, in speaking to a native Austrian, I expressed my surprise at what I had seen.

"Oh, well," he replied, "they are Slovaks."

How vividly this reminded me of a parallel remark with which I was familiar, "Oh, well, they are Negroes!"

It was the tone of this reply that caught my attention. It emphasized what I soon discovered to be another distinguishing feature of life in southern Europe. Everywhere I went in Austria and Hungary I found the people divided according to the race to which they belonged. There was one race at the top, another at the bottom, and then there were perhaps two or three other races which occupied positions relatively higher or lower in between. In most cases it was some section of the Slavic race, of which there are some five or six different branches in the Austrian Empire, which was at the bottom.

Several times, in my efforts to find out something about these so-called "inferior people," I made inquires about them among their more successful neighbours. In almost every case, no matter what race it happened to be to which I referred, I received the same answer. I was told that they were lazy and would not work; that they had no initiative; that they were immoral and not fitted to govern themselves. At the same time, I found them doing nearly all the really hard, disagreeable, and ill-paid labour that was being done. Usually I found, also, that with fewer opportunities than the people around them, they were making progress.

I was frequently surprised at the bitterness between the races. I have heard people talk more violently, but I do not think I have heard any one say anything worse in regard to the Negro than some of the statements that are made by members of one race in Austria in regard to members of some other.

I reached the city of Prague late at night, and awoke next morning in a world that was utterly new to me. It was not that Prague looked so different from other European cities I had seen, but the language sounded more strange than anything else I had ever heard. I do not pretend to understand German, yet it seemed to me that there was something familiar and friendly about that language as compared with Czech.

The Czechs are but one of the seventeen races of Austria-Hungary, each one of which, with the exception of the Jews, who are an exception to everything, is seeking to preserve its own language, and, if possible, compel all its neighbours to learn it. Preserving its own language is not difficult in the country districts, where each race lives apart in its own village and maintains its own peculiar customs and traditions. It is more difficult in the large cities like Vienna and Budapest, where the different nationalities come into intimate contact with each other and with the larger European world.

There is a region in northeastern Hungary where in the course of a day's ride one may pass through, one after another, villages inhabited by as many as five different races — Ruthenians, Jews, Roumanians, Hungarians, and Germans. A racial map of the Dual Empire shows districts in which one race predominates, but these same districts will very likely be dotted with villages in which the fragments of other races still survive, some of them, like the Turks, so few in number that they are not separately counted as part of the population. Under these circumstances travel in this part of the world is made interesting but not easy.

Fortunately, I had letters of introduction to Dr. Albert W. Clarke, head of the Austrian branch of the American Board of Missions at Prague, and he introduced me to some of his native assistants who spoke English, and kindly assisted me in finding what I most desired to see of the city and the people. Through him I had an opportunity to get inside of some of the tenements in which European people live, and to see some of the working people in their homes. I did not have an opportunity to explore the parts of the city in which the very poor people live; in fact, I was told that there was nothing in Prague that corresponded to the slums of our English and American cities. There is much poverty, but it is poverty of a self-respecting sort — not of those who have been defeated and gone under, but of those who have never got up.

I found the average Bohemian workman living in two rooms and working for wages considerably less than the same kind of labour would have brought in England, and very much less than the same kind of labour would have brought in America. There is, however, very little use in comparing the wages that men earn unless you are able to compare all the surrounding conditions.

During my stay in Prague I had an opportunity to see something close at hand of the life of the farming population. Under the guidance of one of Doctor Clarke's assistants I drove out one day to a little village where there were a number of people who had come under the influence of the American Mission in Prague, and where I was assured I should find a welcome.

It was not, perhaps, the best place to get an idea of what is most characteristic in Bohemian country life. I had hoped to see something of the local customs of the country people, but, though it was a holiday when I made my visit, I did not see a single peasant costume.

There are still many places in Bohemia, I understand, where the people take pride in wearing the national costumes, and there are still many parts of the Austrian Empire where relics of the older civilization linger. Indeed, I heard of places where, it is said, the peasants are still paying the old feudal dues; in other places the old unfree condition of the peasants is still continued in the form of peonage, as it may still be sometimes found in our Southern States. In this case the peasants have got themselves into debt for land. They are not allowed to work off this debt, and this serves as a pretence for keeping them bound to the soil. But education and the growth of manufacturing industries have banished the traces of the older civilization from the greater part of Bohemia.

In the village which I visited, as in most of the farming villages in this part of the world, the houses of the farmers stand in a row quite close together on either side of the street. In the rear are the quarters of the servants, the storehouses and the stables, the pig-stys and the cow-stalls, all closely connected, so that it was often a little uncertain to me where the quarters for the servants left off and those for the animals began. In fact, in some places no very definite distinction was made.

One of the most interesting places that I visited during my stay in this village was a dairy farm which was conducted by a Jew. He was evidently one of those of the lower or middle class — a type one hears much of in Europe — who, with very little knowledge or skill in the actual work of agriculture, have succeeded by their superior business skill in getting possession of the land and reducing the peasant to a position not much better than that of a serf. This man not only kept a dairy farm but he operated two or three brickyards besides, and had other extensive business interests in the village. Although he was a man of wealth and intelligence, he had his dwelling in the midst of a compound around which were grouped houses for his labourers, cow-stalls, a wheelwright and blacksmith shop, places for pigs, chickens, and dogs, the whole in a condition of indescribable disorder and filth.

The greater part of the work on the farm seemed to be done by women, most of whom were barefooted or wore wooden shoes. I do not think I have seen any one wearing wooden shoes before since the days of slavery. They had remained in my mind as the symbol of poverty and degradation; but they are worn everywhere in country districts in Europe. In fact, I remember in one instance, when I visited an agricultural school, finding one of the teachers working in the garden wearing wooden shoes. The people who worked on this farm all lived, as far as I could see, in one little ill-smelling and filthy room. There was no sign in the homes which I visited of those household industries for which Hungarian peasants are noted, and which should help to brighten and make comfortable the simplest home.

I believe there are few plantations in our Southern States where, even in the small one-room cabins, one would not find the coloured people living in more real comfort and more cleanliness than was the case here. Even in the poorest Negro cabins in the South I have found evidences that the floor was sometimes scrubbed, and usually there was a white counterpane on the bed, or some evidence of an effort to be tidy.

Prague is one of the most ancient cities in Europe. A thing that impressed me with the antiquity of the town was the fact that before the beginning of the Christian era there was a Jewish quarter in this city. Prague is also one of the most modern cities in Europe. Within a comparatively few years large manufacturing plants have multiplied throughout the country. Bohemia makes, among other things, fezzes, and sells them to Turkey; raises beans, and ships them to Boston.

What is most interesting is the fact that this progress has been, to a very large extent, made possible through the education of the masses of the people. The Bohemians are to-day among the best educated people in Europe. For example, among the immigrants who come from Europe to America, 24.2 per cent. over fourteen years of age are unable to read and write. In the case of the German immigrant not more than 5.8 per cent. are unable to read or write. In the case of the Bohemians the percentage of illiteracy is only 3 per cent. There is only one class of immigrants among whom the percentage of illiteracy is lower. Among the Danish immigrants it is 0.8 per cent.

There is no part of the Austrian Empire where education is more generally diffused or where the schools are so well adapted to the actual needs of the people. In addition to the ordinary primary schools and the gymnasia (which correspond to our high schools) there are several higher institutes of technology which prepare students for industry and commerce. Besides these state schools there are a large number of industrial schools that are maintained by cities or by private associations. Some of these are located in the small towns and are closely connected with the local industries. Sometimes they are organized by the members of the different trades and crafts as a supplement to the apprentice system. For example, in a town where the inhabitants are engaged in the clay industry, there will be found schools which give practical courses in the making of vases and crockery. In some of the larger towns commercial and industrial instruction is given in "continuation schools." In these schools girls who have learned needlework in the elementary schools will be taught sewing, dressmaking, and embroidery and lace work. There are also courses in which boys are prepared to work in the sugar-making, brewing, watchmaking, and other manufacturing industries.

In the two institutes of technology in Prague, one of which is for Bohemians and the other for Germans, courses are given which prepare students to be engineers, chemists, machinists, architects, bookkeepers, etc. In connection with these courses there are also special departments where students are prepared to be master workmen in such trades as bricklaying, carpentry, cabinet-making, and stone masonry.

There is much in the life and history of the Bohemian people that is especially interesting to a race or a people like the Negro, that is itself struggling up to a higher and freer level of life and civilization.

Up to 1848 the masses of the Bohemian people were held in a condition of serfdom. Until 1867 they were not allowed to emigrate from the country, and were thus held, as are the Russian peasants to-day, to a certain degree, prisoners in their own country. Most of the land was in the hands of the nobility, who were the descendants of foreigners who came into the country when it was conquered, a century or more before. Even to-day five families own 8 per cent. of all the land in the kingdom, and one tenth of the population owns 36 per cent. of the area of the country. The Emperor and the Catholic Church are also large landowners.

One of the effects of this new education and the new life that has come with it has been to make the land held in larger estates less productive than that which is divided into smaller holdings and cultivated by the men who own it.

It was interesting to me to learn that the Bohemians in their own country suffer from some of the same disadvantages as the Negro in the South. For example, the educational fund is divided between the races — the Germans and the Czechs — just as the money for education is divided in the South between the whites and the blacks, but, as is true in the South, it is not divided equally between the races.

For example, in the city of Prague there is one gymnasium (school) to every 62,000 Czech inhabitants, while the Germans have one gymnasium for every 6,700 inhabitants. Of what are called the real-schools, in which the education is more practical than that of the gymnasia, there is one for every 62,000 Bohemian inhabitants, while the Germans have one for every 10,000 inhabitants. For a number of years past, although the Bohemians represent 70 per cent. of the population, they have received only a little more than one half of the money appropriated for secondary education, both in the gymnasia and the real-schools. The salaries of teachers in the elementary schools range from $155 to $400 per year; in the schools in which the German language is taught, however, teachers receive an added bonus for their services.

To overcome their disadvantages in this direction the Czechs have supplemented the work of the public schools by industrial schools, which are maintained by the contributions of the people in the same way that the Negroes in many parts of the South have supplemented the work of the public schools in order to increase the terms of the school year and to introduce industrial training of various sorts.

More than this, the masses of the people in Bohemia are limited and restricted in all their movements in ways of which no one in America who has not passed through the hands of the immigration inspectors at Ellis Island has any comprehension. For example, the people of Austria have had for a number of years freedom of conscience, and, in theory at least, every one is allowed to worship according to his own inclination and convictions. Nevertheless, it seems to be as much a crime in Austria to say anything that could be construed as disrespectful to the Catholic Church as it would be to insult the name of the Emperor. I heard a story of a woman who ran a small store in which she was using copies of a Catholic newspaper with which to wrap up articles which she had sold to her customers. She was warned by the police that if she continued to use this paper for that purpose she would be liable to arrest. Afterward packages were found in her store which were wrapped in this paper; she was arrested and the case was carried to the highest court, but the sentence which had been imposed upon her stood, and she was compelled to serve a term in prison as punishment for this offence. It was only with the greatest difficulty, Doctor Clarke informed me, that he succeeded in getting permission from the Government to establish a branch of the Young Men's Christian Association in Prague.

I myself had some experience of these restrictions when I spoke before an audience composed largely of young Bohemian workmen in the rooms of this same Young Men's Christian Association. In order that I might be permitted to make this address it was necessary to announce the subject to the officers of the Government three days before I arrived in the city, and at the meeting I had the unusual experience of having my words taken down by a Government official who was present to see that I did not say anything that would disturb the public peace.

Not knowing what else I could say to this audience that would interest them, I told briefly the story of my own life and of the work that we are trying to do for our students at Tuskegee. I told them also that the institution (Hampton Institute) in which I had gained my education had been established by the same American Board of Missions which was responsible for the existence of the Young Men's Christian Association in Bohemia.

In order that my hearers might understand what I said, it was necessary for the secretary of the association, a Bohemian who spoke very good English, to translate my words sentence by sentence. In spite of these difficulties I do not think I ever spoke to an audience of labouring people who were more intelligent or more appreciative. It was a great pleasure and satisfaction to me to be able to speak to this audience. I felt, as I think they did, that we had something in common which others, perhaps, could not entirely understand, because each of us belonged to a race which, however different in other respects, was the same in this: that it was struggling upward.

CHAPTER V

POLITICS AND RACES

IN PRAGUE, the capital of Bohemia, I came in contact for the first time with the advance guard, if I may use the expression, of a new race, the Slavs. I say a new race, because although the Slavic peoples claim an antiquity as great as that of any other race in Europe, the masses of the race seem just now emerging from a condition of life more primitive than that of almost any other people in Europe.

Many little things, not only what I saw with my own eyes, but what I heard from others, gave me the impression, as I travelled southward, that I was entering into a country where the masses of the people lived a simpler and more primitive existence than any I had seen elsewhere in Europe. I remember, for one thing, that I was one day startled to see, in the neighbourhood of the mining regions of Bohemia, a half-dozen women engaged in loading a coal barge — shovelling the coal into wheelbarrows and wheeling them along a narrow plank from the coal wharf to the ship alongside.

I was impressed, again, by the fact that several of the peoples of the Austrian Empire — the Moravians and Ruthenians are an illustration — still preserve their old tribal names. Certain other of these peoples still keep not only the tribal names, but many of the old tribal customs. Among most of the Slavic peoples, for example, custom still gives to the marriage ceremony the character of barter and sale. In fact, I found that in one of the large provincial towns in eastern Hungary the old "matrimonial fairs" are still kept up. On a certain day in each year hundreds of marriageable young women are brought down to this fair by their parents, where they may be seen seated on their trunks and surrounded by the cattle they expect to have for a dowry. Naturally young men come from all the surrounding country to attend this fair, and usually a lawyer sits out under a tree nearby prepared to draw up the marriage contract. In some cases as many as forty marriages are arranged in this way in a single day.

Divided into petty kingdoms or provinces, each speaking a separate language, living for the most part in the country districts, and held in some sort of political and economic subjection, sometimes by the descendants of foreign conquerors, and sometimes, as in the case of the Poles, by the nobility of their own race, the masses of the Slavic peoples in southern Europe have lived for centuries out of touch with the life of cities, and to a large extent out of touch with the world. Compared, therefore, with the peoples of western Europe, who are living in the centres of modern life and progress, the Slavic peoples are just now on the horizon.

In the course of my travels through Austria and Hungary I think I met, at one time or another, representatives of nearly every branch of the Slavic race in the empire. In Bohemia I became acquainted, as I have said, with the most progressive portion of the race, the Czechs. In Galicia I saw something of the life of the Polish people, both in the towns and in the country districts. Again, in Budapest and Vienna I learned something of the condition of the labouring and peasant classes, among whom the Slavic peoples are usually in the majority. At Fiume, the port of Hungary, from which forty thousand emigrants sail every year for the United States, I met and talked with Dalmatians, Croatians, Slovenes, Ruthenians, and Serbs — representatives, in fact, of almost every race in Hungary. In the plains of central Hungary, and again in eastern Prussia, I saw gangs of wandering labourers, made up of men and women who come to this part of the country from the Slavic countries farther south and east to take part in the harvest on the great estates.

During this time I became acquainted to some extent also with representatives of almost every type of civilization, high and low, among the peoples of southern Europe, from the Dalmatian herdsmen, who lead a rude and semi-barbarous existence on the high, barren mountains along the coast of the Adriatic, to the thrifty and energetic artisans of Bohemia and the talented Polish nobility, who are said to be among the most intellectual people in Europe.

I did not, among these classes I have mentioned, see the most primitive people of the Slavic race, nor the type of the man of that race farthest down. In fact, I have heard that in the mountain regions of southern Galicia there are people who make their homes in holes in the ground or herd together in little huts built of mud. I did not see, either, as I should like to have seen, the life of those Slavic people in southwestern Hungary who still hold their lands in common and live together in patriarchal communities, several families beneath one roof, under the rule of a "house father" and a "house mother," who are elected annually to govern the community.

What little I did see of the life of the different branches of the race gave me the impression, however, of a people of great possibilities, who, coming late into the possession of modern ideas and modern methods, were everywhere advancing, in some places rapidly and in others more slowly, but always making progress.

One thing that has hindered the advancement of the Slavs has been the difference in the languages spoken by the different branches of the race. So great an obstacle is this difference of language that some years ago, when a congress of all the Slavic peoples was held at Prague, the representatives of the different branches of the race, having no common tongue, were compelled to speak to each other in the one language that they all professed to hate — namely, German.

Another thing that has hindered the progress of the Slavs has been the inherited jealousies and the memories they cherish of ancient injuries they have inflicted on one another in times past. In general, it seems to be true of the races of Austria-Hungary that each race or branch of the race hates and despises every other, and this hatred is the more bitter the more closely they are associated. For example, there is a long-standing feud between the

Polish peasants and the Polish nobility. This division is so great that the Polish peasants have frequently sided against the Polish nobility in the contests of the latter with the central government of Austria. However, this sentiment of caste which separates the two classes of the Polish people is nothing compared with the contempt with which every Pole, whether he be peasant or noble, is said to feel for every Ruthenian, a people with whom the Pole is very closely related by blood, and with whom he has long been in close political association. On the other hand, the Ruthenian in Galicia looks upon the Pole just as the Czech in Bohemia looks upon his German neighbour: as his bitterest enemy. The two peoples refuse to intermingle socially; they rarely intermarry; in many cases they maintain separate schools, and are represented separately in the Imperial Parliament, each race electing its own representatives. But all are united in hating and despising the Jew, who, although he claims for himself no separate part of the empire, and has no language to distinguish himself from the other races about him, still clings as tenaciously as any other portion of the population to his own racial traditions and customs.

The Slavic peoples, otherwise divided by language and tradition, are also divided by religion. People speaking the same language, and sharing in other respects the same traditions, are frequently just as widely separated by differences of religion as they could be by differences of race. For example, among the southern Slavs the majority of the Slovenes and the Croatians are Roman Catholics, others are Protestants. On the other hand, the majority of the Serbs, their close neighbours, are members of the Greek Orthodox Church, while others are Mohammedans. So wide is the division between the Roman Catholic and the Orthodox Slavs that in some cases members of the Eastern and Western branches of the Church belonging to the same nationality wear a different costume in order to emphasize the differences of religion that might otherwise be forgotten or overlooked.

In Galicia there are not only the Roman and Orthodox branches of the Church, but there are also three or four other minor branches. One of these, the Uniates, which is a compromise between the two and is intended to be a sort of link between the Eastern and Western churches, is now, it is said, just as distinct from both as any of the other branches of the Church. In this region, which has been the battleground of all the religions in Europe, religious distinctions play a much more important rôle than they do elsewhere, because the masses of the people have not yet forgotten the bitterness and the harshness of the early struggles of the sects. The result is that religious differences seem to have intensified rather than to have softened the racial animosities.

In spite of the divisions and rivalries which exist, there seems to be growing up, under the influence of the struggle against the other and dominant races in the Empire, and as a result of the political agitations to which this struggle has given rise, a sense of common purpose and interest in the different branches of the Slavic race; a sort of racial consciousness, as it is sometimes called, which seems to be one of the conditions without which a race that is down is not able to get the ambition and the courage to rise.

It is the presence of this great Slav race in western Europe, groping its way forward under the conditions and difficulties which I have described, that constitutes, as well as I am able to define it, the race problem of southern Europe.

In many respects the situation of the Slavs in the Austro-Hungarian Empire and in southern Europe generally is more like that of the Negroes in the Southern States than is true of any other class or race in Europe. For one thing, the vast majority of that race are, like the Negroes, an agricultural people. For centuries they have lived and worked on the soil, where they have been the servants of the great landowners, looked down upon by the educated and higher classes as "an inferior race." Although they were not distinguished from the dominant classes, as the Negro was, by the colour of their skin, they were distinguished by the language they spoke, and this difference in language seems to have been, as far as mutual understanding and sympathy are concerned, a greater bar than the fact of colour has been in the case of the white man and the black man in the South.

Up to a comparatively few years ago an educated Slav did not ordinarily speak, at least in public, the language of the masses of the people. Doctor Clarke, the head of the Austrian Mission of the American Board in Prague, told me that as recently as thirty years ago an educated Czech did not care to speak his own language on the streets of Prague. At that time the German language was still the language of the educated classes, and all the learning of Europe was, to a very large extent, a closed book to the people who did not speak and read that language.

To-day conditions have so changed, Doctor

Clarke tells me, that the people in certain quarters of Prague scowl at any one who speaks German on the street.

"When we go to visit an official of the Government," said Doctor Clarke, "we usually inquire, first of all, which language this particular official prefers to speak, German or Czech. It is wise to do this because most of the officials, particularly if they represent the central government of Vienna, speak German; but a Czech who is loyal to his race will not speak the hated German unless he has to do so."

Doctor Clarke told me, as illustrating the fanaticism of the Bohemian people in this matter of language, that his little girls, who had been educated in German schools and preferred to speak that language among themselves, had more than once been hooted at, and even stoned, by young Bohemians in the part of the town where he lives, because they spoke a language which the masses of the people had been brought up to hate.

Another way in which the situation of the Slavic people resembles, to a certain extent, that of the masses of the Negroes in the Southern States, is in the matter of their political relations to the dominant races. Both in Austria and in Hungary all the races are supposed to have the same political privileges, and, in the case of Austria at least, the Government seems to have made a real effort to secure equal rights to all. Here, again, racial and traditional prejudices, as well as the wide differences in wealth and culture of the different peoples, have kept the political power in Austria proper in the hands of the Germans, and in Hungary in the hands of the Magyars.

What makes the situation more difficult for the dominant races in these two countries is the fact that the so-called inferior peoples are increasing more rapidly than the other races in numbers, and the Germans and Magyars are every year becoming a smaller minority in the midst of the populations which they are attempting to control. The result has been that the empire seems to the one who looks on from the outside a seething mass of discontent, with nothing but the fear of being swallowed up by some of their more powerful neighbours to hold the nationalities together.

There is one respect in which the situation of the Negro in America is entirely different from the various nationalities of Austria and Hungary. The Negro is not compelled to get his education through the medium of a language that is foreign to the other people by whom he is surrounded. The black man in the South speaks the same tongue and professes the same religion as the white people. He is not seeking to set up any separate nationality for himself nor to create any interest for himself which is separate from or antagonistic to the interest of the other people of the United States. The Negro is not seeking to dominate politically, at the expense of the white population, any part of the country which he inhabits. Although he has suffered wrongs and injustices, he has not become embittered or fanatical. Competition with the white race about him has given the Negro an ambition to succeed and made him feel pride in the successes he has already achieved; but he is just as proud to be an American citizen as he is to be a Negro. He cherishes no ambitions that are opposed to the interests of the white people, but is anxious to prove himself a help rather than a hindrance to the success and prosperity of the other race.

I doubt whether there are many people in our Southern States who have considered how much more difficult the situation in the Southern States would be if the masses of the black people spoke a language different from the white people around them, and particularly if, at the same time, they cherished political and social ambitions that were antagonistic to the interests of the white man.

On the other hand, I doubt whether the

Negro people realize the advantage which they have in speaking one of the great world languages, the language, in fact, that is more largely used than any other by the people who are most advanced in science, in the arts, and in all that makes the world better. English is not only a great world language, it is the language of a people and a race among whom the highest are neither afraid nor ashamed to reach down and lift up the lowest, and help them in their efforts to reach a higher and a better life.

In the south of Europe conditions are quite different. The languages spoken there, so far from helping to bring people together, are the very means by which the peoples are kept apart. Furthermore, the masses of the people of Austria speak languages which, until a hundred years ago, had almost no written literature. Up to the beginning of the last century the educated people of Hungary spoke and wrote in Latin, and down to the middle of the century Latin was still the language of the Court. Until 1848 there were almost no schools in the Czech language in Bohemia. Up to that time there were almost no newspapers, magazines, or books printed in the language spoken by the masses of the people.

It has been said that the written or literary

languages of the Slavic people have been, with one or two exceptions, almost created during the past hundred years. In fact, some of the Slavs, although they have a rich oral literature, still have, I have been told, no written language of their own.

A great change has been brought about in this respect in recent years. At the present time, of the 5,000 periodicals printed in Austria-Hungary, about 2,000 are printed in German, 938 in Magyar, 582 in Czech, and the remaining 1,480 are in some five or six other languages. The Magyar language is now taught in all the schools of Hungary, whether some other language is taught at the same time or not. Outside of Hungary, in Austria proper, there are some 8,000 exclusively German schools, 5,578 Czech, and 6,632 schools in which are taught other Slav dialects, not to speak of the 645 schools in which Italian is taught, the 162 schools in which Roumanian is taught, and the 5 in which Magyar is taught.

To an outsider it seems as if the purpose of these schools must be to perpetuate the existing confusion and racial animosities in the empire. On the other side, it must be remembered that it has been an enormous advantage to the masses of the people to be able to read the language which they habitually speak. In fact, the multiplication of these different written languages, and of schools in which they are taught, seems to have been the only way of opening to the masses of the people the learning which had been before that time locked up in languages which they sometimes learned to read but rarely spoke.

As I have considered the complications and difficulties, both political and economic, which not merely Austria but Europe has to face as a consequence of the different languages spoken by the different races, I have asked myself what would probably happen in our Southern States if, as some people have suggested, large numbers of these foreign peoples were induced to settle there. I greatly fear that if these people should come in large numbers and settle in colonies outside of the cities, where they would have comparatively few educational advantages and where they would be better able and more disposed to preserve their native customs and languages, we might have a racial problem in the South more difficult and more dangerous than that which is caused by the presence of the Negro. Whatever else one may say of the Negro, he is, in everything except his colour, more like the Southern white man, more willing and able to absorb the ideas and the culture of the white man and adapt himself to existing conditions, than is true of any race which is now coming into this country.

Perhaps my attempt to compare racial conditions in southern Europe with racial conditions in the southern United States will seem to some persons a trifle strange and out of place because in the one case the races concerned are both white, while in the other case one is white and one is black. Nevertheless, I am convinced that a careful study of conditions as they exist in southern Europe will throw a great deal of light upon the situation of the races in our Southern States. More than that, strange and irrational as racial conflicts often seem, whether in Europe or in America, I suspect that at bottom they are merely the efforts of groups of people to readjust their relations under changing conditions. In short, they grow out of the efforts of the people who are at the bottom to lift themselves to a higher stage of existence.

If that be so, it seems to me there need be no fear, under a free government, where every man is given opportunity to get an education, where every man is encouraged to develop in himself and bring to the service of the community the best that is in him, that racial difficulties should not finally be adjusted, and white man and black man live, each helping rather than hindering the other.

CHAPTER V

STRIKES AND FARM LABOUR IN ITALY AND HUNGARY

THERE is one English word which seems to be more widely known and used in Europe than almost any other. It is the word "strike." Labour strikes, I have understood, had their origin with the factory system in England. But the people on the Continent have improved on the original English device, and have found ways of using it of which we in America, I suspect, have rarely if ever heard.

It seems to me that during my short journey in Europe I heard of more kinds of strikes, and learned more about the different ways in which this form of warfare can be used, than I ever learned before in all my life. In Europe one hears, for example, of "political" strikes, of "general" strikes, and of "agricultural" strikes — harvest strikes — which are a peculiar and interesting variety of the ordinary labour strikes. There are rent strikes, "hunger riots," strikes of students, even of legislatures, and when I was in Budapest some one called my attention to an account in one of the papers of what was called a "house strike."

This was a case in which the tenants of one of the large tenement buildings or apartment houses of the city had gone on strike to compel the landlord to reduce the rent. They had hung the landlord in effigy in the big central court around which the building is erected; decorated the walls and balconies with scurrilous placards, and then created such a disturbance by their jeers and outcries, supplemented with fish horns, that the whole neighbourhood was roused. The house strikers took this way to advertise their grievances, gain public sympathy, and secure reduction of the rent.

I had an opportunity, during my stay in Europe, to get some first-hand information in regard to these continental strikes. I was in Berlin just before and after the three days' battle between the striking coalyard men of Moabit and the police, in the course of which several of the officers and hundreds of the people were wounded. For several days one section of Berlin was practically in a state of siege. The police charged the crowd with their horses, trampled the people under foot, and cut them down with their swords. The soldiers hunted the strikers into the neighbouring houses, where they attempted to barricade themselves and replied to the attacks of the police by hurling missiles from the windows of the houses into the streets below. At night the streets were in darkness, because the strikers had cut the electric wires, thus shutting off the lights, so that the police were compelled to carry torches in order to distinguish friends from foes.

At another time, while I was in Fiume, Hungary, I had an opportunity to see for myself the manner and spirit in which these strikes are conducted, or, rather, the way in which they are put down by the police.

I had gone out one day to visit the emigrant station, which is situated on the outskirts of the city, and noticed, on my way thither, a number of policemen on the car. Then, apparently at a signal from a man in charge, they seemed to melt away. Half an hour later, while I was at the emigrant station, I was startled by loud cries outside the building. Every one rushed to the windows. The street was crowded with men, women, and children, all running helter-skelter in the direction of the city. Some of the hands in a nearby factory had gone on strike. I could not at first understand why every one seemed in such a state of terror. Very soon I learned, however, that they were running from the police, and a moment later the police themselves moved into view.

They were formed in a broad double line across the avenue, and, marching rapidly, simply swept everything before them. At their head, bearing a heavy cane, was a man in plain clothes. I do not know whether he was an officer or the proprietor of the factory, but I was struck with the haughty and contemptuous air with which he surveyed the rabble as it melted away from in front of him. In a few minutes the street was empty and, so far as I could see, the strike was over.

It was a small affair in any case. There was no bloodshed and almost no resistance on the part of the strikers, so far as I could see. It was sufficient, however, to give me a very vivid notion of the ruthless way in which the governments of these stern military powers deal with rebellious labourers. European governments seem to have the habit of interfering, in a way of which we have no conception in this country, in all the small intimate affairs of life. So it is not to be expected that they would be able, like the police in this country, to act as a neutral party or referee, so to speak, in the struggles of labour and capital. That is the reason, I suspect, why in Europe strikes almost always turn out to be a battle with the police or an insurrection against the Government.

Almost anything may be made the occasion of a strike in Europe, it seems. Sometimes in Austria and Hungary, as I learned, members of the local diets or provincial legislatures go on a strike and refuse to make any laws until certain demands have been complied with by the central government at Vienna. Sometimes the students in one or more of the national universities go on a strike because a favourite professor has been removed by the Government, or because they are opposed to some particular measure of the Government. Not infrequently, in France or Italy, labour disturbances are fomented for political or party purposes, particularly among the employees of the state railways.

Strikes are a favourite weapon of the Socialists when they are seeking to force some political measure through parliament. Until a few years ago it seemed that the "general strike," in which all the labourers of a city or several cities, by suddenly laying down their tools and refusing to return to their work, sought to force some concession by the Government, was the means by which the Socialists proposed to overturn all the existing governments in Europe. Since the failure of the revolution in Russia and of similar movements on a smaller scale in Italy and elsewhere, this form of strike seems to have fallen into disrepute.

The most novel and interesting form of labour insurrection which I found while I was in Europe was the "strike of the agricultural labourers." In both Hungary and Italy the agricultural labourers have for some years past been organized into more or less secret societies, and the outbreaks which have been fomented by these secret societies have been, I understand, the most bloody and the most far-reaching in influence of any labour strikes in Europe.

The possibility that farm hands might be organized into labour unions, and make use of this form of organization in order to compel landowners to raise wages, had never occurred to me, and I took some pains to learn the conditions in Hungary and Italy under which these organizations have grown up.

I found that while the situation of the farm hands in Hungary differs from that of the farm hands in Italy in many ways, there are two important respects in which the situation of each is the same: First, a large part of the land of both countries is held in large estates; second, farm labourers, as a rule, particularly in Hungary, do not live, as is the case in America, on the land. On the contrary, they dwell apart in villages, so that they are hardly any more attached to the soil they cultivate than the factory hand is attached to the factory in which he is employed. In Hungary, for example, it is the custom for a group of labourers to enter, during the spring and summer, into a contract with a landowner to harvest his crop in the fall. A contractor, who either represents or employs the farm hands, will look over the field and bargain with the owner to do the work for a certain per cent. of the crop. At the harvest time the contractor will arrive with his labourers just as he would come with a gang of men to build a house or dig a ditch. While the work is going on the labourers, men and women together, practically camp in the fields, sleeping sometimes in the open or in such scant shelter as they are able to find.

It happened that I was in Hungary at the harvest time, and in the course of my journey through the country I have several times seen these gangs of men and women going to their work at daybreak. In this part of the country the strangest costumes are worn by the peasant people, and the women especially, with their bright kerchiefs over their heads, their short skirts and high boots, when they were not barefoot, were quite as picturesque as anything I had read had led me to expect. The labourers go to work at early dawn, because during the harvest season the field hands work sometimes as much as fourteen to sixteen hours a day, and then throw themselves down to rest for the night on a truss of straw or under a single blanket. After the harvest is over they return again to their villages.

Working in this way in troups of wandering labourers, there was no room for any permanent human relationships between themselves and their employers; such relationships, for example, as exist, in spite of the differences of race and colour, between every white planter in the South and his Negro tenants. On the other hand, the labourers, working and living together in the way I have described, come to have a strong sense of their common interest, all the stronger, perhaps, because they are looked down upon by the rest of the population, and particularly by the small landowners with whom they were associated up to the time of their emancipation, in 1848.

About 1890 a series of bad harvests — coming on the heels of other changes which, for a number of years, had made their lives steadily harder — helped to increase the discontent of the farm hands. Thus it was that when, about this time, the Socialists turned their attention to the agricultural population of Hungary, they found the people prepared to listen to their doctrines.

What made Socialism the more popular among the lowest farming classes was the fact that it not only promised to teach the farm labourers how they might increase their wages, but declared that the state was going to take the land out of the hands of the large landowners and divide it among the people who cultivated it.

What made the situation the more difficult was the fact that the agricultural labourers, as soon as they were thoroughly organized, had the landowners, during the harvest time, at a peculiar disadvantage, because when work in the fields stopped, the standing grain ripened and spoiled and the landowner was ruined.

In the emergency created by these strikes the Government came to the rescue of the landowner by establishing recruiting stations for farm labourers in different parts of the country. Collecting labourers in those parts of the country where labour was abundant, they shipped it to other parts of the country where, because of strikes, labourers were scarce and crops were in danger. Thus, the Government had at one time a reserve force of not less than 10,000 strike-breakers with which it was at any moment able to come to the rescue of a landowner who was threatened.

In many cases the Government undertook to regulate wages between landowners and their hands. In some cases they even sent troops into the fields, and in the course of the struggle there were frequent bloody collisions between the labourers and the troops.

One effect of these disturbances was to greatly increase the amount of immigration to America. In 1904, when the struggle was at its height, no less than 100,000 persons, mostly from the country districts, emigrated from Hungary. Thousands of others left the country and moved into the cities.

Hungary is about half the size of Texas, and it has nearly five times its population. Those who remember the "Negro exodus" of thirty years ago, and the apprehension that was created when some 40,000 Negroes left the plantations in Mississippi and Louisiana, will be able to understand the effect if for a number of years the South should lose annually by emigration to the cities or to other parts of the country 100,000 of its labourers in the cotton fields.

The exodus of the farm labourer from Hungary threatened, in spite of the rapid increase of the population, to permanently check the rising prosperity of the country. It was soon found that the great landowners could not rely upon repressive measures alone to solve their labour problems. Something must be done to redress the grievances and to improve the condition of the agricultural population. As a matter of fact, a very great deal was done by the state for agriculture, and something was done for the agricultural labourers. For example, relief funds were organized in sixty-four counties and boroughs to aid temporarily disabled workmen. Public prizes and diplomas were offered to labourers who were faithful to their masters.

Something was done to brighten the monotony of the agricultural labourer's life and to strengthen the ties between the labourers and their employers. At the suggestion of the Minister of Agriculture, an attempt was made to revive the harvest feasts, which brought the farmer and his labourers together. Workingmen's clubs, libraries, friendly and coöperative societies were encouraged by the Government. A popular weekly paper, printed in seven different languages, was started for the benefit of agricultural labourers and as a means of agricultural education. A bill for insurance against accidents and old age for the benefit of agricultural labourers provided that if a labourer loses more than a week's time he shall receive, in addition to the expenses of doctor and medicine, a sum amounting to about 25 cents a day for sixty days. In case of death of an agricultural labourer, his family receives a sum amounting to something between $40 and $50.

In Italy, the Socialistic movement among the agricultural classes took a somewhat different course. For one thing, it was not confined merely to the poorest class — namely, those labourers who live in the villages and go out at certain seasons to assist in the work on the farms — but extended to the small proprietors also, and those who rented land. In many cases the large estates in Italy are not managed as in Hungary, by the proprietor, but by middlemen and overseers, who pay a certain amount of rent to the proprietor and then sublet to tenants. Sometimes, particularly in southern Italy, lands are sublet a second and third time.

In many cases the terms upon which the land was held and worked by the small farmer were terribly oppressive, even in northern Italy, where conditions are incomparably better than in the south.

Although the peasants in northern Italy were nominally given their freedom in 1793, their condition, until a few years ago, has been described by one who was himself a large land proprietor as "little better than if they were slaves." In addition to the high rents, the tenant farmer was compelled to furnish the overseer with a certain number of chickens and eggs, and a certain amount of peaches, nuts, figs, hemp and flax, in proportion to the amount of land he rented.

The overseer claimed, also, just as the overlord did in the days of feudalism, the rights to the labour of the peasant and his ox-cart for a certain part of every year. His children were expected to work as servants in his household at a nominal price. The overseer sold the crop of the tenant farmer, and, after deducting all that was coming to him for rent and for other charges, returned the remainder to the tenant farmer as his share of the year's work.

In one case where, as a result of the revolt of his tenants the middleman was driven out, the tenant farmer, under the direction of the Socialist leaders, undertook to rent the land directly from the landowners, it was found that the middleman had been appropriating not less than 48 per cent. of the profits, which, under the new arrangement, went directly into the hands of the man who tilled the soil.

For a number of years there had existed among the small farmers numerous societies for mutual aid of various kinds. After the Socialists began to turn their attention to the agricultural population they succeeded in gaining leadership in these societies and used them as a means of encouraging agricultural strikes. It was from these same societies also that they recruited the members of those organizations of farm labourers and tenants which have attempted to form large estates on a coöperative basis. By this means the small farmer has been able to do away with the middleman and still retain the advantages which result, particularly in harvesting and marketing the crops, from conducting the operations on a large scale.

In recent years coöperative organizations of all kinds have multiplied among the small farmers of northern Italy. There are societies for purchasing supplies as well as for disposing of the products of the small farmers; the most important of these societies have been, perhaps, the coöperative credit organizations, by means of which small landowners have been able to escape the burden of the heavy interest charges they were formerly compelled to pay.

I was interested to learn that both the Government and the Socialists were at different times opposed to these coöperative societies, although for different reasons. The Socialists were opposed to coöperation because by removing the causes of discontent it sapped the revolutionary spirit of the farming classes. The Government, on the other hand, was opposed to the coöperative societies because their leaders were so frequently revolutionists who were using the society to stimulate discontent and organize the movement to overthrow the Government.

The great general strike of September, 1904, which resulted in practically putting an end, for five days, to all kinds of business industries in the city of Milan, was provoked by the state police firing upon some peasants who were holding a meeting to pay their shares and take their lots in an agricultural coöperative society.

I have attempted to describe at some length the character of the Socialistic movement as I found it in Hungary and Italy, because it represents on the whole the movement of the masses at the bottom of life in Europe. Through this party, for the first time, millions of human beings who have had no voice in and no definite ideas in respect to the Government under which they lived are learning to think and to give expression to their wants.

Few people, I venture to say, have any definite notion to what extent the most remote parts of Europe, from which the majority of our immigrants now come, have been penetrated by the ideas and the sentiments of the Socialistic party. There are, for example, some five or six different branches of the party in Bohemia. Socialism, I learn, has made its way even into such countries as Roumania, Servia, Bulgaria, and Dalmatia, where perhaps three fourths of the population are engaged in agriculture.

There are, however, as I discovered, various kinds and types of Socialism. I think I saw during my journey across Europe as many different kinds of Socialists as I did kinds of Jews, which is saying a good deal. In Denmark and Italy, for example, I met men of the very highest type who were members of the Socialist party. In Copenhagen I was entertained by the editors of the Socialistic paper, *The Politiken*, which is perhaps the most ably edited and influential paper in Denmark. In Italy many of the most patriotic as well as the most brilliant men in the country, writers, students, and teachers, are members of the Socialist party.

In Poland, on the other hand, I met other Socialists who had taken an active part in the revolution in Russia and who, for aught I know, were members of that group of desperate men who are said even now to be plotting from Cracow, Austria, a new revolutionary movement among the agricultural classes in Russia.

In short, I found that where the masses of the people are oppressed, where the people at the bottom are being crushed by those who are above them, there Socialism means revolution. On the other hand, where governments have shown a liberal spirit, and especially where the Socialists have had an opportunity to participate in the Government, or have been able, by means of the coöperative societies I have described, to do constructive work for the benefit of the masses, they have ceased to be revolutionists, have no longer sought to overturn the Government, but have patriotically striven to strengthen the existing order by freeing it from those defects that were dangerous to its existence.

In saying this, I do not mean to imply that I in any way favour the Socialistic programme of reform. I live in the Southern States, a part of the country which, more than any other part of the civilized world, still believes that the best government is the government that governs least; the government that you can wear like an old coat, without feeling it. More than that, I believe that the best and only fundamental way of bringing about reform is not by revolution, not through political machinery that tries to control and direct the individual from the outside, but by education, which gets at the individual from within; in short, fits him for life but leaves him free.

There is much in the history of the agricultural labourers of Hungary and Italy that is interesting to any one who has studied the condition of the Negro farm labourer in the South. In many respects their history has been the same. There is, however, this difference: When the serfs were freed in Hungary, as in most other parts of Europe, provision was made to give them land, though to a very large extent they were denied the political privileges enjoyed by the upper classes.

In Italy also it was intended, in giving the serfs freedom, to give them likewise land. Again, when the vast estates of the Church were taken over by the State, an attempt was made to increase the class of small owners and to give the land to the people who tilled it. In both cases, however, it was but a few years before the greater portion of the peasant owners were wiped out and their lands absorbed into the large estates. At the present time the small landowners, under the influence of education and agricultural organization, are gaining ground, and both countries, in the interest of agriculture, are seeking to encourage this movement.

The case of the Negro was just the opposite. When the masses of the Negro people were turned loose from slavery they carried in their hands the ballot that they did not know how to use, but they took no property with them. At the present time, I believe, by a conservative estimate, that the Negroes in the South own not less than twenty million acres of land, an area equal to the five New England States of Vermont, New Hampshire, Massachusetts, Rhode Island, and Connecticut.

On the other hand, the Negroes have largely lost, at least temporarily, many of the political privileges which were given them at emancipation. The experience of the peasants of Europe, just as the experience of the Negro in America, has served to confirm an opinion I have long held — namely, that it is very hard for a man to keep anything that he has not earned or does not know how to use. And in most cases, the best way and, in fact, the only way to insure any people in the possession either of property or political privileges is to fit them by education to use these gifts for their own good and for the highest good of the community in which they live.

The peasants were given land without effort on their part and soon lost it. The masses of the Negroes were given the ballot without effort on their part and they soon lost it. The peasants are now gradually gaining the land through their own effort and are keeping it. The masses of Negroes are gradually gaining the ballot through their own effort, and are likely to keep it when so gained.

CHAPTER VII

NAPLES AND THE LAND OF THE EMIGRANT

I HAD crossed Europe from north to south before I got my first glimpse of an emigrant bound for America. On the way from Vienna to Naples I stopped at midnight at Rome, and in the interval between trains I spent an hour in wandering about in the soft southern air — such air as I had not found anywhere since I left my home in Alabama.

In returning to the station my curiosity was aroused, as I was passing in the shadow of the building, by what seemed to me a large vacant room near the main entrance to the station. As I attempted to enter this room I stumbled over the figure of a man lying on the stone floor. Looking farther, I saw something like forty or fifty persons, men as well as women, lying on the floor, their faces turned toward the wall, asleep.

The room itself was apparently bare and empty of all furniture. There was neither a bench nor a table, so far as I could see, in any part of the room. It seems that, without any expectation of doing so, I had wandered into the room reserved for emigrants, and came accidentally upon one of the sights I most wanted to see in Italy — namely, a party of emigrants bound for America.

As near as I could learn, these people were, for the most part, peasants, who had come in from the surrounding country, carrying what little property they possessed on their backs or tied up in little bundles in their arms, and were awaiting the arrival of the train that was to take them to the port from which they could take ship for America.

I confess it struck me as rather pathetic that, in this splendid new and modern railway station, in which the foreign traveller and the native Italian of the upper classes were provided with every convenience and luxury, so little thought had been given to the comfort of these humble travellers, who represent the people in Italy who pay proportionately most of the taxes, and who, by their patient industry and thrift, have contributed more than any other class to such progress as Italy has made in recent years.

Later on I had an opportunity to pass through the country from which perhaps the majority of these emigrants had come. I travelled through a long stretch of country where one sees only now and then a lonesome shepherd or a wretched hut with one low room and a cow-stall. I also visited some of the little villages which one sees clinging to the barren hilltops, to escape the poisonous mists of the plains below. There I saw the peasants in their homes and learned something of the way in which the lowly people in the rural districts have been neglected and oppressed. After that I was able to understand that it was no special hardship that these emigrants suffered at Rome. Perhaps many of them had never before slept in a place so clean and sanitary as the room the railway provided them.

Early the next morning, as my train was approaching Naples, my attention was attracted by the large number of women I saw at work in the fields. It was not merely the number of women but the heavy wrought-iron hoes, of a crude and primitive manufacture, with which these women worked that aroused my interest. These hoes were much like the heavy tools I had seen the slaves use on the plantations before the Civil War. With these heavy instruments some of the women seemed to be hacking the soil, apparently preparing it for cultivation; others were merely leaning wearily upon their tools, as if they were over-tired with the exertion. This seemed quite possible to me, because the Italian women are slighter and not as robust as the women I had seen at work in the fields in Austria.

I inquired why it was that I saw so many women in the fields in this part of the country, for I had understood that Italian women, as a rule, did not go so frequently into field work as the women do in Austria and Hungary. I learned that it was because so many of the men who formerly did this work had emigrated to America. As a matter of fact, three fourths of the emigration from Italy to America comes from Sicily and the other southern provinces. There are villages in lower Italy which have been practically deserted. There are others in which no one but women and old men are left behind, and the whole population is more than half supported by the earnings of Italian labourers in America. There are cities within twenty miles of Naples which have lost within ten years two thirds of their inhabitants. In fact, there is one little village not far from the city of which it is said that the entire male population is in America.

Ten days later, coming north from Sicily, I passed through the farming country south of Naples, from which large numbers of emigrants go every year to the United States. It is a sad and desolate region. Earthquakes, malaria, antiquated methods of farming, and the general neglect of the agricultural population have all contributed to the miseries of the people. The land itself — at least such portion of it as I saw — looks old, wornout, and decrepit; and the general air of desolation is emphasized when, as happened in my case, one comes suddenly, in the midst of the desolate landscape, upon some magnificent and lonely ruin representing the ancient civilization that flourished here two thousand years ago.

Statistics which have been recently collected, after an elaborate investigation by the Italian Government, show that, in a general way, the extent of emigration from southern Italy is in direct ratio to the neglect of the agricultural classes. Where the wages are smallest and the conditions hardest, there emigration has reached the highest mark. In other words, it is precisely from those parts of Italy where there are the greatest poverty, crime, and ignorance that the largest number of emigrants from Italy go out to America, and, I might add, the smallest number return. Of the 511,935 emigrants who came to North and South America from Italy in 1906, 380,615 came from Sicily and the southern provinces.

One of the most interesting experiences I had while in Europe was in observing the number of different classes and races there are in Europe who look down upon, and take a hopeless view of, certain of their neighbours because they regard them as inferior. For example, one of the first things I learned in Italy was that the people in northern Italy look down upon the people of southern Italy as an inferior race. I heard and read many times while I was in Italy stories and anecdotes illustrating the childishness, the superstition, and the ignorance of the peasant people and the lower classes generally in southern Italy. In fact, nothing that I have known or heard about the superstition of the Negro people in America compares with what I heard about the superstition of the Italian peasants. What surprised me more was to learn that statistics gathered by the Italian Government indicate that in southern Italy, contrary to the experience of every other country, the agricultural labourers are physically inferior to every other class of the population. The people in the rural districts are shorter of stature and in a poorer condition generally than they are in the cities.

For all these reasons I was the more anxious to learn for myself what these people were like. I wanted to find out precisely in what this inferiority of the southern Italian consisted, because I knew that these people were very largely descended from the ancient Greeks, who, by reputation at least, were the most gifted people the world has ever known.

The city of Naples offers some advantages for studying the southern population, since it is the port at which the stream of emigration from the small towns and farming districts of the interior reaches the sea. The exportation of labourers to America is one of the chief businesses of that city. It was at Naples, then, that I gained my earliest first-hand acquaintance with the Italians of the south.

I think the thing that impressed me most about Naples was the contrast between the splendour of its natural surroundings, the elegance and solidity of its buildings, and the dirt, disorder, and squalor in which the masses of the people live. It was early morning when I arrived in the city for the first time. The sun, which was just rising over the black mass of Vesuvius, flooded the whole city and the surrounding country with the most enchanting light. In this soft light the gray and white masses of the city buildings, piled against the projecting hillside to the right and stretching away along the curving shores to the left, made a picture which I shall never forget.

Some of this sunshine seemed to have got into the veins of the people, too, for I never saw anywhere so much sparkle and colour, so much life and movement, as I did among the people who throng the narrow streets of Naples. I never heard before so many curious human noises or saw such vivid and expressive gestures. On the other hand, I never saw anywhere before so many beggars, so many barefooted men, so many people waiting at the station and around the streets to pick up a casual job. It seemed to me that there were at least six porters to every passenger who got off the train, and these porters were evidently well organized, for I had the experience of seeing myself and my effects calmly parcelled out among half a dozen of them, every one of whom demanded, of course, a separate fee for his services.

My experience in Europe leads me to conclude that the number of casual labourers, hucksters, vagabonds, and hunters of odd jobs one meets in a city is a pretty good index of the condition of the masses of the people. By this measure I think that I should have been able to say at the outset that there was in Naples a larger class living in the dirt, degradation, and ignorance at the bottom of society than in any other city I visited in Europe. I make this statement even though cities like Catania and Palermo, in Sicily, which are surrounded by an agricultural population just as wretched, are little, if any, better than Naples in this respect.

Very few persons who go to Naples merely as sightseers ever get acquainted, I suspect, with the actual conditions of the people. Most travellers who see Naples are carried away by the glamour of the sunshine, the colour, and the vivacity of the Italian temperament. For that reason they do not see the hard struggle for existence which goes on in the narrow streets of the city, or, if they do, they look upon the shifts and devices to which this light-hearted people are driven in order to live as merely part of the picturesqueness of the southern life and people.

I have been more than once through the slums and poorer quarters of the coloured people of New Orleans, Atlanta, Philadelphia, and New York, and my personal observation convinces me that the coloured population of these cities is in every way many per cent. better off than the corresponding classes in Naples and the other Italian cities I have named. As far as the actual hardships they have to endure or the opportunities open to them, the condition of the Negroes in these cities does not compare, in my opinion, with that of the masses of the Italians in these southern Italian cities.

There is this difference also: the majority of the Negroes in the large cities of the South and North in the United States are from the country. They have been accustomed to range and wander in a country where life was loose and simple, and existence hardly a problem. They have not been accustomed to either the comforts or the hardships of complex city life. In the case of the Italians, life in the crowded, narrow streets, and the unsanitary intimacy and confusion in which men, goats, and cattle here mingle, have become the fixed habit of centuries.

It is not an unusual thing, for instance, to find a cow or a mule living in close proximity, if not in the same room, with the rest of the family, and, in spite of the skill and artistic taste which show themselves everywhere in the construction and decoration of the buildings, the dirt and disorder in which the people live in these buildings are beyond description. Frequently, in passing through the streets of these southern cities, one meets a herd of goats wandering placidly along over the stone pavements, nibbling here and there in the gutters or holding up in front of a house to be milked.

Even where the city government has made the effort to widen and improve the streets, let in air and sunlight, and maintain sanitary conditions, the masses of the people have not yet learned to make use of these conveniences. I recall, in passing along one of these streets, in the centre of the city, which had been recently laid out with broad stone sidewalks and built up with handsome three and four story stone buildings, seeing a man and a cow standing on the sidewalk at the corner of the street. It seemed to me that the natural thing would have been to let the cow stand in the street and not obstruct the sidewalk. But these people evidently look upon the cow as having the same rights as other members of the population. While the man who owned the cow was engaged in milking, a group of women from the neighbouring tenements stood about with their pitchers and gossiped, awaiting their turn at the cow.

This method of distributing milk — namely, by driving the animal to the front door and milking while you wait — has some advantages. It makes it unnecessary to sterilize the milk, and adulteration becomes impracticable. The disadvantage is that, in order to make this method of milk delivery possible, the cow and the goat must become city dwellers and live in the same narrow streets with the rest of the population. Whatever may be true of the goat, however, I am sure that the cow is not naturally adapted to city life, and where, as is true in many instances, whole families are forced to crowd into one or two rooms, the cow-stall is likely to be still more crowded. Under these conditions I am sure that the average cow is going to be neither healthy nor happy.

For my purposes it is convenient to divide the life of Naples into three classes. There is the life of the main avenues or boulevards, where one sees all that is charming in Neapolitan life. The buildings are handsome, streets are filled with carriages, sidewalks are crowded with handsomely dressed people. Occasionally one sees a barefooted beggar asleep on the marble steps of some public building. Sometimes one sees, as I did, a woman toiling up the long street side by side with a donkey pulling a cart. There are a good many beggars, but even they are cheerful, and they hold out their hands to you with a roguish twinkle in their eyes that somehow charms the pennies out of your pocket.

Then there is the life of the narrower streets, which stretch out in an intricate network all over the older part of the city. Many of these streets contain the homes as well as the workshops of the artisan class. Others are filled with the petty traffic of hucksters and small tradesmen. In one street you may find a long row of pushcarts, with fish and vegetables, or strings of cheap meat dangling from cords, surrounded by a crowd, chaffering and gesticulating — Neapolitan bargain-hunters. In another street you will find, intermingled with the little shops, skilled artisans with their benches pushed half into the street, at work at their various tasks. Here you will see a wood-carver at his open doorway, busily engaged in carving out an elegant bit of furniture, while in the back of the shop his wife is likely to be engaged in getting the midday meal. A little farther along you may meet a goldsmith, a worker in iron or in copper. One is making a piece of jewellery, the other is mending a kettle. In these streets one sees, in fact, all the old handicrafts carried on in much the same manner and apparently with the same skill that they were carried on three hundred years ago.

Finally, there are the narrower, darker, dirtier streets which are not picturesque and into which no ordinary traveller ventures. This seldom-visited region was, however, the one in which I was particularly interested, for I had come to Naples to see the people and to see the worst.

In the neighbourhood of the hotel where I stayed there was a narrow, winding street which led by a stone staircase from the main thoroughfare up the projecting hillside to one of those dark and obscure alleyways for which Naples, in spite of the improvements which have been made in recent years, is still noted. Near the foot of the stairs there was a bakery, and not far away was the office of the State Lottery. The little street to which I refer is chiefly inhabited by fishermen and casual labourers, who belong to the poorest class of the city. They are the patrons also of the lottery and the bakery, for there is no part of Naples that is so poor that it does not support the luxury of a lottery; and, I might add, there are few places of business that are carried on in a filthier manner than these bakeries of the poorer classes.

I was passing this place late in the afternoon, when I was surprised to see a huckster — I think he was a fish vender — draw up his wagon at the foot of this stone staircase and begin unhitching his mule. I looked on with some curiosity, because I could not, for the life of me, make out where he was going to put that animal after he had unhitched him. Presently the mule, having been freed from the wagon, turned of his own motion and began clambering up the staircase. I was so interested that I followed.

A little way up the hill the staircase turned into a dark and dirty alleyway, which, however, was crowded with people. Most of them were sitting in their doorways or in the street; some were knitting, some were cooking over little charcoal braziers which were placed out in the street. One family had the table spread in the middle of the road and had just sat down very contentedly to their evening meal. The street was strewn with old bottles, dirty papers, and all manner of trash; at the same time it was filled with sprawling babies and with chickens, not to mention goats and other household appurtenances. The mule, however, was evidently familiar with the situation, and made his way along the street, without creating any surprise or disturbance, to his own home.

I visited several other streets during my stay in Naples which were, if possible, in a worse condition than the one I have described. In a city where every one lives in the streets more than half the time, and where all the intimate business of life is carried on with a frankness and candour of which we in America have no conception, there is little difficulty in seeing how people live. I noted, for example, instances in which the whole family, to the number of six or seven, lived in a single room, on a dirt floor, without a single window. More than that, this one room, which was in the basement of a large tenement house, was not as large as the average one-room Negro cabin in the South. In one of these one-room homes I visited there was a blacksmith shop in one part of the room, while the family ate and slept in the other part. The room was so small that I took the trouble to measure it, and found it 8 x 13 feet in size.

Many of these homes of the poorer classes are nothing better than dark and damp cellars. More than once I found in these dark holes sick children and invalid men and women living in a room in which no ray of light entered except through the open door. Sometimes there would be a little candle burning in front of a crucifix beside the bed of the invalid, but this flickering taper, lighting up some pale, wan face, only emphasized the dreary surroundings. It was a constant source of surprise to me that under such conditions these people could be so cheerful, friendly, and apparently contented.

I made some inquiry as to what sort of amusements they had. I found that one of the principal forms of amusement of this class of people is gambling. What seems stranger still, this vice is in Italy a Government monopoly. The state, through its control of the lottery, adds to the other revenue which it extracts from the people not less than five million dollars a year, and this sum comes, for the most part, from the very poorest part of the population.

There are, it seems, something like 1,700 or 1,800 offices scattered through the several large cities of Italy where the people may buy lottery tickets. It seemed to me that the majority of these offices must be in Naples, for in going about the city I saw them almost everywhere, particularly in the poorer quarters.

These lottery offices were so interesting that I determined to visit one myself and learn how the game was played. It seems that there is a drawing every Saturday. Any one may bet, whatever amount he chooses, that a number somewhere between one and ninety will turn up in the drawing. Five numbers are drawn. If you win, the lottery pays ten to one. You may also bet that any two of the five numbers drawn will turn up in succession. In that case, the bank pays the winner something like fifty to one. You may also bet that three out of five will turn up, and in case you win the bank pays 250 times the amount you bet. Of course the odds are very much against the player, and it is estimated that the state gets about 50 per cent. of all the money that is paid in. The art of the game consists, according to popular superstition, in picking a lucky number. In order to pick a lucky number, however, one must go to a fortune-teller and have one's dreams interpreted, or one must pick a number according to some striking event, for it is supposed that every event of any importance suggests some lucky number. Of course all this makes the game more interesting and complicated, but it is, after all, a very expensive form of amusement for poor people.

From all that I can learn, public sentiment in Italy is rapidly being aroused to the evils which cling to the present system of dealing with the agricultural labourer and the poorer classes. But Italy has not done well by her lower classes in the past. She has oppressed them with heavy taxes; has maintained a land system that has worn out the soil at the same time that it has impoverished the labourer; has left the agricultural labourers in ignorance; has failed to protect them from the rapacity of the large landowners; and has finally driven them to seek their fortunes in a foreign land.

In return, these emigrants have repaid their native country by vastly increasing her foreign commerce, by pouring back into Italy the earnings they have made abroad, by themselves returning with new ideas and new ambitions and entering into the work of building up the country.

These returned emigrants have brought back to the mother country improved farming machinery, new methods of labour, and new capital. Italian emigrants abroad not only contribute to their mother country a sum estimated at between five and six million dollars annually, but Italian emigration has awakened Italy to the value of her labouring classes, and in doing this has laid the foundation for the prosperity of the whole country. In fact, Italy is another illustration that the condition of the man at the bottom affects the life of every class above him. It is to the class lowest down that Italy largely owes what prosperity she has as yet attained.

CHAPTER VIII

THE LABOURER AND THE LAND IN SICILY

AMONG the things that make Sicily interesting are its ruins. There are dead cities which even in their decay are larger and more magnificent than the living cities that have grown up beside them — larger and more magnificent even than any living city in Sicily to-day. There are relics of this proud and ancient past everywhere in this country.

In the modern city of Catania, for example, I came suddenly one day upon the ruins of the forum of a Roman city which was buried under the modern Italian one. At Palermo I learned that when the members of the Mafia, which is the Sicilian name for the "Black Hand," want to conceal a murder they have committed, they put the body in one of the many ancient tombs outside the city, and leave it there for some archæologist to discover and learn from it the interesting fact that the ancient inhabitants of Sicily were in all respects like the modern inhabitants.

Among the other antiquities that one may see in Sicily, however, is a system of agriculture and method of tilling the soil that is two thousand years old. In fact, some of the tools still in use in the interior of the island are older than the ruins of those ancient heathen temples, some of which were built five centuries before Christ. These living survivals, I confess, were more interesting to me than the dead relics of the past.

These things are not easy to find. The guide-books mention them, but do not tell you where to look for them. Nevertheless, if one looks long enough and in the right place it is still possible to see in Sicily men scratching the field with an antique wooden plow, which, it is said, although I cannot vouch for that, is mentioned in Homer. One may see a Sicilian farmer laboriously pumping water to irrigate his cabbage garden with a water-wheel that was imported by the Saracens; or one may see, as I did, a wine press that is as old as Solomon, and men cutting the grapes and making the wine by the same methods that are described in the Bible.

It was my purpose in going to Sicily to see, if possible, some of the life of the man who works on the soil. I wanted to get to the people who lived in the little villages remote from the larger cities. I was anxious to talk with some of these herdsmen I had seen at a distance, wandering about the lonesome hillsides, tending their goats and their cows and perhaps counting the stars as the shepherds did in the time of Abraham. As there are some 800,000 persons engaged in agriculture in one way or another, it did not seem to me that this would be difficult. In spite of this fact, if I may judge by my own experience, one of the most difficult persons to meet and get acquainted with in this country, where many things are strange and hard to understand, is the man who works out in the open country on the land.

Even after one does succeed in finding this man, it is necessary to go back into history two or three hundred years and know a great deal about local conditions before one can understand the methods by which he works and thinks. In fact, I constantly had the feeling while I was in Sicily that I was among people who were so saturated with antiquity, so out of touch, except on the surface, with modern life, so imbedded in ancient habits and customs, that it would take a very long time, perhaps years, to get any real understanding of their ways of thinking and living.

In saying this I do not, of course, refer to the better classes who live in the cities, and especially I do not refer to the great landowners, who in Sicily do not live on the land, but make their homes in the cities and support themselves from the rents which are paid them by overseers or middlemen, to whom they usually turn over the entire management of their properties.

Nevertheless, in spite of the difficulties I have mentioned, I did get some insight into the condition of the rural agricultural classes in Sicily — namely, the small landowner and the agricultural labourer — and I can perhaps best tell what I learned by starting at the beginning.

The first thing I remember seeing of Sicily was a long black headland which stretches out into the sea like a great black arm toward the ships that approach Palermo from Naples. After that the dark mass of the mainland, bare and brown and shining in the morning light, seemed to rise suddenly out of the smooth and glittering sea. A little later, the whole splendid panorama of the beautiful bay of Palermo lay stretched out before me.

I recall this picture now because it suggests and partly explains the charm which so many travellers find in this island, and because it stands out in contrast with so much that I saw later when I visited the interior.

Sicily is, in this, like a great many other

places I saw in Europe: it looks better on the outside than it looks on the in. All the large cities in Sicily are situated on a narrow rim of fertile land which encircles the island between the mountains and the sea. Palermo, for example, is situated on a strip of this rim which is so rich that it is called the "Shell of Gold." In this region, where the soil is constantly enriched from the weathering of the neighbouring mountains, and where agriculture has been carried to the highest perfection that science and the skill of man can bring it, are situated those wonderful orange and lemon groves for which Sicily is famous. As an illustration of what irrigation and intensive culture can do in this soil, it is stated that the value of the crop in this particular region has been increased by irrigation from $8 to $160 an acre.

When one goes to Sicily to look at the agriculture it is this region that one sees first. During my first day in Palermo I drove through miles of these magnificent fruit farms, all laid out in the most splendid style, surrounded by high stone walls, the entrance guarded by heavy iron gates, and provided with extensive works for supplying constant streams of water to the growing fruit. The whole country, which is dotted with beautiful villas and winter palaces, is less like a series of fruit farms than it is like one vast park. Here the fruit ripens practically the whole year round. The trees are heavy all winter with growing fruit, and one can wander for hours through a forest of lemon and orange trees so closely crowded together that the keen rays of the southern sun can scarcely penetrate their foliage.

Palermo, however, like many other European cities in which the masses of the people are just now emerging out of the older civilization into the newer modern life, is divided into an old and a new city. There is the northern end, with broad streets and handsome villas, which the people call the "English Garden." This is the new city and the quarter of the wealthy classes. Then at the southern end there is the old city, with crowded, narrow and often miserably dirty streets, which is the home of the poorer class.

After visiting one or two of the estates in the suburbs at the northern end of the city, I determined to see some of the truck farms of the smaller farmers which I had heard were located at the south end of the city. I made up my mind, also, if possible, to get out into the country, into the wilder and less settled regions, where I could plainly see from my hotel window the olive groves creeping up the steep mountainside and almost visibly searching out the crevices and sheltered places on the steep slopes in search of water, which is the one missing ingredient in the soil and climate of this southern country.

Now one of the singular things about Palermo and some other cities in Sicily is that, as soon as you get to the edge of the town, you find yourself driving or walking between high stone walls which entirely shut out the view in every direction. We drove for an hour through these blind alleys, winding and twisting about without seeing anything of the country except occasionally the tops of the trees above the high stone walls that guarded the farms on either side. Occasionally we passed heavy iron gates which looked like the gates of a prison. Now and then we came upon a little group of houses built into the walls. These barren little cells, lighted only by an open door, looked as if they might be part of a prison, except for the number of sprawling children, the goats, and the chickens, and the gossiping housewives who sat outside their houses in the shadow of the wall sewing, or engaged in some other ordinary household task. There was scarcely a sprig of grass anywhere to be seen. The roads frequently became almost impassable for wagons, and eventually degenerated into mere mule paths, through which it seemed almost impossible, with our carriage, to reach the open country.

What added to the prison-like appearance of the place was the fact that, as soon as we approached the edge of the town, we met, every hundred yards or more, a soldier or a police officer sitting near his sentry box, guarding the approaches to the city. When I inquired what the presence of these soldiers meant, I was told that they were customs officers and were stationed there to prevent the smuggling of food and vegetables into the city, without the payment of the municipal tax which, it seems, is levied on every particle of produce that is brought into the city. I am sure that in the course of half an hour we met as many as twenty of these officers watching the highway for smugglers.

As we proceeded, our driver, who had made several fruitless attempts to turn us aside into an old church or cemetery, to see the "anteechee," as he called it, grew desperate. When I inquired what was the trouble I learned that we had succeeded in getting him into a part of the city that he had never before visited in his whole life, and he was afraid that if he went too far into some of the roads in which we urged him to go he would never be able to get back. Finally we came to a road that appeared to lead to a spot where it seemed one could at least overlook the surrounding country. We urged him to go on, but he hesitated, stopped to inquire the way of a passing peasant and then, as if he had made a mighty resolve, he whipped up his horse and said he would go on even if that road took him to "paradise." All this time we were not a quarter of a mile beyond the limits of the customs zone of the city.

Finally we came, by good fortune, to a hole in one of the walls that guarded the highway. We stopped the carriage, got out, clambered up the steep bank and made our way through this hole into the neighbouring field. Then we straightened up and took a long breath because it seemed like getting out of prison to be able to look about and see something green and growing again.

We had hardly put our heads through the hole in this wall, however, when we saw two or three men lying in the shade of a little straw-thatched hut, in which the guards sleep during the harvest season, to keep the thieves from carrying away the crops. As soon as these men saw us, one of them, who seemed to be the proprietor, arose and came toward us. We explained that we were from America and that we were interested in agriculture. As soon as this man learned that we were from

America he did everything possible he could to make us welcome. It seems that these men had just sat down to their evening meal, hich consisted of black bread and tomatoes. Tomatoes seemed to be the principal part of the crop that this farmer was raising at that time. He invited us, in the politest manner possible, to share his meal with him and seemed greatly disappointed that we did not accept. Very soon he began telling the same story, which I heard so frequently afterward during my stay in Sicily. He had a son in America, who was in a place called Chicago, he said, and he wanted to know if I had ever heard of such a place and if so perhaps I might have met his son.

The old man explained to me all about his farm; how he raised his crop and how he harvested it. He had about two acres of land, as well as I could make out, for which he paid in rent about $15 per acre a year. This included, as I understood, the water for irrigation purposes. He admitted that it took a lot of work to make a living for himself, and the others who were helping him, from this small piece of land. It was very hard to live anywhere in Sicily, he said, but the people in Palermo were much better off than they were in other places.

I asked him what he would do if his son should come back from America with a bag of money.

The old man's face lighted up and he said promptly, "Get some land and have a little home of my own."

Many times since then I have asked the same or similar questions of some man I met working on the soil. Everywhere I received the same answer. Everywhere among the masses of the people is this desire to get close to the soil and own a piece of land of their own.

From where we stood we could look out over the country and see in several places the elaborate and expensive works that had been erected for pumping water by steam for the purposes of irrigation. One of the small farmers I visited had a small engine in the back of his house which he used to irrigate a garden of cauliflower about four acres in extent. This man lived in a little low stone and stucco house, but he was, I learned, one of the well-to-do class. He had an engine for pumping water which cost him, he said, about $500. I saw as I entered his place a little stream of water, not much larger than my thumb, drizzling out of the side of the house and trickling out into the garden. He said it cost him between $4 and $5 a day to run that engine. The coal he used came from England.

I had seen, as I entered the Palermo harbour, the manner in which this coal was unloaded, and it gave me the first tangible evidence I had found of the cheapness of human labour in this over-populated country. Instead of the great machines which are used for that purpose in America and England, I learned, this work was all done by hand.

In order to take this coal from the ship it was first loaded into baskets, which were swung over the side of the vessel and there piled upon a lighter. This lighter was then moved from the ships to the shore. The baskets were then lifted out by hand and the coal dumped on the wharf. From these it was reloaded into carts and carried away. It was this coal, handled in this expensive way, that this farmer was using to pump the water needed to irrigate his land.

After leaving Palermo I went to Catania, at the other side of the island. The railway which climbs the mountains in crossing the island took me through a very different country and among very different people than those I had seen at Palermo. It was a wild, bare, mountainous region through which we passed; more bare, perhaps, at the time I saw it than at other times, because the grain had been harvested and plowing had not begun. There were few regular roads anywhere. Now and then the train passed a lonely water-wheel; now and then I saw, winding up a rocky footpath, a donkey or pack-mule carrying water to the sulphur mines or provisions to some little inland mountain village.

Outside of these little villages, in which the farm labourers live, the country was perfectly bare. One can ride for miles through this thickly populated country without seeing a house or a building of any kind, outside of the villages.

In Sicily less than 10 per cent. of the farming class live in the open country. This results in an enormous waste of time and energy. The farm labourer has to walk many miles to and from his labour. A large part of the year he spends far away from his home. During this time he camps out in the field in some of the flimsy little straw-thatched shelters that one sees scattered over the country, or perhaps he finds himself a nest in the rocks or a hole in the ground. During this time he lives, so to speak, on the country. If he is a herdsman, he has his cows' or goats' milk to drink. Otherwise his food consists of a piece of black bread and perhaps a bit of soup of green herbs of some kind or other.

During my journey through this mountain district, and in the course of a number of visits to the country which I made later, I had opportunity to learn something of the way these farming people live. I have frequently seen men who had done a hard day's work sit down to a meal which consisted of black bread and a bit of tomato or other raw vegetable. In the more remote regions these peasant people frequently live for days or months, I learned, on almost any sort of green thing they find in the fields, frequently eating it raw, just like the cattle.

When they were asked how it was possible to eat such stuff, they replied that it was good; "it tasted sweet," they said.

I heard, while I was in Sicily, of the case of a woman who, after her husband had been sent to prison, supported herself from the milk she obtained from a herd of goats, which she pastured on the steep slopes of the mountains. Her earnings amounted to not more than 12 to 14 cents a day, and, as this was not sufficient for bread for herself and her four children, she picked up during the day all sorts of green stuff that she found growing upon the rocks, and carried it home in her apron at night to fill the hungry mouths that were awaiting her return. Persons who have had an opportunity to carefully study the condition of this country say it is incredible what sort of things these poor people in the interior of Sicily will put into their stomachs

One of the principal articles of diet, in certain seasons of the year, is the fruit of a cactus called the Indian fig, which grows wild in all parts of the island. One sees it everywhere, either by the roadside, where it is used for hedges, or clinging to the steep cliffs on the mountainside. The fruit, which is about the size and shape of a very large plum, is contained in a thick, leathern skin, which is stripped off and fed to the cattle. The fruit within is soft and mushy and has a rather sickening, sweetish taste, which, however, is greatly relished by the country people.

One day, in passing through one of the suburbs of Catania, I stopped in front of a little stone and stucco building which I thought at first was a wayside shrine or chapel. But it turned out to be a one-room house. This house had a piece of carpet hung as a curtain in front of the broad doorway. In front of this curtain there was a rude table made of rough boards; on this table was piled a quantity of the Indian figs I have described and some bottles of something or other that looked like what we in America call "pop."

Two very good-looking young women were tending this little shop. I stopped and talked with them and bought some of the cactus fruit. I found it sold five pieces for a cent. They told me that from the sale of this fruit they made about 17 cents a day, and upon this sum they and their father, who was an invalid, were compelled to support themselves. There were a few goats and chickens and two pigs wandering about the place, and I learned that one of the economies of the household consisted in feeding the pigs and goats upon the shells or husks of the Indian figs that were eaten and thrown upon the ground.

As near as I could learn, from all that I heard and read, the condition of the agricultural population in Sicily has been growing steadily worse for half a century, at least.

Persons who have made a special study of the physical condition of these people declare that this part of the population shows marked signs of physical and mental deterioration, due, they say, to the lack of sufficient food. For example, in respect to stature and weight, the Sicilians are nearly 2 per cent. behind the population in northern Italy. This difference is mainly due to the poor physical condition of the agricultural classes, who, like the agricultural population of the southern mainland of Italy, are smaller than the population in the cities.

In this connection, it is stated that considerably less than one third as much meat is consumed per capita in Sicily as in northern Italy. Even so, most of the meat that is eaten there is consumed in the hotels by the foreigners who visit the country.

In looking over the budgets of a number of the small landowners, whose position is much better than that of the average farm labourer, I found that as much as $5 was spent for wine, while the item for meat was only $2 per year. There are thousands of people in Sicily, I learned, who almost never taste meat. The studies which have been made of the subject indicate that the whole population is underfed.

Upon inquiry I found it to be generally admitted that the condition of the population was due to the fact that the larger part of the land was in the hands of large landowners, who have allowed the ignorant and helpless peasants to be crushed by a system of overseers and middlemen as vicious and oppressive as that which existed in many parts of the Southern States during the days of slavery.

This middleman is called by Italians a gobellotto, and he seems to be the only man in Sicily who is getting rich out of the land. If a gobellotto has a capital of $12,000 he will be able to rent an estate of 2,500 acres for a term of six to nine years. He will, perhaps, work only a small portion of this land himself and sublet the remainder.

Part of it will go to a class of farmers that correspond to what are known in the South as "cash renters." These men will have some stock, and, perhaps, a little house and garden. In a good season they will be able to make enough to live upon and, perhaps, save a little money. If the small farmer is so unfortunate, however, as to have a bad season; if he loses some of his cattle or is compelled to borrow money or seed, the middleman who advances him is pretty certain to "clean him up," as our farmers say, at the end of the season. In that case, he falls into the larger and more unfortunate class beneath him, which corresponds to what we call in the Southern States the "share cropper." This man, corresponding to the share cropper, is supposed to work his portion of land on half-shares, but if, as frequently happens, he has been compelled to apply to the landlord during the season for a loan, it goes hard with him on the day of settlement. For example, this is the way, according to a description that I received, the crop is divided between the landlord and his tenants: After the wheat has been cut and thrashed — thrashed not with a machine, nor yet perhaps with flails, but with oxen treading the sheaves on a dirt floor — the gobellotto subtracts from the returns of the harvest double, perhaps triple, measure of the seed he had advanced. After that, according to the local custom, he takes a certain portion for the cost of guarding the field while the grain is ripening, since no man's field is safe from thieves in Sicily.

Then he takes another portion for the saints, something more for the use of the threshing floor and the storehouse and for anything else that occurs to him. Naturally he takes a certain portion for his other loans, if there have been any, and for interest. Then, finally, if there is nothing further to be subtracted, he divides the rest and gives the farmer his half.

As a result the poor man who, as some one has said, "has watered the soil with his sweat," who has perhaps not slept more than two hours a night during the harvest time, and that, too, in the open field, is happy if he receives as much as a third or a quarter of the grain he has harvested.

In the end the share cropper sinks, perhaps, still lower into the ranks of day labourer and becomes a wanderer over the earth, unless, before he reaches this point, he has not sold what little property he had and gone to America.

I remember meeting one of these outcasts and wornout labourers, who had become a common beggar, tramping along the road toward Catania. He carried, swung across his back in a dirty cloth of some indescribable colour, a heavy pack. It contained, perhaps, some remnants of his earthly goods, and as he stopped to ask for a penny to help him on his way, I had a chance to look in his face and found that he was not the usual sort. He did not have the whine of the sturdy beggars I had been accustomed to meet, particularly in England. He was haggard and worn; hardship and hunger had humbled him, and there was a beaten look in his eyes, but suffering seemed to have lent a sort of nobility to the old man's face.

I stopped and talked with him and managed to get from him some account of his life. He had been all his life a farm labourer; he could neither read nor write, but looked intelligent. He had never married and was without kith or kin. Three years before he had gotten into such a condition of health, he said, that they wouldn't let him work on the farm any more, and since that time he had been wandering about the country, begging, and living for the most part upon the charity of people who were almost as poor as he.

I asked him where he was going. He said he had heard that in Catania an old man could get a chance to sweep the streets, and he was trying to reach there before nightfall.

Several hours later, in returning from the country, I turned from the highway to visit the poorer districts of the city. As I turned into one of the streets which are lined with grimy little hovels made of blocks hewn from the great black stream of lava which Mt. Ætna had poured over that part of the city three hundred and fifty years before, I saw the same old man lying in the gutter, with his head resting on his bundle, where he had sunken down or fallen.

I have described at some length the condition of the farm labourers in Italy because it seems to me that it is important that those who are inclined to be discouraged about the Negro in the South should know that his case is by no means as hopeless as that of some others. The Negro is not the man farthest down. The condition of the coloured farmer in the most backward parts of the Southern States in America, even where he has the least education and the least encouragement, is incomparably better than the condition and opportunities of the agricultural population in Sicily.

The Negro farmer sometimes thinks he is badly treated in the South. Not infrequently he has to pay high rates of interest upon his "advances" and sometimes, on account of his ignorance, he is not fairly treated in his yearly settlements. But there is this great difference between the Negro farmer in the South and the Italian farmer in Sicily: In Sicily a few capitalists and descendants of the old feudal lords own practically all the soil and, under the crude and expensive system of agriculture which they employ, there is not enough land to employ the surplus population. The result is the farm labourers are competing for the privilege of working on the land. As agriculture goes down and the land produces less, the population increases and the rents go up. Thus between the upper and the nether millstone the farmer is crushed.

In the South we have just the contrary situation. We have land crying for the hand to till it; we have the landowners seeking labour and fairly begging for tenants to work their lands.

If a Negro tenant does not like the way he is treated he can go to the neighbouring farm; he can go to the mines or to the public works, where his labour is in demand. But the only way the poor Italian can get free is by going to America, and that is why thousands sail from Palermo every year for this country. In certain places in Sicily, in the three years including 1905 and 1907, more than four persons in every hundred of the population left Sicily for America.

One thing that keeps the Sicilian down is the pride with which he remembers his past and the obstinacy with which he clings to his ancient customs and ways of doing things. It is said by certain persons, as an excuse for backward conditions of the country, that even if the landlords did attempt to introduce new machinery and modern methods of cultivation the people would rebel against any innovation. They are stuck so fast in their old traditional ways of doing things that they refuse to change.

I have sometimes said that there was a certain advantage in belonging to a new race that was not burdened with traditions and a past — to a race, in other words, that is looking forward instead of backward, and is more interested in the future than in the past. The Negro farmer certainly has this advantage over the Italian peasant.

If you ask a Sicilian workman why he does something in a certain way, he invariably replies: "We have always done that way," and that is enough for him. The Sicilian never forgets the past until he leaves Sicily, and frequently not even then.

The result is that while the Negro in Africa

is learning, as I saw from a recent report of the German Government, to plow by steam, the Sicilian farmer, clinging proudly to his ancient customs and methods, is still using the same plow that was used by the Greeks in the days of Homer, and he is threshing his grain as people did in the time of Abraham.

CHAPTER IX

WOMEN AND THE WINE HARVEST IN SICILY

IT WAS late in September when I reached Catania, on the eastern side of Sicily. The city lies at the foot of Mt. Ætna on the edge of the sea. Above it looms the vast bulk of the volcano, its slopes girdled with gardens and vineyards that mount, one terrace above the other, until they lose themselves in the clouds. A wide and fertile valley below the city to the south, through which the railway descends from the mountain to the sea, seemed, as did Mt. Ætna itself, like one vast vineyard.

This was the more noticeable and interesting because, at the time I reached there, the harvest was in progress; the vineyards were dotted with women carrying baskets; the wine presses were busy, and the air was filled with the fumes of the fermenting grape juice.

Although it was Sunday morning and the bells in a hundred churches were calling the people to prayers, there was very little of the Sunday quiet I had somehow expected to meet. Most of the shops were open; in every part of the city men were sitting in their doorways or on the pavement in front of their little cell-like houses, busily at work at their accustomed crafts. Outside the southern gate of the city a thrifty merchant had set up a hasty wine shop, in order to satisfy the thirst of the crowds of people who were passing in and out of the city and also, perhaps, to escape the tax which the city imposes upon all sorts of provisions that enter the city from the surrounding country. Country wine was selling here at a few pennies a litre — I have forgotten the exact sum — and crowds of people from the city celebrated, something after the ancient custom of the country, I suppose, the annual harvest of the grapes.

Out of the southern gate of the city, which leads into the fertile vine-clad plain, a dusty and perspiring procession — little two-wheeled carts, beautifully carved and decorated, carrying great casks of grape juice, little donkeys with a pigskin filled with wine on either flank and a driver trotting along beside them — pushed and crowded its way into the city. At the same time a steady stream of peasants on foot, or city people in carriages, mingling with the carts and pack-animals, poured out of the gate along the dusty highway, dividing and dwindling, until the stream lost itself among the cactus hedges that mark the winding country roads.

It was to me a strange and interesting sight and, not only on this particular Sunday but afterward, almost every day I was in the city, in fact, I spent some time studying this procession, noting the different figures and the different types of which it was made up. It was at this gate that I observed one day a peasant woman haggling with the customs officer over the tax she was to pay for the privilege of bringing her produce to town. She was barefoot and travel-stained and had evidently come some distance, carrying her little stock of fruit and vegetables in a sack slung across her back. It seemed, however, that she had hidden, in the bottom of the sack, a few pounds of nuts, covering them over with fruit and vegetables. Something in her manner, I suppose, betrayed her, for the customs officer insisted on thrusting his hand down to the very bottom of the little sack and brought up triumphantly, at last, a little handful of the smuggled nuts. I could not understand what the woman said, but I could not mistake the pleading expression with which she begged the officer to let her and her little produce through because, as she indicated, showing him her empty palms, she did not have money enough to pay all that he demanded.

I had heard and read a great deal about the

hardships and cruelties of the tariff in America, but I confess that the best argument for free trade that I ever met was that offered by the spectacle of this poor woman, with her little store of fruit and nuts, trying to get to market with her goods.

Not far outside the city the highway runs close beside a cemetery. From the road one can see the elegant and imposing monuments that have been erected to mark the final resting places of the wealthy and distinguished families of the city. The road to this cemetery passes through a marble archway which is closed, as I remember, by massive iron gates. Standing by this gate, I noticed one day a young peasant woman silently weeping. She stood there for a long time, looking out across the fields as if she were waiting for some one who did not come, while the tears streamed down her face. She seemed so helpless and hopeless that I asked the guide who was with me to go across the street and find out what her trouble was. I thought there might perhaps be something that we could do for her.

The guide, with the natural tact and politeness of his race, approached the woman and inquired the cause of her grief. She did not move or change expression, but, while the tears still streamed down her face, pointed to a pair of high-heeled slippers which she had taken off and placed beside her on the ground.

"They hurt my feet," she said, and then smiled a little, for she, too, saw that there was a certain element of humour in the situation. I looked at her feet and then at her shoes and made up my mind that I could not help her.

Farther on we passed some of the large estates which are owned generally by some of the wealthy landed proprietors in the city. The corresponding region outside of Palermo is occupied by orange and lemon groves, but around Catania all the large estates, apparently, are given up to the culture of the vine.

A large vineyard in the autumn or the time of the grape harvest presents one of the most interesting sights I have ever seen. The grapes, in thick, tempting clusters, hang so heavy on the low vines that it seems they must fall to the ground of their own weight. Meanwhile, troops of barefooted girls, with deep baskets, rapidly strip the vines of their fruit, piling the clusters in baskets. When all the baskets are full, they lift them to their heads or shoulders and, forming in line, march slowly in a sort of festal procession in the direction of the wine press.

At the plantation which I visited the wine house was a large, rough building, set deep in the ground, so that one was compelled to descend a few steps to reach the ground floor. The building was divided so that one room contained the huge casks in which the wine was stored in order to get with age that delicate flavour that gives it its quality, while in the other the work of pressing the grapes was carried on.

There was at one side of the room a press with a great twisted arm of a tree for a lever, but this was only used, I learned, for squeezing dry the refuse, from which a poorer and cheaper sort of wine was made. Directly in front as one entered the building, and high up under the roof, there was a huge, round, shallow tub-like vat. In this vat four or five men, with their trousers rolled up above their knees and their shoes and stockings on, were trotting about in a circle, and, singing as they went, tramping the grapes under their feet.

Through an open space or door at the back I caught a glimpse now and then of the procession of girls and men as they mounted the little stairs at the back of the wine house to pour fresh grapes into the press. In the light that came in through this opening the figures of the men trampling the grapes, their bare legs stained with wine, stood out clear and distinct. At the same time the fumes which arose from the grapes filled the wine house so that the air, it almost seemed, was red with their odour. It is said that men who work all day in the wine press not infrequently become intoxicated from merely breathing the air saturated with this fermenting grape juice.

I imagine that the harvest season has always been, in every land and in every time, a period of rejoicing and gladness. I remember it was so among the slaves on the plantation when I was a boy. As I watched these men and listened to the quaint and melancholy little songs they sang, while the red wine gushed out from under their trampling feet, I was reminded of the corn-huskings among the slaves, and of the songs the slaves sang at those times.

I was reminded of it the more as I noticed the way in which the leader in the singing bowed his head and pressed his temples, just as I have seen it done before by the one who led the singing at the corn-husking. I recall that, as a boy, the way this leader or chorister bowed his head and pressed his hands against his temples made a deep impression. Perhaps he was merely trying in this way to remember the words, but it seemed as if he was listening to music that welled up inside of him, seeking in this way, not merely to recall the words, but catch the inspiration of the song. Sometimes, after he had seemed to listen this way for a few minutes, he would suddenly fling back his head and burst into a wilder and more thrilling strain.

All this was strangely interesting and even thrilling to me, the more so, perhaps, because it seemed somehow as if I had seen or known all this somewhere before. Nevertheless, after watching these men, stained with wine and sweat, crushing the grapes under shoed and stockinged feet, I had even less desire to drink wine than ever before. It perhaps would not have been so bad if the men had not worn their socks.

One thing that impressed me in all that I saw was the secondary and almost menial part the women took in the work. They worked directly under an overseer who directed all their movements — directed them, apparently, with a sharp switch which he carried in his hand. There was no laughter or singing and apparently little freedom among the women, who moved slowly, silently, with the weary and monotonous precision in their work I have frequently noted in gang labour. They had little if any share in the kind of pleasurable excitement which helped to lighten the work of the men.

Once or twice every year, at the time of the grape and olive harvests, the girls and women come down from their mountain villages to share with the men in the work of the fields. For these two brief periods, as I understand it, the women of each one of these little country villages will be organized into a gang, just as is true of the gangs of wandering harvesters in Austria and Hungary. I had seen, on the Sunday I arrived in Catania, crowds of these women trooping, arm in arm, through the streets of the city. A party of them had, in fact, encamped on the pavement in the little open square at the southern gate of the city. They were there nearly all day and, I suppose, all night, also. I was interested to observe the patience with which they sat for hours on the curb or steps, with their heads on their bundles, waiting until the negotiations for hiring them were finished.

This brief period of the harvest time is almost the only opportunity that the majority of these country women have to get acquainted with the outside world. For the remainder of the year, it seems, they are rarely allowed to venture beyond the limits of the street or village in which they live.

In the course of my journey across the island I had seen, high up in the mountains, some of these inaccessible little nests from which, perhaps, these girls had come. In one or two cases, and especially at the time I visited the sulphur mines, I had an opportunity to see something of the life of these mountain villages. Now that I have come to speak especially of the women of the labouring and agricultural classes, I may as well tell here what I saw and learned of the way they live in their homes.

Such a village as I have referred to consists, for the most part, of rows of low, one-story stone buildings, ranged along a street that is dirty beyond description. The wells are frequently built without mortar or plaster, and roofed sometimes with wood, but more frequently with tiles. In a corner there is a stone hearth upon which the cooking is done, when there is anything to cook. As there is no chimney, the smoke filters out through the roofing.

I remember well a picture I saw in passing one such house. In front of the house a woman was standing holding in her arms a perfectly naked child. Another child, with nothing on but a shirt, was standing beside her holding her skirt. Through the open door I could see the whole of the single room in which this family lived. Back of the living-room and connected with it was a stall for the cattle. This was typical of many other homes that I saw.

During the day the women, the children, the pigs, and the chickens spend most of their time in the dirty, crowded street. As a rule the men, unless they are engaged in some sort of handicraft, are away in the fields at work. In many cases they do not come home once a month.

In my journeys through these villages and the poor streets of the larger cities one question constantly arose in my mind for which I was never able to find an answer. It was this: What becomes of these people, together with their pigs, goats, chickens, and other animals, at night? How does the interior of these homes look after sundown?

I have gone through some of the poorer streets of Catania at night, but invariably found them in almost total darkness. I could hear the people talking as they sat in their doorways, but I could not see them. In fact, I could not see anything but the dim outlines of the buildings, because nowhere, apparently, were there any lights.

A German author, Mr. S. Wermert, who has studied conditions closely in Sicily, and has written a great book on the social and economic conditions of the people, says, in regard to the way the people live in the little villages:

"In the south, as is well known, people live for the most part out of doors. Every one sits in the street before the house door; there the craftsman works at his trade; there the mother of the family carries on her domestic labours. At evening, however, all crowd into the cave, parents and children, the mule or the donkey. The fattening pig, which, decorated with a collar, has been tied during the day in front of the house, where, with all the affection of a dog, it has glided about among the children, must also find a place in the house. The cock and hens betake themselves at sunset into this same space, in which the air is thick with smoke, because there is no chimney to the house. All breathe this air. One can imagine what a fearful atmosphere pervades the place. Every necessity of physical cleanliness and moral decency is lacking. In the corner there is frequently only one bunk, upon which the entire family sleeps, and for the most part it consists of nothing more than a heap of straw. In the fierce heat of the summer one naturally sleeps without a cover; in winter every one seeks to protect himself under the covers. Even when there are separate sleeping places all the most intimate secrets of family life become known to the children at an early age. Brothers and sisters almost always sleep in the same bed. Frequently a girl sleeps at the feet of her parents. The stupidity and coarseness of such a family existence is beyond description. There is naturally no such thing as a serious conception of morality among a people that for generations has grown up without education. For that reason, it frequently happens that the most unspeakable crimes are committed. It is, therefore, frequently difficult to determine with exactness the parentage of the children born into the family. The saying of the Romans, that 'paternity is always uncertain,' holds good here. In fact, it is quite possible that this legal conception owes its origin to observations in regard to the condition of the rural population of that period. It is, however, probable that in the country districts of Sicily conditions have changed very little since Roman times."

From all that I can learn, the filthy promiscuity of these crowded houses and dirty streets have made the Sicilian rural villages breeding places of vices and crimes of a kind of which the rural Negro population in the United States, for example, probably never heard. There are some things, in connection with this ancient civilization, concerning which it is better the Negro should not know, because the knowledge of them means moral and physical degeneration, and at the present time, whatever else may be said about the condition of the Negro, he is not, in the rural districts at least, a degenerate. Even in those parts of the Southern States where he has been least touched by civilization, the Negro seems to me to be incomparably better off in his family life than is true of the agricultural classes in Sicily.

The Negro is better off in his family, in the first place, because, even when his home is little more than a primitive one-room cabin, he is at least living in the open country in contact with the pure air and freedom of the woods, and not in the crowded village where the air and the soil have for centuries been polluted with the accumulated refuse and offscourings of a crowded and slatternly population.

In the matter of his religious life, in spite of all that has been said in the past about the ignorance and even immorality of certain of the rural Negro preachers, I am convinced, from what I learned while I was in Sicily, that the Negro has a purer type of religion and a better and more earnest class of ministers than is true of the masses of these Sicilian people, particularly in the country districts.

In this connection, it should not be forgotten also that the Negro is what he is because he has never had a chance to learn anything better. He is going forward. The people of Sicily, who have been Christians almost since the time that the Apostle Paul landed in Syracuse, have, on the other hand, gone backward. All kinds of barbarous superstitions have grown up in connection with their religious life and have crowded out, to a large extent, the better elements.

While the condition of Negro education in the Southern States is by no means perfect, the Negro, and particularly the Negro woman, has some advantages which are so far beyond the reach of the peasant girl in Sicily that she has never dreamed of possessing them. For example, every Negro girl in America has the same opportunities for education that are given to Negro boys. She may enter the industrial school, or she may, if she choose, as she frequently does, go to college. All the trades and the professions are open to her. One of the first Negro doctors in Alabama was a woman. Every year there are hundreds and, perhaps, thousands of Negro girls who go up from the farming districts of the Southern States to attend these higher schools, where they have an opportunity to come under the influence of some of the best and most cultivated white people in the United States. In the country villages, I venture to say, not one girl in a hundred ever learns so much as to read and write.

I was much impressed, as I went about in Sicily, with the substantial character of the buildings and improvements, such as they were. Everything is of stone. Even the most miserable house is built as if it were expected to last for centuries, and an incredible amount of labour has been spent everywhere throughout the country in erecting stone walls.

One reason for this is that there is almost no wood to be had for building. Everything is necessarily built of stone and tiles. Another reason, I suspect, why Sicilian people build permanently is because they never expect any change in their condition. If one asks them why they have built their villages on the most inconvenient and inaccessible places, they do not know. They know only that these towns have always been there and they haven't the least idea but what they will remain always where they are. As a matter of fact, in order to find an explanation for the location of these towns, students, I learned, have had to go back several centuries before Christ to the time when the Greeks and the Phœnicians were contending for the possession of the island. At that time the original population took refuge in these mountain fastnesses, and through all the changes since, these towns, with, perhaps, some remnants of the race that originally inhabited the island, have remained.

Everywhere in Sicily one is confronted with the fact that he is among a people that is living among the ruins and remains of an ancient civilization. For example, in seeking to understand the difference in the position of women in Sicily from that of other parts of Europe I learned that one had to go back to the Greeks and the Saracens, among whom women held a much lower position and were much less free than among the peoples of Europe. Not only that, but I met persons who professed to be able to distinguish among the women Greek and Saracen types. I remember having my attention called at one time to a group of women, wearing very black shawls over their heads, who seemed more shrinking and less free in their actions than other women I had seen in Sicily. I was informed that these women were of the Saracen type and that the habit of wearing these dark shawls over their heads and holding them tight under their chins was a custom that had come from the Arabs. The shawls, I suppose, took the place in a sort of way of the veils worn by Oriental women.

Now all these ancient customs and habits, and all the quaint superstitions with which life among the ignorant classes is overgrown, have, I suppose, the same kind of interest and fascination as some of the ancient buildings. But very few people realize, I am convinced, to what degree these ancient customs weigh upon the people, especially the women, and hinder their progress.

In the midst of these conditions the Sicilian women, who are looked upon by the men as inferior creatures and guarded by them as a species of property, live like prisoners in their own villages. Bound fast, on the one hand, by age-long customs, and on the other surrounded by a wall of ignorance which shuts out from them all knowledge of the outer world, they live in a sort of mental and moral slavery under the control of their husbands and of the ignorant, and possibly vicious, village priests.

For this reason, the journey to America is for the woman of Sicily a real emancipation. In fact, I do not know of any more important work that is going on for the emancipation of women anywhere than that which is being done, directly and indirectly, through the emigration from Sicily and Italy to the United States, in bringing liberty of thought to the women of Southern Italy.

CHAPTER X

THE CHURCH, THE PEOPLE, AND THE MAFIA

ONE of the interesting sights of Catania, Sicily, as of nearly every other city I visited in Europe, is the market-place. I confess that I have a fondness for visiting markets. I like to wander through the stalls, with their quantities of fruit, vegetables, meat and bread, all the common, wholesome and necessary things of life, piled and ranged in bountiful profusion.

I like to watch the crowds of people coming and going, buying and selling, dickering and chaffering. A market, particularly an old-fashioned market, such as one may see almost anywhere in Europe, in which the people from the town and the people from the country, producer and consumer, meet and bargain with each other, seems a much more wholesome and human place than, for example, a factory. Besides that, any one who goes abroad to see people rather than to see things will, I believe, find the markets of Europe more interesting and more instructive than the museums.

During my journey across Europe I visited the markets in nearly every large city in which I stopped. I saw something of the curious Sunday markets of Bethnal Green and Whitechapel, London, with their long lines of shouting hucksters and their crowds of hungry shoppers, and the Jewish market in the Ghetto of Cracow, Poland, where pale-faced rabbis were slaughtering, according to the strict ritual of the Jewish law, droves of squawking geese. Among others, I visited the Monday market in Catania, which differs from the markets I had seen elsewhere in the multitudes of articles of household manufacture offered for sale, and in the general holiday character of the proceedings.

It was like a country fair in one of our Southern cities, only cruder and quainter. For example, instead of the familiar shooting gallery, with painted targets, one enterprising man had set up a dozen painted sticks on a rough box, and offered to the public, for something less than a cent, the opportunity to shoot at them with an ancient cross-bow, such as I did not imagine existed outside of museums. Then there were all sorts of curious and primitive games of chance. Among other devices for entertaining and mystifying the people I noticed a young woman seated in a chair, blindfolded. A crowd surrounded her while she named various objects belonging to the crowd, which her companion, a man, held in his hands. At the same time she told the colour of the hair and eyes, and reeled off a prophecy in regard to the future of the different persons to whom the article belonged.

More interesting still were the public story-tellers, who seemed to take the place, to a certain extent, of the daily newspaper among the masses of the people, so many of whom can neither read nor write.

The story-tellers stood upon little platforms, which they carried about with them like portable pulpits, in order that they might be plainly visible to the crowd. Each carried a large banner on which were painted a series of pictures representing the scenes in the stories which they told.

These stories, together with the pictures which illustrated them, had apparently been composed by the men who told them, for they all touched upon contemporary events. In fact, most of them referred in some way to America. Like those songbirds that have only one constantly repeated note, each story-teller had but one story, which he told over and over again, in the same tones, with the same attitudes, and same little dramatic surprises.

Although I was not able to understand what was said, it was not difficult to follow the narrative from the pictures. One story told the fortunes of a young girl who had been lured away to America. Perhaps she was one of those "white slaves" to which I noticed a good many references in Italy, and in other of the emigrant countries. At any rate, she was imprisoned in a very dark and dismal place in some part of New York which I was not able to locate from the picture. Then her brother, or perhaps it was her lover, whom she had left behind in Sicily, saw a vision. It was a vision of St. George and the dragon, and after seeing this vision he rose up and went to America and rescued her. The touching thing about it all, the thing that showed how realistic this whole tale was to the crowd that stood and listened to it in rapt attention, was that when the story reached the point where the picture of St. George and the dragon is referred to, the men simultaneously raised their hats. At the same time the speaker assumed a more solemn tone, and the crowd listened with a reverential awe while he went on to relate the miracle by which the young woman had been saved.

The sight of this crowd of people, standing bareheaded in an open square, listening reverentially to the story of a street fakir, struck me, like so much else that I saw of the life of the common people in Catania and elsewhere in Sicily, as strangely touching and pathetic. It reminded me of all that I had read and heard of the superstitions of the common people of the country and gave me as insight, such as I had not had before, into the way in which the masses of the people feel toward the Catholic Church, with all its religious ceremonies and symbols. It led me to suspect, also, that much in the religious life of the Sicilian people which looks, perhaps, to those who have had a different training, like superstition, is in fact merely the natural expression of the reverence and piety of a simple-minded and, perhaps, an ignorant people.

I was told, while I was in that city, that Catania has two hundred and fifty churches, and though I do not know that this statement is correct, I could easily believe it from the interminable clanging church bells that smote upon my ears the first Sunday morning I was in the city. At any rate, no one can go through the city and look at the public buildings, or study the people in their homes, without meeting abundant evidence of the all-pervading influence of the Church. Everywhere, built into the buildings, on the street corners, and in every possible public place, one sees little images of the Virgin, with perhaps a burning lamp before them. Once I ran across one such image, with a lamp before it, planted in a field. I was told it was there to protect the crops from the influence of evil spirits.

It did not seem to have occurred to any one that the image of the Virgin and the blessing of the Church, which were intended to protect the fields from evil spirits, might protect them also from thieves, or banish from the community the evil spirits that inspired men to rob and steal. If this opinion had been very widely held among the masses of the people it would hardly have been necessary to guard the fields night and day during the harvest season, by men armed with shotguns.

This brings me to another point in which I should like to compare the masses of the Sicilian people with the masses of the Negroes in the Southern States — namely, in respect to their religious life.

Naturally, the first thing that strikes one, in attempting to make such a comparison, is the wide difference in the situation of the average black man in the Southern States and the corresponding class in Sicily. In all the externals of religious life, at least, the Sicilian is far ahead of the Negro.

Sicily was one of the first countries in the world in which Christianity was planted. St. Paul stopped three days in Syracuse on his way to Rome, and there is still standing a building in Catania in which St. Peter is said to have preached.

Sicily has inherited the traditions, the organization and the splendid churches and buildings which have grown up and accumulated through a thousand years and more. The black man, on the contrary, gained his first knowledge of Christianity in slavery and in a very imperfect and unsatisfactory form. It is only since freedom came that the Negro church has had an opportunity to extend and establish its influence among the masses of the people, while out of their poverty Negroes, who are even yet struggling to build and own their own homes, and so establish family life, have had to build churches and training schools for their ministers, to establish a religious press, to support missionary societies and all the other aids and accessories of organized religion.

In view of the wide difference between the people of Sicily and the Negroes in America, so far as concerns the external side of their religious life, it struck me as curious that I should hear almost exactly the same criticism of the people in Sicily, in respect to their religion, that I have frequently heard of the Negroes in America. A very large number of the popular superstitions of Sicily, what we sometimes call the folklore of a country, are very much like many of the notions that the Negroes are supposed to have imported to America from Africa. Any one who has listened to any of the older generation of coloured people tell of the various ways of "working the roots," as they call it, will learn a great many things that can be almost exactly duplicated in the popular notions about drugs and philters among the people of Sicily.

It is said of the Sicilians, among other things, that their Christianity is saturated with pagan superstitions and that, for the average Sicilian, religion has no connection with moral life.

In many cases it seems as if the image of the Virgin has become, among the lower class of people, little more than a fetish, a thing to conjure with. For example, the peasant who, in order to revenge himself upon his landlord, and perhaps to compensate himself for what he believes has been taken from him by fraud or extortion, determines to rob his landlord's field or flock, will pray before one of these images, before starting out, for success. If he is really "pious" he may offer to the saints, in case he is successful, a portion of what he has stolen. If, however, he fails and is merely superstitious, he will sometimes curse and revile, or even spit upon, the image to which he previously prayed.

I have heard that the savages in Africa will

sometimes behave in the same way toward the object of which they have made a fetish, but I have never heard of anything like that among my own people in the South. The Negro is frequently superstitious, as most other ignorant people are, but he is not cynical, and never scoffs at anything which has a religious significance.

One thing that indicates the large part that religion plays in the lives of the Sicilian people is the fact that out of the 365 days in the year 104 are sacred to the Church. The large amounts of money expended annually by the different cities of Sicily upon processions and celebrations in honour of the local saints is one of the sources of complaint made by those who are urging reforms in the local administrations. They say that the money expended in this way might better be used in improving the sanitary condition of the cities.

As indicating how little all this religious activity connects itself with practical and moral life it is stated that, while Sicily supports ten times as many churches and clergy in proportion to its population as is true of Germany, for instance, statistics show that it suffers from eleven times as many murders and crimes of violence. In quoting these statements I do not intend to suggest a comparison between the form of religion that prevails in Germany with that in Sicily. Religion, like everything else in Sicily, is deeply rooted in the past. It has shared all the changing history of that island, and naturally reflects the conditions, sentiments, and prejudices of the people.

If the Catholic Church is in any way to blame for the existing conditions in Sicily it seems to me it is in the fact that during the long period of years in which the education of the people has been almost wholly in its hands, the Church has held fast to the old medieval notion that education was only for the few, and for that reason has done little or nothing to raise the standard of intelligence among the masses.

It has been a great mistake on the part of the Church, it seems to me, to permit it to be said that the Socialists, many of whom are not merely indifferent but openly opposed to the Church, represent the only party that has sincerely desired and striven for the enlightenment and general welfare of the people at the bottom. Such a statement could not, of course, be so easily made of the Church in its relations to the masses of the people elsewhere in Italy.

The fact about the Sicilian seems to be, however, not that he is, as is sometimes said of the Negro, unmoral, but that the moral code by which he governs himself sometimes makes him a menace to public order.

One of the first things that impressed me, while I was in Sicily, was the enormous and expensive precautions that were necessary to guard the fields from thieves. Hundreds of miles of high stone walls have been erected in different parts of the island to protect property from vandalism and thieves. In the harvest time it is necessary to practically garrison the island with armed guards to preserve the crops. The cost of putting a private policeman in every field and garden is very heavy, and this expense, which is imposed upon the land, falls in the long run upon the labourer.

The reason for this condition rests in the conviction, which every farm labourer shares, that for his long and crushing labour on the land he does not receive a sufficient wage. In many cases it is likely enough that he is driven by hunger to steal. Under such circumstances it is not difficult to understand that stealing soon ceases to be looked upon as a crime, and seems to be regarded as a kind of enterprise which is only wrong when it is unsuccessful. But there is something further, I learned, in the back of the head of almost every Sicilian which explains many things in the Sicilian character and customs that strike strangers as peculiar. I refer to what goes in Sicily under the name of the *omerta*, and is, like some of the customs that exist in the Southern States, part of the unwritten law of the country. The principle of this unwritten law is silence. If any one is robbed, wounded, or injured in any way he remains silent. If the police seek to find out who is his enemy he will answer, "I do not know."

In some provinces in Sicily it is said to be almost impossible to arrest and convict criminals, because no one will hesitate to go into court and perjure himself for a friend. It is considered a point of honour to do so. On the other hand, to assist the police in any way in the prosecution of crime is looked upon as a disgrace. The ordinary man may be a thief, a robber, or a murderer and be forgiven, but there is no comfort in heaven or earth for the man who betrays a neighbour or a friend.

Complaint is sometimes made that the coloured people in the Southern States will protect and conceal those among their number who are accused of crime. In most cases where that happens I believe it will be found that the real reason is not the desire to save any one of their number from a just and deserved punishment, but rather the feeling of uncertainty, because of what they have heard and seen of lynchings in different parts of the country, as to whether the accused will have the benefit of a full and fair investigation in a court of law.

There is among the Negro population of the United States, even though the administration of the law is almost entirely in the hands of another race, no settled distrust of the Government and the courts and no disposition, as is true of the Sicilian, to resort to private justice and revenge. In spite of the fact that he frequently gets into trouble with the police and the courts the Negro is, by disposition at least, the most law-abiding man in the community. I mean by this, the Negro is never an anarchist, he is not opposed to law as such, but submits to it when he has committed a crime.

This brings me to another feature of Sicilian life — namely, the Mafia.

I had heard a great deal about the Mafia in Italy, and about the criminal political organizations in other parts of Italy, before I came to Europe, and was anxious, if possible, to learn something that would give me an insight into the local causes and conditions which had produced them.

One of the professional story-tellers whom I encountered while I was wandering about in the market in Catania recalled the subject to my mind. He was retailing to a crowd in the market square a story that was even more exciting and interesting to me, at least, than the one which I have already mentioned. It was, in fact, nothing less than an account of the murders and outrages of the Black Hand in New York City.

At first it struck me as very curious that I should meet in Italy, the home of the Mafia and the Camorra, a crowd of people in the public square listening with apparent wonder and awe to an account of the fabulous crimes and misdeeds of their fellow countrymen in another part of the world. I had a sort of notion that the Black Hand operations would be so familiar to Sicilians that they would have no curiosity about them. It was not so, however, and after I learned that New York had an Italian population larger than Rome, larger, in fact, than any Italian city, with the exception of Naples, this did not seem so strange. There are, as a matter of fact, more than 500,000 Italians in New York City, and 85 per cent. of them are from southern Italy. Among this 85 per cent. are very many who belong to the criminal classes. The result is that the Mafia, under the name of the Black Hand, is probably as active and, perhaps, as powerful among the Italian population in New York to-day as it ever was in Italy.

While I was in Palermo I had the place pointed

out to me where Petrosino, the Italian detective from New York, who went to Sicily to secure the records of some of the noted Italian criminals then living in America, was shot and killed. Petrosino was killed March 12, 1909. The killing of this American officer in the streets of Palermo served to call attention to the number of Black Hand crimes committed by Italians in this country. During the next nine months after Petrosino's death it was reported that no less than fifty "Italian killings," as they were called, took place either in New York City itself or in the surrounding territory, and from 1906 to 1909, according to statistics prepared by the New York *World*, of the 112 unexplained murders committed in and around New York, 54 were those of Italians. This suggests, at least, the manner in which our own country is affected by the conditions of the masses in southern Italy and Sicily.

The Mafia, the Black Hand, as it is called in America, is a kind of institution which is so peculiar and to such an extent the product of purely local conditions that it seems difficult even for those who know most about it to explain its existence. One statement which I heard in regard to the matter was especially interesting to me. It was said that the condition of mind which made the Mafia possible, the fear and distrust which divide the masses of the people from the ruling classes and the Government, was the result of the mingling of the races in the island; that the Mafia was, in short, Sicily's race problem.

It is certainly true that in no other part of Europe, with the possible exception of Spain, have the different peoples of Europe and Africa become so intermingled as they have in this island, which is one of the natural bridges between Europe and Africa. In addition to the Arabs and Saracens from Africa, nearly all the races of Europe, Germans, Latins, Greeks, have all at different times lived and ruled on the island. Near Palermo, for example, there are still the remnants of a colony of Albanians, a Slavic people who speak modern Greek, and worship after the fashion of the Eastern Church, and there are fragments and remnants of many other races still preserved in different parts of the island.

My own experience has taught me, however, to distrust what I may call "racial explanations." They are convenient and easy to make, but too sweeping, and, practically, the effect of them is to discourage any effort to improve. For example, if some one discovers that the condition in which a people happens to be found at any given time is due to race, that it is constitutional, and in the blood, so to speak, then, of course, there is nothing to do. If, however, it is due to environment, education may help. The discussion and emphasis on the fact of race have been made the excuse, in the Southern States, for a good deal of apathy and indifference in regard to the hopes and progress of the Negro. In fact, whenever I hear a politician in the South ask the rhetorical question, "Can the leopard change his spots?" I usually find that he is opposing the establishment of a Negro school or is discouraging some other effort to improve the condition of the Negro people.

The real trouble with explanations of this kind is that as soon as a man has made up his mind, for example, that a people, or class of people, belongs to a so-called "inferior race," he is not inclined to support any kind of experiment, like the building of a school, that may prove that his explanation was mistaken.

The real reason for the backward condition of Sicily is, in my opinion, not so much the intermixture of races as the neglect and oppression of the masses of the people. In 1861, when Sicily became a part of the Italian Confederation, 90 per cent. of the population were wholly unable to read or write. This means that at this time the people of Sicily were not much better off, as far as education is concerned, than the Negro slaves at the time of emancipation. It has been estimated that between 5 and 10 per cent. of the slaves could read and write.

One of the first things the Italian Government attempted to do, after annexation, was to reorganize the school system of Sicily. But even under the new Government, and with a compulsory education law on the statute books, progress has been slow. In 1881, twenty years later, more than 84 per cent. of the population could neither read nor write, and as late as 1901, for every hundred inhabitants of school age, more than seventy were illiterate.

In practically the same period — that is, from 1866 to 1900 — the Negro population in the United States reduced its illiteracy to 44.5 per cent. of the population of school age, and for every one hundred Negroes in the Southern States, fifty-two could read and write.

Sicily has three universities, one in each of its three largest cities, Palermo, Catania, and Messina, but they are for the few, and have in no way connected themselves with the practical interests and the daily life of the people. One result of the ignorance of the people is that in Sicily, where the educational qualifications exclude more persons than elsewhere from the suffrage, not more than 3.62 persons in every hundred of the population vote. This is according to statistics, which go back, however, to 1895.

As near as I can make out, the Mafia seems to have grown up, in the first place, like the White Caps, the Night Riders, and the lynchers in our own country, as a means of private vengeance. The people, perhaps because they despised and hated the Government, preferred to settle their scores in the old barbaric fashion of private warfare. The consequence was that the small towns were divided by tribal and family feuds. Under such circumstances professional outlaws became of service either for the purposes of attack or defence. From conditions something like this what is known as the Mafia sprang.

It is said that it was the rich fruit gardens of the "Shell of Gold" outside of Palermo which gave the Mafia its first secure foothold and eventually made that city the centre of its activity. In that region field guards were necessary, in addition to the high walls, to keep thieves out of the plantations where the golden fruit ripened almost all the year round. In the course of time these field guards became associated in a sort of clan or guild. In these guilds the most enterprising of the guards eventually became the leaders, and ruled those under them like the tribal chiefs.

Once established, these bands soon dominated the situation. No property owner dared install a guard without the consent of the chief. If he did, he was likely to have his trees destroyed or his whole crop stolen. A guard who was not a member of the band was likely to be brought down some night with a shot from a hedge. On the other hand, the mere knowledge that a certain plantation was under the protection of the Mafia was in itself almost sufficient to insure it from attack, and this because the Mafia, through all its devious connections with the lower and criminal classes, was much better able to ferret out and punish the criminals than the police.

By making himself at the same time useful and feared in the community, the chief of the Mafia soon began to get his hand in almost everything that was going on. He found himself called on to settle disputes. He mixed in politics and was secretly in the employ of rich and powerful men. In this way the Mafia, which was at bottom largely a criminal organization, gained in time standing and recognition in the community, in some respects, not unlike, I imagine, that of Tammany Hall in New York. When the Mafia, under the name of the Black Hand, reached New York, however, it seems to have become a criminal organization, pure and simple.

Those who have studied the history of this peculiar organization much farther than I have been able to do say that in their opinion the Mafia, or Black Hand, will not long survive in America because there is in this country no such oppression of the poor by the rich and no such hatred and suspicion of the high by the low as is the case in Sicily, to give it general support. In other words, the Mafia is dependent on class hatred and class oppression for its existence.

Perhaps I can give some idea of what it is that embitters the poor man in Sicily, who is without property, education, or opportunity, against the large property owners, the rich, educated, and ruling class.

It is estimated by the Socialists that in Italy the labouring man pays 54 per cent. of the taxes; business men and the professional classes pay 34 per cent., while the class which lives upon rents and the income from investments of various kinds furnishes but 12 per cent. of the revenues of the state.

Italy has, I think, every kind and method of taxation which has ever been invented. There is an income tax, which varies between 7½ and 20 per cent., though small incomes of less than one hundred dollars a year are exempt. The tax on landed property amounts to 30, 40, or even 50 per cent. In addition to these there is the lottery, the state monopolies, the stamp tax and dog tax. Finally the municipal taxes on all kinds of foodstuffs which are brought into the town. This tax absorbs from 20 to 30 per cent. of the labouring man's income.

All these taxes, direct and indirect, are so arranged that the heaviest burden falls upon that portion of the community which is least able to bear it. For example, salt is a Government monopoly in Italy, and in 1901 the people of Italy paid $15,000 for salt which cost the Government $1,200 to manufacture. The Italian Government ships salt to America for the use of the Gloucester fishermen for 50 cents a barrel of 280 pounds, or five and three-fifth pounds for a cent. This same salt costs the Italian, because of the monopoly of the Government, 4 cents a pound — that is to say, twelve times what it costs in America. In order to protect this monopoly the Government even goes so far as to station guards along the whole seacoast to prevent people from "stealing" sea water in buckets, to obtain salt.

Fortunately the state monopoly of salt does not extend to Sicily, but the principle of taxing the people according to their necessities, rather than according to their ability to pay, is the same there as elsewhere in Italy. As an illustration of the unfair way in which the taxes are levied in some parts of the country it is said that the donkey of the poor farmer is compelled to pay a tax, while the saddle-horse of the rich landlord goes free.

In comparison with this, the Negro in the South hardly knows what taxes are. The Negro farmer, for example, has an inexhaustible market for his cotton, corn, pork, and vegetables, and all the other farm vegetables that he can raise. Land is so cheap that a thrifty farmer can buy and pay for a farm within five or six years. Taxes on farm land are so low that the farmer hardly considers them in his yearly budget.

Poor as some of the Negro schools are in some parts of the South, they are vastly better and more numerous than those of the country people in Sicily. More than that, the Government puts no tax either on rain or sunshine, and the Negro in the Southern States has plenty of both, which is not true of the Sicilian farmer, who has too much sunshine and not enough rain. So much is the farmer in Sicily in need of water that at certain times in the year it is said that wine is cheaper than water. Finally, the Negro farmer, if he desires to take a load of produce to the town, does not, as is the case of the Sicilian, meet a policeman on the outskirts of the city who takes one fifth of his cotton, corn, eggs, or whatever he happens to have, away from him, before he will allow him to enter the town.

One day, while I was walking along the edge of the harbour in Catania, I noticed a man who was at work mending a high wire netting, about twenty or thirty feet high, which extended along the edge of the water. I saw that it extended as far as I could see. Upon inquiry I learned that it was placed there to prevent the fishermen, whom I noticed constantly coming and going with their little sailing boats, from bringing their fish into the city without paying the tax.

At the custom house, where the fishermen land, I observed one of these fishermen, who had landed with a small quantity of fish, which he was carrying to the market nearby, stop and fumble in his clothes, trying to find money enough to pay the tariff. When he could not find sufficient money to pay the sum demanded, he left two small fishes behind with the collector to cover the amount of the tax.

Fish is the cheapest and most abundant food the poor in the city can get to eat. The sea, just beyond their doors, is swarming with this kind of food. Nevertheless the city maintains an expensive army of officials to collect this miserable little tax upon the necessities of the poor.

The yearly income of a labourer's family in Catania is about 750 lire, or $170 a year. Of this amount it has been reckoned that in the way of taxes upon foodstuffs brought into the city the labourer pays 150 lire, or one fifth of his whole income.

In spite of all that has been proposed and attempted to improve conditions in Sicily since that island became a part of the Italian Confederation, the Government has failed, so far as I can learn, to gain the confidence, respect, and coöperation of the masses of the people. Naturally, conditions which have grown up in the course of hundreds of years and have become fixed in the minds and habits of all classes of the people cannot be changed suddenly. The farther I have looked into the situation in Sicily the more I am convinced that, different as it is in details, the problem of Sicily is fundamentally the same as that which we have here to face in the Southern States since the war. It is, in short, a problem of education, and by that I mean education which seeks to touch, to lift and inspire the man at the bottom, and fit him for practical daily life.

In this opinion I find that I am in agreement with the members of the commission which was appointed by the Italian Government in 1896 to investigate the condition of the peasants in southern Italy, particularly in their relation to the landed proprietors. The report of the commission, which has been recently made, fills several large volumes, but the substance of it seems to be, as far as I can learn, that the root of the evil is in the ignorance of the rural population. One of the effects of Italian immigration to America will probably be the establishment of a popular school system for the people on the land.

CHAPTER XI

CHILD LABOUR AND THE SULPHUR MINES

THERE is one street in Catania, Sicily, which seems to be given over to the trade and industry of the poorer people of the city. It is not mentioned in the guide-books, and there is perhaps no reason why it should be. Nevertheless, there are a great many interesting things to be seen in that street — strange, quaint, homely things — that give a stranger intimate glimpses into the life of the people.

For exampie, on a street corner, tucked away in one of those snug spaces in which one sometimes finds a crowded fruit-stand, I discovered, one day, a macaroni factory. Within a space perhaps three feet wide and ten or twelve feet in length one man and a boy conducted the whole business of the sale as well as the manufacture of macaroni, from the raw grain to the completed article of trade. The process, as it was carried on in this narrow space, was necessarily a simple one. There was a bag of flour, a box in which to mix the paste, and a press by which this paste was forced through holes that converted it into hollow tubes. Afterward these hollow tubes were laid out on a cloth frame which, because there was no room inside, had been set up in the street. After leaving this cloth frame the macaroni was hung up on little wooden forms for inspection and for sale.

One of the most curious and interesting places on the street was an apothecary's shop in which the apothecary manufactured all his own drugs, and acted at the same time as the poor man's physician or medical adviser. This man had never studied pharmacy in a college. His knowledge of drugs consisted entirely of the traditions and trade secrets which had come down to him from his predecessor in the business. His shop was filled with sweet-smelling herbs, gathered for him by the peasants, and from these he brewed his medicines. The skeleton of a fish hung over the counter from which medicines were dispensed, and the shelves behind were filled with many curious and musty bottles.

The apothecary himself was a very serious person, with a high, pale forehead and the absorbed air of a man who feels the weight of the knowledge he carries around with him. All these things, especially the smell of the herbs, were quite awe-inspiring, and undoubtedly contributed something to the efficacy of the medicines.

It is a very busy street in which the apothecary, the macaroni manufacturer, and the others are located. In fact, it seems as if work never stopped there, for it is full of little shops where men sit in their doorways or at the open windows until late at night, working steadily at their various trades, making the things they sell, and stopping only now and then to sell the things they make. The whole region is a hive of industry, for it is the neighbourhood where the artisans live, those skilled workmen who make everything by hand that, in our part of the world, we have long since learned to make by machine. In fact, in this street it is possible to get a very good picture, I suspect, of the way in which trade and industry were carried on in other parts of Europe before the age of steam.

About nine o'clock Saturday night — the night upon which I arrived in Catania — I was walking down one of the side streets in this part of the city, when my attention was attracted to a man, sitting in his doorway, working by the light of a little smoky lamp. He was engaged in some delicate sort of iron work, and, as near as I could make out, he seemed to be a tool-maker.

What particularly attracted my attention was a little girl, certainly not more than seven years of age, who was busily engaged in polishing and sharpening the stamps he used. I stopped for a moment and watched this man and child, working steadily, silently, at this late hour of the night. I could but marvel at the patience and the skill the child showed at her work. It was the first time in my life that I had seen such a very little child at work, although I saw many others in the days that followed.

I have often heard it said that people who are born under the soft southern skies are habitually indolent, and never learn to work there, as they do in more northern latitudes. This is certainly not true of Sicily, for, so far as my experience goes, there is no other country in Europe where incessant labour is so largely the lot of the masses of the people. Certainly there is no other country where so much of the labour of all kinds, the skilled labour of the artisan as well as the rough labour of digging and carrying on the streets and in the mines, is performed by children, especially boys.

There is a law against Sunday labour in Catania, but the next morning, as I passed through this same quarter of the city, I found the majority of the people still busily at work. I stopped to watch a man who was making mandolins. This man lived in one room, which was at the same time a workshop, kitchen, and bedroom. There was a great heap of mattresses piled high upon the bed in one corner. A little charcoal brazier, on which the cooking for the family was performed, stood upon the workbench. The ceiling was hung with finished instruments, and the pavement in front of the house was piled with others in various stages of completion. This room was occupied by a family of five, all of whom, with the exception of the wife and mother, were engaged, each in their different ways, in the work of manufacturing mandolins. All the skilled work (the setting of the decorations and the polishing of the frames) was performed by the boys, but a little girl who was standing near seemed to be making herself handy as a helper in the work of the others.

In this treeless country, where there is almost no wood of any kind to be had, the most useful building material, after stone and plaster, seems to be tile. Not only the roofs but the floors of most of the buildings are made of this material, and its manufacture is consequently one of the principal minor industries of the country. One day, while I was wandering about in the outskirts of Catania, I ran across a plant where two men and three little boys were at work mixing the clay, forming it into octagonal shapes, and piling it out in the sun to dry. The two men were at work in the shade of a large open shed, but I could not make out what they were doing. As nearly as I could see, almost all of the actual work was performed by the children, who ranged, I should say, from eight to twelve years of age. The work of carrying the heavy clay, and piling it up in the sun after it had been formed into tiles, was done by the younger children.

I am certain that if I had not seen them with my own eyes I would never have believed that such very little children could carry such heavy loads, or that they could work so systematically and steadily as they were compelled to do in order to keep pace with the rapid movements of the older boy, who was molding the tiles from the soft clay. The older boy could not have been, as I have said, more than twelve years of age, but he worked with all the skill and the rapidity of an experienced piece-worker driven at the top of his speed. I was so filled with pity and at the same time with admiration for this boy that, as I was unable to speak to him, I ventured to offer him a small coin in token of my appreciation of the skill with which he worked. So intent was he on his task, however, that he would not stop his work even to pick up the money I proffered him, but simply thanked me and nodded his head for me to place it on the bench beside him.

These instances of skilled labour among children are by no means exceptional. At another time I remember stopping to look at a little boy who, it seemed to me, could not be more than eight or nine years of age, working side by side with a man, evidently his father, together with several other men, all of them engaged in building a boat. The boy I speak of was engaged in finishing off with a plane the hardwood rail of the sides of the boat, and as I watched him at his task I was again compelled to wonder at the ease and skill with which these little fellows use their tools.

All these things, as I have said, gave me an idea of the manner in which the trades were carried on before the extensive use of machinery had brought the factory system into existence. It showed me also the easy way in which, in those days, the industrial education of children was carried on. When the work in the handicrafts was performed in the house, or in a shop adjoining the house, it was an easy thing for the father to hand down to the son the trade he himself had practised. Under the conditions in which trades are carried on in Sicily to-day children are literally born to the trade which their fathers practise. In these homes, where the shop and the home are crowded together in one or two rooms, children see their fathers and mothers at work from the time they are born. As soon as they are able to handle a tool of any kind the boys, at any rate, and frequently the girls also, are set to work helping their parents. As the father, in his turn, has probably inherited the accumulated traditions and skill of generations that preceded him in the same trade, his children are able to get from him, in the easiest and most natural way, an industrial education such as no other kind of school can give.

Whatever may be the disadvantages of the people of Sicily in other respects, they have an advantage over the Negro in learning the skilled trades, the value of which it is difficult to estimate. Everywhere one sees the evidences of this skill with the hand, not only in the public buildings, but in some of the common objects of daily use. I have already referred to the way in which the ordinary little two-wheeled carts, which take the place of the ordinary farmer's wagon in this country, are decorated. I have seen in Catania men at work practically hewing these carts out of the log. I do not know to what extent the frame of the wagon is hewn out in this way, but, at any rate, the spokes are. Every detail is worked out with the greatest possible skill, even to the point of carving little figures or faces at the ends of the beams that make the frames. Likewise the harness of the donkeys that draw these carts is an elaborate and picturesque affair which must require a vast amount of patience and skill to make. The point I wish particularly to emphasize here is that all this skill in the handicrafts, which has become traditional in a people, is the best kind of preparation for every kind of higher education. In this respect the Italian, like the Japanese and Chinese, as well as every other race which has had centuries of training in the handicrafts, has an advantage over the Negro that can only be overcome when the masses of the Negro people have secured a training of the hand and a skill in the crafts that correspond to those of other races.

Not only are children, especially boys, employed at a very early age in all the trades I have mentioned, but young boys from fourteen to sixteen perform, as I have said, in the mines and elsewhere an incredible amount of the crude, rough work of the community.

I remember, one day in Palermo, seeing, for the first time in my life, boys, who were certainly not more than fourteen years of age, engaged in carrying on their backs earth from a cellar that was being excavated for a building. Men did the work of digging, but the mere drudgery of carrying the earth from the bottom of the excavation to the surface was performed by these boys. It was not simply the fact that mere children were engaged in this heavy work which impressed me. It was the slow, dragging steps, the fixed and unalterable expression of weariness that showed in every line of their bodies. Later I learned to recognize this as the habitual manner and expression of the *carusi*, which is the name that the Italians give to those boys who are employed in the sulphur mines to carry the crude ore up from the mines where it is dug and to load it into the cars by which it is conveyed to the surface.

The work in a sulphur mine is organized in many respects, I learned, like that of a coal mine. The actual work of digging the sulphur is performed by the miner, who is paid by the amount of crude ore he succeeds in getting out. He, in his turn, has a man or a boy, sometimes two or three of them, to assist him in getting the ore out of the mine to the smelter, where it is melted and refined. As I myself had had some experience as a boy in work similar to this in the mines of West Virginia, I was interested in learning all I could in regard to these boys and the conditions under which they worked.

In the case of boys employed for this work, the Sicilians have a custom of binding out their children to the miner, or *picconiero*, as he is called. Such a boy is then called, in the language of the country, a *caruso*. As a matter of fact, a *picconiero* who buys a boy from his parents to employ him as a *caruso* actually purchases a slave. The manner in which the purchase is made is as follows: In Sicily, where the masses of the people are so wretchedly poor in everything else, they are nevertheless unusually rich in children, and, as often happens, the family that has the largest number of mouths to fill has the least to put in them. It is from these families that the *carusi* are recruited. The father who turns his child over to a miner receives in return a sum of money in the form of a loan. The sum usually amounts to from eight to thirty dollars, according to the age of the boy, his strength and general usefulness. With the payment of this sum the child is turned over absolutely to his master. From this slavery there is no hope of freedom, because neither the parents nor the child will ever have sufficient money to repay the original loan.

Strange and terrible stories are told about the way in which these boy slaves have been treated by their masters. Before coming to Sicily I had met and talked with persons who described to me the processions of half-naked boys, their bodies bowed under the heavy weight of the loads they carried, groaning and cursing as they made their way up out of the hot and sulphurous holes in the earth, carrying the ore from the mine to the smelter. All that I had heard elsewhere was confirmed later by the details furnished by official reports and special studies of conditions in the mining regions, made at different times and by different persons. In these reports I learned that the mines had been in the past the refuge of a debased and criminal population, whose vices made the bleak, sulphur-smitten region where the mines are located as much like hell as it looks.

The cruelties to which the child slaves have been subjected, as related by those who have studied them, are as bad as anything that was ever reported of the cruelties of Negro slavery. These boy slaves were frequently beaten and pinched, in order to wring from their overburdened bodies the last drop of strength they had in them. When beatings did not suffice, it was the custom to singe the calves of their legs with lanterns to put them again on their feet. If they sought to escape from this slavery in flight, they were captured and beaten, sometimes even killed.

As they climbed out of the hot and poisonous atmosphere of the mines their bodies, naked to the waist and dripping with sweat, were chilled by the cold draughts in the corridors leading out of the mines, and this sudden transition was the frequent cause of pneumonia and tuberculosis.

In former years children of six and seven years of age were employed at these crushing and terrible tasks. Under the heavy burdens (averaging about forty pounds) they were compelled to carry, they often became deformed, and the number of cases of curvature of the spine and deformations of the bones of the chest reported was very large. More than that, these children were frequently made the victims of the lust and unnatural vices of their masters. It is not surprising, therefore, that they early gained the appearance of gray old men, and that it has become a common saying that a *caruso* rarely reaches the age of twenty-five.

It was with something of all this in my mind that I set out from Palermo a little before daylight one morning in September to visit the mines at Campofranco, on the southern side of the island, in the neighbourhood of Girgenti. My misgivings were considerably increased when, upon reaching the railway station to take the train, I found that the guide and interpreter who had been employed the night before to accompany us on the trip had not made his appearance. We waited until all the porters at the station and the guards on the train were fairly in a fever of excitement in their well-meant efforts to get us and our baggage on the train. Then, at the last moment, with the feeling that we were taking a desperate chance, we scrambled aboard and started off into a wild region, which no guide-book had charted and, so far as I knew, no tourist had ever visited.

The train carried us for some distance along the fertile plain between the sea and the hills. It was just possible to make out in the twilight of the early morning the dim outlines of the little towns we passed. At length, just as we were able to catch the first gleams of the morning sun along the crests of the mountains, the railway turned abruptly southward and the train plunged into a wide valley between the brown and barren hills.

At Roccapalumba we left the main line of the railway, which turns eastward from there in the direction of Catania, and continued our journey with the somewhat ruder comforts of an accommodation train. From this point on the way grew rougher, the country wilder, and the only companions of our journey were the rude country folk, with an occasional sprinkling of miners. At the little town of Lercara we entered the zone of the sulphur mines. From now on, at nearly every station we passed, I saw great masses of the bright yellow substance, piled in cars, waiting to be carried down to the port of Girgenti for shipment to all parts of the world, and particularly to the United States, which is still the largest market for this Sicilian gold.

The nearer the train approached our destination, the more uncomfortable I grew about the prospect that was before us. I felt very sure that I should be able to reach Campofranco and perhaps see something of the mines, but whether I should ever be able to get out again and what would become of me if I were compelled to seek shelter in some of the unpromising places I saw along the way was very uncertain.

Fortunately, Dr. Robert E. Park, of Boston, who was travelling with me, and who accompanied me on nearly all of my excursions of this kind, was with me on this trip. Doctor Park had a pretty thorough mastery of the German language, and could speak a little French, but no Italian. He had, however, an Italian grammar in his satchel, and when we finally found ourselves at sea, in a region where neither English, German, nor French was of any help to us, he took that grammar from his satchel and set to work to learn enough Italian between Palermo and Campofranco to be able to make at least our most urgent wants known. For four hours he devoted himself industriously to the study of that beautiful and necessary language. It was a desperate case, and I think I am safe in saying that Doctor Park studied grammar more industriously during those four hours than he ever did before in his life. At any rate, by the time the train had crossed the rocky crest of the mountains which divide the north and south sides of Sicily, and before we disembarked at the lonesome little station of Campofranco, he could speak enough Italian, mixed with German, French, and English, to make himself understood. Perhaps another reason for Doctor Park's success was the fact that the Italians understand the sign language pretty well.

The mines at Campofranco are on the slope of the mountain, just above the railway station. A mile or more across the great empty valley, high up on the slope of the opposite mountain, is the village from which the mines get their name, a little cluster of low stone and cement buildings, clinging to the mountainside as if they were in imminent danger of slipping into the valley below.

A few hundred yards above the station great banks of refuse had been dumped into the valley, and a place levelled off on the side of the mountain, where the furnaces and smelters were located. There were great rows of kilns, like great pots, half buried in the earth, in which the ore is melted and then run off into forms, where it is cooled and allowed to harden.

I confess that I had been very dubious as to the way that we were likely to be received at the mines, seeing that we did not know the customs nor the people, and had very scant supply of Italian in which to make known our wants. The manager, however, who proved to be a very polite and dignified man, could speak a little French and some English. He seemed to take a real pleasure in showing us about the works. He explained the methods by which the sulphur was extracted, insisted upon our drinking a glass of wine, and was even kind enough to loan me a horse and guide when I expressed a desire to rent one of the passing donkeys to convey me to some of the more inaccessible places, farther up the mountain, where I could see the miners had burrowed into the earth in search of sulphur. On the vast slope of the mountain and at a distance they looked like ants running in and out of little holes in the earth.

It was at the mouth of one of these entrances

to the mines that I got my first definite notion of what sulphur miners look like — those unfortunate creatures who wear out their lives amid the poisonous fumes and the furnace heat of these underground hells. There was a rumble of a car, and presently a man, almost stark naked, stepped out of the dark passageway. He was worn, haggard, and gray, and his skin had a peculiar grayish-white tinge. He spoke in a husky whisper, but I do not know whether that is one of the characteristic effects of the work in the mines or not. I was told that, in addition to other dangers, the sulphur has a bad effect upon the lungs. It was explained to me that the sulphur dust gets into the lungs and clogs them up, and that is what accounts for the groans of the *carusi*, so frequently spoken of, when they are tugging up the steep and winding passageways with the heavy burdens of crude ore on their backs.

It had been many years since I had been in a mine, but as I entered the dark, damp gallery and felt the sudden underground chill, the memories of my early experiences all came back to me. As we got farther into the mine, however, the air seemed to grow warmer. Suddenly a door at the side of the gallery opened; a blast of hot air, like that from a furnace, burst out into the corridor, and another of those half-naked men, dripping with perspiration, stepped out.

We passed at intervals along the main corridor a number of these doors which, as I discovered, led down into parts of the mine where the men were at work. It seemed incredible to me that any one could live and work in such heat, but I had come there to see what a sulphur mine was like, so I determined to try the experiment.

The side passage which I entered was, in fact, little more than a burrow, twisting and winding its way, but going constantly deeper and deeper into the dark depths of the earth. I had known what it was to work deep down under the earth, but I never before so thoroughly realized what it meant to be in the bowels of the earth as I did while I was groping my way through the dark and winding passages of this sulphur mine.

It is down at the bottom of these holes, and in this steaming atmosphere, that the miners work. They loosen the ore from the walls of the seams in which it is found, and then it is carried up out of these holes in sacks by the *carusi*.

In the mine which I visited the work of getting the ore to the surface was performed in a modern and comparatively humane way.

It was simply necessary to carry the ore from the different points where it is mined to the car, by which it is then transported to the smelter. In those mines, however, where the work is still carried on in the old, traditional fashion, which has been in vogue as far back as any one can remember, all the ore is carried on the backs of boys. In cases where the mine descended to the depth of two, three, or four hundred feet, the task of carrying these loads of ore to the surface is simply heartbreaking. I can well understand that persons who have seen conditions at the worst should speak of the children who have been condemned to this slavery as the most unhappy creatures on earth.

From all that I can learn, however, the conditions have changed for the better in recent years. In 1902 a law was passed which forbade the employment of children under thirteen years in underground work, and to this was added, a little later, a provision which forbade, after 1905, the employment of children under fifteen in the mines.

So far as I am able to say, this provision was carried out in the mine I visited, for I did not see children at work anywhere inside the mine. I saw a number of the poor little creatures at work in the dumps outside the mine, however. They were carrying refuse ore in bags on their backs, throwing it on screens, and then loading the finer particles back into the cars. Once having seen these gangs of boys at work, I could never mistake their slow, dragging movements and the expression of dull despair upon their faces.

It is said that the employment of boys in the sulphur mines is decreasing. According to law, the employment of children under fifteen years of age has been forbidden since 1905. As is well known, however, in Italy as in America, it is much easier to make laws than to enforce them. This is especially true in Sicily. The only figures which I have been able to obtain upon the subject show that from 1880 to 1898 there was an enormous increase in the number of children employed in and about the mines. In 1880 there were 2,419 children under fifteen years working there, among whom were eight girls. Of this number 88 were seven and 163 were eight years of age, while 12 per cent. of the whole number were under nine years of age. In 1898, however, the number of children under fifteen years of age was 7,032, of whom 5,232 were at work inside the mines. At this time the Government had already attempted to put some restrictions on the employment of children in the mines, but the age limit had not been fixed as high as fifteen years.

The sulphur mines are located on the southern slopes of the mountains that cross Sicily from east to west. About ten miles below Campofranco the two branches of the railway, one running directly south from Roccapalumba, and the other running southwest from Caltanisetta, come together a few miles above Girgenti. On the slopes of the broad valleys through which these two branches of the railway run are located nearly all the sulphur mines in Sicily. From these mines, which furnish something like 70 per cent. of the world's supply of sulphur, a constant stream of this yellow ore flows down to the sea at the port of Girgenti.

After leaving Campofranco I travelled through this whole region. In many places the mountain slopes are fairly honeycombed with holes where the miners in years past have dug their way into the mountain in search of the precious yellow mineral. For many miles in every direction the vegetation has been blasted by the poisonous smoke and vapours from the smelters, and the whole country has a blotched and scrofulous appearance which is depressing to look upon, particularly when one considers the amount of misery and the number of human lives it has cost to create this condition. I have never in my life seen any place that seemed to come so near meeting the description of the "abomination of desolation" referred to in the Bible. There is even a certain grandeur in the desolation of this country which looks as if the curse of God rested upon it

I am not prepared just now to say to what extent I believe in a physical hell in the next world, but a sulphur mine in Sicily is about the nearest thing to hell that I expect to see in this life.

As I have already said, however, there are indications that in the sulphur mines, as elsewhere in Sicily, the situation of the man farthest down is improving. I pray God that it is so, for I could not picture an existence more miserable than the slow torture of this crushing labour in the hot and poisonous air of these sulphur mines.

Let me say also that I came away from the sulphur mines and from Sicily with a very much better opinion of the people than when I entered. I went to Italy with the notion that the Sicilians were a race of brigands, a sullen and irritable people who were disposed at any moment to be swept off their feet by violent and murderous passions. I came away with the feeling that, whatever might be the faults of the masses of the people, they were, at the very least, more sinned against than sinning, and that they deserve the sympathy rather than the condemnation of the world.

The truth is that, as far as my personal experience goes, I was never treated more kindly in my whole life than I was the day when, coming as a stranger, without an introduction of any kind, I ventured to visit the region which has the reputation of being the most wicked, and is certainly the most unfortunate, in Europe. I mean the region around and north of Girgenti, which is the seat at once of the sulphur mines and the Mafia.

If any one had told me before I went to Sicily that I would be willing to intrust my life to Sicilians away down in the darkness of a sulphur mine, I should have believed that such a person had lost his mind. I had read and heard so much of murders of the Mafia in Sicily, that for a long time I had had a horror of the name of Sicilians; but when I came in contact with them, before I knew it, I found myself trusting them absolutely to such an extent that I willingly followed them into the bowels of the earth; into a hot, narrow, dark sulphur mine where, without a moment's warning, they might have demanded my life or held me, if they cared to, for a ransom. Nothing of this kind occurred; on the other hand, I repeat, every Sicilian with whom I came in contact in the sulphur mine treated me in the most kindly manner, and I came away from their country having the highest respect for them.

I did not meet, while I was there, a single person, from the superintendent to the lowest labourer at the mines, who did not seem, not only willing, but even anxious, to assist me to see and learn everything I wanted to know. What is more, Campofranco was the only place in Europe where I met men who refused to accept money for a service rendered me.

CHAPTER XII

FIUME, BUDAPEST, AND THE IMMIGRANT

IT WAS a cold, cloudy, windy, rainy day when the little coasting vessel that was to take us across the Adriatic drew out from the gray and misty harbour of the ancient city of Ancona and started in the direction of Fiume, the single point at which the Kingdom of Hungary touches the sea. I had read of the hardships of the early immigrants, and I heard once an old coloured man, who had been carried to America as a slave, tell of the long journey of himself and some fifty others, all crowded together in a little sailing vessel. It was not, however, until this trip of a few hours on the Adriatic in a dirty, ill-smelling little vessel that I began to understand, although I had crossed the ocean several times, how uncomfortable a sea voyage might be.

Fortunately the journey was not a long one, and after the vessel found itself in the shelter of one of the beautiful green islands which are stationed like sentinels along the Dalmatian coast, it was possible to go on deck and enjoy the view of the rugged and broken coast line.

It was indeed a splendid sight, in the clear light of the late afternoon, to watch the great blue-gray clouds roll up over the green and glistening masses of the islands, which lifted themselves on every side out of the surrounding sea.

What I had heard and read of the Dalmatian coast had led me to look for the signs of an ancient civilization, not unlike that which I had left in Italy. What impressed me at first sight about Fiume, however, was the brand-new and modern character of everything in view. I do not mean that the city had any of the loose-jointed and straggling newness of some of our western American towns. It had rather the newness and completeness of one of those modern German cities, which seem to have been planned and erected out of hand, at the command of some higher authority. In that part of Germany which I visited I noticed that nothing was allowed to grow up naturally, in the comfortable and haphazard disorder that one finds in some parts of America. This is particularly true of the cities. Everything is tagged and labelled, and ordered with military precision. Even the rose-bushes in the gardens seem to show the effect of military discipline. Trimmed and pruned, they stand up straight, in long and regular rows, as if they were continually presenting arms.

The impression which I got of modern Hungary at Fiume was confirmed by what I saw a few days later at Budapest, the capital. There was the same air of newness and novelty, as if the city had been erected overnight, and the people had not yet grown used to it.

A little further acquaintance with the cities of Fiume and Budapest made it plain, however, in each case, that the new city which filled the eye of the stranger had been, as a matter of fact, built over, or, rather, added to, a more ancient one.

In Fiume, for example, somewhat hidden away behind the new buildings which line the broad avenue of the modern Magyar city, there is still preserved the outlines of the ancient Italian town, with its narrow, winding streets, crowded with all the quaint and vivid life, the petty traffic, and the varied human sights and sounds with which I had become familiar during my journey through Italy.

So in Budapest, across the river from the modern Hungarian, or, rather, Magyar city of Pest, there is the ancient German city of Buda, with its castle and palace, which dates back into the Middle Ages.

What is still more interesting is that in these two modern cities of Fiume and Pest, in which one sees and feels the impress of a strong and masterful people, one meets everywhere, in the midst of this feverish and artificial modern life, evidences of the habit and manners which belong to an older and simpler age.

For example, it struck me as curious that in a city which is so well provided with the latest type of electric street cars one should see peasant women trudging in from the country with heavy loads of vegetables on their backs; and, in a city where the Government is seeking to provide modern houses for the labouring classes, with all the conveniences that invention can supply, one should see these same peasant women peacefully sleeping on the pavement or under the wagons in the public square, just as they have been so long accustomed to sleep, during the harvest times, in the open fields.

In the same way, in another connection, it seemed strange to read in the report of the Minister of Agriculture that an agricultural school at Debreczen, which had been carried on in connection with an agricultural college at the same place, had been closed because "the pupils of this school, being in daily contact with the first-year pupils of the college, boarding at the Pallag, attempted to imitate their ways, wanted more than was necessary *for their future social position*, and at the same time they aimed at a position they were not able to maintain."

All this suggests and illustrates the rapidity with which changes are going on in Hungary and the haste with which the leaders in the Government and in social life are moving to catch up with and, if possible, get ahead of the procession of progress in the rest of Europe.

The trouble seems to be that in Hungary progress has begun at the top, with the Government, instead of at the bottom, with the people. The Government, apparently, desires and hopes to give the masses of the people an education that will increase their usefulness, without at the same time increasing their wants and stimulating their desire to rise. Its efforts to improve the condition of the masses are further confused by a determination to suppress the other nationalities and preserve the domination of the Magyar race. In short, I think I might sum up the situation by saying that Hungary is trying the doubtful experiment of attempting to increase the efficiency of the people without giving them freedom.

The result is that while the Government is closing up the schools because, as the Minister of Agriculture says, "an important political and social principle is endangered" when students begin to hope and dream of a higher and better situation in life than that in which they were born, the masses of the people are emigrating to America in order to better their condition.

At Fiume I had an opportunity to study at close range what I may call the process of this emigration. I had, in other words, an opportunity to see something, not merely of the manner in which the stream of emigration, flowing out from the little inland villages, is collected and cared for at Fiume until it pours into and is carried away in the ships, but also to get a more definite idea of the motives and social forces that are working together to bring about this vast migration of the rural populations of south-eastern Europe.

In no country in Europe, not even in Italy, has emigration been so carefully studied, and in no country has more been done to direct and control emigration than in Hungary. At the same time I think it is safe to say that nowhere else has emigration brought so many changes in the political and social life of the people. At one time, indeed, it seemed as if Hungary proposed to make emigration a state monopoly. This was when the Government, in granting to the Cunard Steamship Company a monopoly of the emigrant business at Fiume, made a contract to furnish that line at least 30,000 emigrants a year. At that time there were between one hundred and two hundred thousand emigrants leaving Hungary every year, most of whom were making the journey to America by way of the German lines at Hamburg and Bremen.

It is said that the Hungarian Government, in order to turn the tide of emigration in the direction of Fiume and swell the traffic at that port, directed that all steamship tickets should be sold by Government agents, who refused permission to emigrants to leave the country by other than the Fiume route.

Since then, however, Hungary has, I understand, modified its contract with the Cunard Company in such a manner that it does not appear as if the Government had actually gone into the business of exporting its own citizens, and, instead of attempting to direct emigration through Fiume by something amounting almost to force, it has rather sought to invite traffic by creating at this post model accommodations for emigrants.

As a matter of fact the Government has, as a rule, attempted to discourage emigration rather than increase it. Where that was not possible it has still tried to maintain its hold upon its citizens in America; to keep alive their interest in their native land and make the emigration, as far as possible, a temporary absence, in order that the state should not suffer a permanent loss of its labouring population, and in order, apparently, that the stream of gold which had poured into the country as a result of this emigration might not cease.

The actual amount of money which is brought back by returning emigrants, or those living temporarily in America, cannot be definitely determined. For example, not less than 47,000 emigrants returned to Hungary in 1907. It is estimated, if I remember rightly, that each returned emigrant brought home at least $200, while the average immigrant, not permanently settled in America, sends back every year about $120, which is probably more money than he could earn at home. In the years 1900 to 1906, inclusive, there was sent to Hungary by money orders alone, $22,917,566. In the year 1903 an official investigation shows that, in addition to the money which went from America in other ways, $17,000,000 was sent to Hungary through banks.

One result of this influx of money from America has been that the peasant has been able to gratify his passion to obtain for himself a little strip of land or increase the size of the farm he already possesses. In fact, in certain places mentioned by Miss Balch in her book, "Our Slavic Fellow Citizen," the demand for land has been so great that it has increased in value between 500 and 600 per cent.*

In one year, 1903, according to Miss Balch, 4,317 emigrants from one county in Croatia sent home $560,860, which is an average of not quite $130 per immigrant. With this money 4,116 homes were bettered, by paying debts, buying more land, or making improvements.

These facts give, however, but a small indication of the influence which immigration has had, directly and indirectly, upon the conditions of life among the masses of the people in Hungary and other portions of southeastern Europe. For one thing, in arousing the hopes, ambitions, and discontent of the so-called "inferior" peoples, it has added fuel to the racial conflicts of the kingdom.

The Slovak or the Croatian who comes to America does not at once lose his interest in the political and social struggles of his native land. On the contrary, in America, where he has opportunity to read newspapers printed in his own language, and to freely discuss racial policies in the societies and clubs which have been formed by the different nationalities in many parts of the United States, the average Slovak or Croatian in America is likely to take a more intelligent interest in the struggle for national

*Charities Publication Committee, 1910.

existence of his own people than he took at home.

In the case of members of some of the minor nationalities it has happened that, owing to the persistence with which the Hungarian Government had discouraged their efforts to teach their own languages, it is not until they have reached America that they have had opportunity to read their mother-tongue.

Some indication of the interest which the different immigrant peoples take in the struggles of the members of their own race, in their native land, is given by the work which several of these nationalist societies are doing in America. The National Slavonic Society organizes political meetings, raises funds for Slovak political prisoners in Hungary, and scatters Slovak literature for the purpose of arousing sympathy and interest in the Slovak cause.

In his book, "Racial Problems in Hungary," Seton-Watson, who has made a special study of the condition of the Slovaks, says:

"The returned Slovak emigrants who have saved money in the United States are steadily acquiring small holdings in Hungary, and helping to propagate ideas of freedom and nationality among their neighbours. . . . They speedily learn to profit by the free institutions of their adopted country, and to-day the 400,000 Slovaks of America possess a national culture and organization which present a striking contrast to the cramped development of their kinsmen in Hungary. There are more Slovak newspapers in America than in Hungary; but the Magyars seek to redress the balance by refusing to deliver these American journals through the Hungarian post-office. Everywhere among the emigrants, leagues, societies, and clubs flourish undisturbed; . . . these societies do all in their power to awaken Slovak sentiment, and contribute materially to the support of the Slovak press in Hungary.*

Seton-Watson adds that "the independence and confidence of the returned emigrants are in striking contrast with the pessimism and passivity of the elder generation." It is for this reason, perhaps, that the Magyars, who represent the "superior race" in Hungary, say that "America has spoiled the Slovak emigrant."

In travelling across Hungary from Fiume to Budapest, and thence to Cracow, Poland, I passed successively through regions and districts inhabited by many different racial types, but I think I gained a more vivid notion of the strange mixture of races which make up the population of the Dual Monarchy from what I saw in Fiume than in any other part of the country. In Budapest, which is the great melting pot of the races in Hungary, there is much the same uniformity in the dress and manners of the different races that one meets in any other large and cosmopolitan city. Fiume, on the contrary, has a much larger number of people who seem to be still in touch

*Quoted by Miss Balch in "Our Slavic Fellow Citizens," p. 116.

with the customs and life of their native villages, and have not yet learned to be ashamed to wear the quaint and picturesque costumes of the regions to which they belong.

Among the most striking costumes which I remember to have seen were those of the Montenegrin traders, with their red caps, embroidered vests, and the red sashes around their waists, which made them look like brigands. After these, perhaps the most picturesque costumes which I saw were worn by a troop of Dalmatian girls, the most striking feature of whose costume was the white woollen leggings, tied at the knee with ribbons. One figure in particular that I recall was that of a little woman striding through the streets of Fiume, driving a little train of beautiful cream-coloured oxen.

All these distinctions of costume emphasized each other by contrast, and as they each signified differences in traditions, prejudices, and purposes of the people to whom they belonged, they gave one a sort of picture of the clash of races in this strange and interesting country.

Even among those races which are no longer divided by costume and habits, racial distinctions seem to be more clearly drawn than at Budapest. For example, to a large extent the business of the city seems to be monopolized by Germans and Jews. The Government officials are Magyars, but the bulk of the population are Italians and Croatians. As a matter of fact there are three distinct cities, which commonly go under the name of Fiume. There is the modern city, with its opera house, its handsome official buildings, which is Magyar; the elder city, with its narrow, gossiping streets and Roman triumphal arch, which is Italian, and, finally, just across the canal, or "fiume," which seems to have given the name to the city, is a handsome new Croatian town which is officially distinct from the rest of the city, having its own mayor and town officials.

Fiume itself has an exceptional position in the Kingdom of Hungary. It is what was known in the Middle Ages as a "free city," with a governor and representatives in the Hungarian Parliament. The mayor, I understand, however, is an Italian, who has married a Croatian wife. This alliance of two races in one family seems to have a certain advantage in the rather tumultuous politics of the city, for I was told that when the Croatians, as sometimes happens, go to the mayor's house in procession, with their grievances, the mayor's wife has been able to help her husband by addressing her own people in their native language.

The most interesting thing I saw in Fiume,

however, was the immense emigration building, which has accommodations, as I remember, for something like 3,000 emigrants. Here are the offices of the Hungarian emigration officials, and in this same building are received and cared for, until the next succeeding sailing, the accumulations of the stream of emigration which flows steadily out at this port from every part of the kingdom.

Here the emigrants, after they have been medically examined, given a bath and their clothes disinfected, are detained until the time of embarkation. In company with United States Consul Slocum, from whom I received much valuable information, I visited the emigration building and spent a large part of one day looking into the arrangements and talking, through an interpreter, with emigrants from different parts of the country who were waiting there to embark.

Under his guidance I inspected the barracks, furnished with rows upon rows of double-decked iron beds, observed the machinery for disinfecting the clothing of emigrants, visited the kitchen, tasted the soup, and finally saw all the different nationalities march in together to dinner, the women in one row and the men in another. The majority of them were of Magyar nationality; good, wholesome, sturdy, and thrifty people they seemed. They were from the country districts. Some of them were persons of property, who were going to America to earn enough money to pay off mortgages with which their lands were burdened. Very many of them had relatives, a brother, a sister, or a husband already in America, and they seemed to be very well informed about conditions in the new country where they were going.

The two most interesting figures that I noticed among the intended emigrants were a tall, pallid, and barefooted girl, with rather delicate and animated features, and a man in a linen blouse which hung down to his knees, his feet and legs incased in a kind of moccason, surmounted with leggings, bound with leather thongs. The girl was a Ruthenian, who was going to meet relatives in America. The man, whom I noticed looking, with what seemed to me rather envious interest and curiosity, at a pair of American shoes on sale at one of the booths in the big common hall, was a Roumanian.

Two of the emigrants with whom I talked had been in America before. One of these, who understood a little English, seemed to be a leader among the others. When I asked him the reason why he was going back to America he spoke quite frankly and disparagingly about conditions in the old country.

He said it was not so much the wages that led people to emigrate, though they were small enough. But the worst of it was that there were long intervals when it was not possible to get any work. Besides that, the taxes were high.

"And then," he added, shrugging his shoulders and throwing out his arm with a gesture of impatience, "it is too tight here."

I suspect that this expresses the feeling of a good many emigrants who, returning to their native country, have emigrated a second time. They have found things in the old country "too tight" for comfort. There is still room in America for people to spread out, and grow and find out for themselves what they are capable of. As long as people find things "too tight" they will move on. The plant stretches always toward the light.

Among the emigrants with whom I had an opportunity to talk was a group of Roumanians who had come up from Transylvania, or Siebenbürgen, as they called it. They were a dark, silent sort of people, who hung very closely together and looked at us out of the corners of their eyes. When I sought to talk with them they seemed indisposed to answer my questions, and finally one of them told the interpreter that they had been instructed not to talk with any one until they reached America.

Considering the elaborate regulations which their Government has imposed upon people seeking to leave Hungary, and the still more elaborate regulations which our Government has imposed upon people seeking to enter the United States, this did not particularly surprise me.

Since these people were Roumanians, or Wallachs, from Siebenbürgen, they may have had other reasons for not telling why they were leaving the country. The Roumanians, although they proudly claim descent from the Roman conquerors of this part of the world, are, nevertheless, classed among the "inferior," as they are, in fact, among the most ignorant, races in Hungary. As they have been particularly persistent in advertising their wrongs to the rest of Europe, and have been frequently punished for it, they may, perhaps, have learned that silence is golden, particularly in the presence of Magyar officials.

When in Vienna I was seeking for information that would help me to understand the racial situation in the Dual Monarchy, I found that one of the most learned and brilliant writers on that subject was a Roumanian who, while he was a student in a Roumanian academy in 1892, had been arrested with other students and condemned to four years' imprisonment for writing and circulating a pamphlet in which were enumerated "acts of violence" committed against the other races of Hungary by the "superior" Magyars.

The superiority of the dominant race seems, as a matter of fact, to be the foundation stone of the political policy of the present government in Hungary. In the last analysis it seems to be the major premise, so to speak, of every argument which I happen to have heard or read in justification of the policy which the Government has pursued in reference to the other races of the monarchy. In fact, the "superiority of the Magyar" race is responsible for most that is good and evil in the history of Hungary for the past seventy years. It seems, for example, to have been the chief source of inspiration for the heroic struggle against Austria which began in 1848 and ended with the independence of Hungary in 1867. It seems, also, to have been the goad which has spurred on the impatient leaders of modern Hungary in their hurry to overtake and surpass the progress of civilization in the rest of Europe.

Unfortunately the ambition and success of

the Magyars in their effort to gain their political independence and preserve their peculiar racial type from being lost and swallowed up by the other and "inferior" peoples by whom it is surrounded have encouraged every other nationality in a similar desire and determination.

"If it is good for the Magyars to preserve their language, customs, and racial traditions," say the other races, in effect, "why is it not just as important for us that we preserve ours?"

The reply of the Magyars is, in effect: "You have no language, no history, no tradition worth keeping. In short, you are an inferior race."

Naturally the argument does not end there. The other nationalities reply by founding national schools and colleges to study and preserve their peculiar language, traditions, and customs, while these nationalities who have previously had no history proceed to make some. Thus the doctrine of superiority of the Magyar race, which has been so valuable in stimulating the Magyars to heroic efforts in behalf of their own race, seems to have been just as valuable in stinging into life the racial pride and loyalty of the other races. And thus, on the whole, in spite of its incidental cruelties, the conflict of the races in Hungary, like the struggle of the white and black races in the South, seems to have done less harm than good.

At least this is true so far as it concerns the races which are down and are struggling up, because oppression, which frequently stimulates the individual or the race which suffers from it, invariably injures most the individual or the race which inflicts it.

Most of the "acts of violence" of which the subordinate nations complain are committed in the name of what is known as the "Magyar State Idea," which seems to be little more, however, than the idea that the Magyars must dominate, although they represent but 51 per cent. of the population in Hungary proper and 45 per cent. of the total population, including that of the annexed territory, Croatia-Slavonia.

So far is the Magyar race identified with the Government in Hungary that it is punished as a kind of treason to say anything against the Magyars. Most of the persons who are persecuted for political crimes in Hungary seem to be charged either with panslavism, which is usually little more than a desire of the Slavs to preserve their own national existence, or with "incitement against the Magyar nationality."

On the part of the Magyars it does not seem to be any crime to speak disrespectfully, or even contemptuously, of the other races. I have observed that those writers who have sought to defend the "Magyar State Idea" refer quite frankly to the Roumanians and the Slovaks as "inferior races," who are not competent to govern themselves.

There is, likewise, a saying among the Magyars to the effect that "a Slovak is not a human being," a notion that seems to spring up quite naturally in the mind of any race which has accustomed itself to the slavery and oppression of another race.

It is, however, all the more curious that such a saying should gain currency in Hungary in view of the fact that Kossuth, the great national hero of Hungary, was himself a Slovak.

One hears strange stories in Hungary of the methods which the dominant race has employed to hold the other races in subjection. For example, in the matter of elections, bribery, intimidation, and all the other familiar methods for exploiting the vote of ignorant and simple-minded people are carried on in a manner and to an extent which recalls the days of Reconstruction in the Southern States.

In order to maintain the superior race in power, newspapers are suppressed, schools are closed and the moneys for their support, which have been collected for educational purposes, are confiscated by the Government.

As an illustration of the lengths to which

Hungary has gone in order to maintain Magyar domination, it is said that when the Catholic clergy, seeing the ravages which drink had made among Slovaks, attempted to organize temperance societies among them, the Government suppressed these organizations on the ground that they tended to foster the sentiment of panslavism and so were in opposition to the "Magyar State Idea." It is known, however, that the chief complaints against these societies were from liquor dealers.

Apparently it is just as easy in Hungary as in America for selfish persons to take advantage of racial predjuice and sentiment in order to use it for their own ends. In fact, all that I saw and learned in regard to the relation of the races in Hungary served to show me that racial hatred works in much the same way, whether it exists among people of the same colour but different speech, or among people of different colour and the same speech.

If there are some points in which the relations of the races in Hungary and the United States are similar, there are others in which they differ. While Hungary is seeking to solve its racial problem by holding down the weaker races and people, America is seeking to accomplish the same result by lifting them up. In Hungary every effort seems to be made to compel the so-called "inferior race" to give up their separate language, to forget their national history, traditions, and civilization—everything, in fact, which might inspire them, as a people, with a desire or a proper ambition to win for themselves a position of respect and consideration in the civilized world.

In America, on the contrary, each race and nationality is encouraged to cultivate and take pride in everything that is distinctive or peculiar, either in its traditions, racial traits, or disposition. I think I am safe in saying that there is no country in the world where so many different races of such different colours, habits, and traditions live together in such peace and harmony as is true in the United States. One reason for this is that there is no other country where "the man farthest down" has more opportunity or greater freedom than in the United States.

CHAPTER XIII

CRACOW AND THE POLISH JEW

EVER since I can remember I have had a special and peculiar interest in the history and the progress of the Jewish race. The first book that I knew, the Bible, was a history of the Jews, and to my childish mind the most fascinating portion of that book was the story of the manner in which Moses led the children of Israel out of the house of bondage, through the wilderness, into the promised land. I first heard that story from the lips of my mother, when both she and I were slaves on a plantation in Virginia. I have heard it repeated and referred to many times since. In fact, I am certain that there is hardly a day or a week goes by that I do not meet among my people some reference to this same Bible story.

The Negro slaves were always looking forward to the time when a Moses should arise from somewhere who would lead them, as he led the ancient Hebrews, out of the house of bondage. And after freedom, the masses of the Negro people have still continued to look to some great leader, some man inspired of God, who would lead them out of their difficulties into the promised land, which, somehow, they never seem able to reach.

As I learned in slavery to compare the condition of the Negro with that of the Jews in bondage in Egypt, so I have frequently, since freedom, been compelled to compare the prejudice, even persecution, which the Jewish people have to face and overcome in different parts of the world with the disadvantages of the Negro in the United States and elsewhere.

I had seen a good deal of the lower classes of the Jews in New York City before going to Europe, and when I visited Whitechapel, London, I had an opportunity to learn something of the condition of the Polish and Russian Jews who, driven from their native land, have found refuge in England. It was not until I reached Cracow, in Austrian Poland, or Galicia, however, that I really began to understand what life in the Ghetto, of which I had heard so much, was really like. It was not until then that I began to comprehend what the wear and tear of centuries of persecution, poverty, and suffering had meant in the life of the Jews.

One of the first things I observed in regard to the Jews abroad was the very different forms which racial prejudice takes in the different countries that I visited. For example, in East London, which has long been the refuge for the poor and oppressed of other countries, the Jew is tolerated, although he is not liked. It is not clear just what is the source of the English prejudice. Complaint is sometimes made that the Jewish immigrant has driven out the native Briton from certain parts of East London, but it is admitted at the same time that in such cases it is because the Jew has proven a better tenant. He does not drink, he is law-abiding, and he pays his rent regularly. It seems to be true in London, also, as it is in New York, that as soon as the Jewish immigrant has made a little success he does not remain in the same quarter of the city. He soon moves out and his place is taken by some new and half-starved fugitive from Russia or Roumania, so that there is a constant stream of "greeners," as they are called, coming in, and another, perhaps somewhat smaller, stream of those who have been successful moving out. In spite of this fact, it is generally admitted that general conditions have improved under the influence of the Jews. English prejudice where it exists seems to be due, therefore, partly to economic causes and partly to the general distrust of the alien that seems to be gaining in England with the influx of immigration from southern Europe. In Denmark, on the contrary, where the Jews seem to be very largely represented among the educated and well-to-do classes, I discovered a great deal of prejudice against the Germans but almost none against the Jews. In fact, one of the most distinguished men in Denmark, outside of the King, a man who has been a leader in the intellectual life of that country during the past thirty years, Prof. Georg Brandes, is a Jew.

In Germany I learned that, while the Jews are prominent not only in business but in the professions, it was still difficult for them to rise in the army or to advance to the position of professor in the universities, unless they have first been baptized.

In speaking about this matter to a German whom I met at one of the hotels in Vienna, I called to mind the name of a distinguished professor whose name I had heard as an instance of a Jew gaining a high position in a German university.

"Oh, well," he replied, "he has been baptized."

That recalls to my mind a conundrum which an acquaintance proposed while we were discussing some of the peculiarities of race prejudice in Europe.

"When is a Jew not a Jew?" he asked. The

answer is of course, "When he is a Christian." In other words, prejudice in Germany seems to be directed only against the Jew who clings to his religion.

When I reached Prague in Bohemia I learned that among the masses of the people there is little distinction made between Jews and Germans, since both speak the same language, and the Czechs, confusing the one with the other, hate both with a double hatred, first, for what they are, and then for what they seem to be.

In Vienna and Budapest the Jews, through the newspapers which they control, seem to exercise a powerful influence on politics. I remember hearing repeated references while I was there to the "Jewish press." In Prague it is said that every German paper but one is controlled by Jews. Jews are represented, however, not only in the press in Austria-Hungary, but in the army and in all the other professions. They are not only financiers and business men, but doctors, lawyers, artists, and actors, as elsewhere in Europe where they have gained their freedom. Nevertheless it is still against the law for Jews and Christians to intermarry in Austria-Hungary.

I have referred at some length to the condition of the Jews in other parts of Europe where they have profited by the social and political freedom which was granted them in the course of the nineteenth century, because their progress there is in such striking contrast with their condition as I saw it in and around Cracow, in Galicia; as it is, also, just across the borders of Austria-Hungary, in Russian Poland and Roumania, and as it seems to have been in other parts of Europe seventy-five or a hundred years ago, before the gates of the Ghetto were opened and the inhabitants emancipated.

Some notion of the conditions under which the Jews lived, in almost every part of Europe, a hundred years ago, may be gathered from the restrictions which are imposed upon them to-day in Russia and Roumania. In Roumania a Jew can neither vote nor hold office in the civil service. He is excluded from the professions; he is not permitted, for example, to become a physician or even open a pharmacy; he is not permitted to live in the rural districts; he may neither own land outside of the town nor work as an agricultural labourer. In the mills and factories not more than 25 per cent. of the employees may be Jews. Although they are practically restricted to business enterprises, Jews may not become members of chambers of commerce. Jews are bound to serve in the army, they pay heavier taxes, proportionately, than other portions of the community, but they are classed under the laws as "aliens not subject to alien protection."

In Russia, Jews are not allowed to live outside of what is called the "Pale of Settlement," which includes twelve provinces on the western and southwestern borders which Russia has annexed during the past two hundred years. Only merchants who pay a special license of 1,000 rubles, or about $500, university graduates, and a few others may live outside the pale. A Jew is not even permitted to live in Siberia unless he has been sent there in punishment for crime.

Inside the pale, Jews are not allowed to live outside the cities and incorporated towns. Although Jews are allowed to vote in Russia and send representatives to the Duma, they are not permitted to hold office or to be employed in the public service. They are compelled to pay in addition to the ordinary taxes, which are heavy enough, taxes on the rents they receive from property owned by them, or inheritances, on the meat killed according to the Jewish law, on candles used in some of their religious observances, and on the skull caps they wear during religious services. In spite of this they are excluded from hospitals, schools, and public functions, which, in the pale, are mainly paid for out of the extra taxes imposed upon them.

The most singular thing about it all is that the disabilities under which the Russian Jew now labours are at once removed by baptism. Not only that, but every Jew who allows himself to be sprinkled with holy water, in sign of the renunciation of his religion and his people, receives thirty rubles, "thirty pieces of silver," as a reward.

The Jews whom I saw in Galicia are not subject to any of the medieval restrictions which are imposed upon members of their race in Russia and Roumania. They enjoy, in fact, all the political rights of other races. Nevertheless, Jews in Galicia are said to be poorer than they are in some parts of Russian Poland, although very much better off than in some parts of southern Russia.

Elsewhere in Europe, where they have had their freedom, Jews are as a rule more prosperous than the people by whom they are surrounded. In Berlin, Germany, for instance, where Jews represent 4.88 per cent. of the total population, 15 per cent. of those who had an income of 1,500 marks, or more, were Jews. Statistics show that similar conditions exist in other parts of Europe.*

When I asked an acquaintance, who had lived a number of years in Austria, why this was so,

*M. Fishberg, "The Jews," p. 366,

he replied that there were so many Jews in Galicia that there were not enough other people to support them. He then went on to explain that between the two classes, the nobility who owned the land and the peasant who cultivated it, the Jew represented the trader, or middleman. It was, therefore, literally true that there were not enough other people in the country to support the Jew, who represents, however, not more than 11 per cent. of the total population.

One of the first persons I met in Galicia was a representative of this poorer class of Jews. I reached Cracow late one afternoon in the latter part of September. There was a cold wind blowing and, for the first time since I had left Scotland, I noticed an uncomfortable keenness in the evening air, which was an indication, I suppose, that I was on the northern and eastern or the Russian side of the Carpathian Mountains. One of the first persons I encountered as I was standing shivering at the entrance of the hotel was a pale-faced, brown-eyed little boy, who spoke to me in English and seemed to want to establish some sort of friendship with me on the basis of our common acquaintance with the English language. He was unmistakably a Jew and, as we walked down the street together, he told me something of his life in London and then in Cracow. I gathered from what he was able to tell me that his father, who was a cabinetmaker and, as he said, "very poor," had found it harder to live in the fierce competition of the London sweatshops, where he had been employed, than in the Ghetto at Cracow, and so had grown discouraged and returned.

I learned from him, as I did later from others of his race, that not all the Jews who came to England and America succeed and get rich in a few years, as seems to be commonly supposed. Some of them fail, and some get into unexpected troubles, and frequently families who immigrate are broken up and some of them sent back as a consequence of the enforcement of the immigration regulations, so that there is not so much eagerness to go to America as there was a few years ago.

In spite of this fact the Jews of Galicia, nearly every one of whom probably has friends or relatives either in England or America, seem to look with peculiar interest upon every one who speaks the English language, because they regard them as representatives of a people who, more than any other in the world, have tried to be just to the Jews.

A few days later I met in a little village a few miles from Cracow a Jewish trader who, like most of the Jews in this part of the country, spoke German as well as Polish, so that with the assistance of Doctor Park I was able to speak with him. He said that his business was to buy grain and fodder from the large landowners in different parts of Galicia and sell it again to the peasants, who used it to feed their stock. When he learned that I was from America and that I wanted to see something of the life of the peasant people he volunteered to be my guide. It was a very fortunate meeting for me, for I found that this man not only knew about the condition of nearly every family in the village, but he understood, also, exactly how to deal with them so that, at his touch, every door flew open, as if by magic, and I was able to see and learn all that I wanted to know.

In the meantime I noticed that our guide and interpreter seemed to be quite as interested in learning about America as I was interested in getting acquainted with Galicia. He interlarded all his information about the condition of the peasants in different parts of the country with questions about conditions in America. As it turned out, he not only had relatives in America, but he had a cousin in New York who had got into trouble and been sent to prison for three years on account of some business irregularity. It was a small matter, according to my Jewish friend, that would not have cost more than eight days' imprisonment in Galicia. He could not understand, therefore, how a poor man should be treated more harshly in a free country like America, where all are equal, than he was at home, where he was the underdog and did not expect consideration. What seemed to trouble him most, however, was the fact that he had not heard from his cousin for a year and no one knew what had become of him.

When the matter was explained to me, I told the man that if he would give me the name and last address of his cousin, when I returned to New York I would look the matter up and, if possible, learn what had become of the missing cousin.

This seemed to me a very natural proposal, under the circumstances, but it evidently took the poor man by surprise, for he stopped, stared at me an instant, and then in the most humble manner knelt down and kissed my hand. I confess that at first I was a little shocked and rather disgusted. Afterward I learned that it is a common habit, more especially in Russia, for peasants to kiss the hands and even the feet of their superiors. The thought that occurred to me, however, was that it must have taken many centuries of subjection and oppression to make this attitude of humility a familiar and natural way, as it seemed to be in this case, of expressing gratitude.

The singular thing about it all was that this Jew who had shown himself so humble toward me looked down upon and despised the Polish peasants among whom he trades. He referred to them as "ignorant and dirty creatures." For all that, he seemed to have learned their ways of expressing himself to those to whose power or influence he looked for help or protection.

Under these circumstances, with these ingrained habits in the masses of the people, I found it hard to imagine just what the right of manhood suffrage, which has recently been conferred upon the people in all the provinces of Austria, was likely to mean in actual practice.

Nothing was impressed more forcibly upon me during my study of conditions in Europe than this — namely, that we can tell very little from the mere fact that this or that political institution exists in a country just what privileges or disadvantages these institutions bring to the masses of the people. In fact, it seems to be just as true in Europe as it is in America, that mere legislative enactments can of themselves no more produce justice and freedom than they can produce industry and thrift. After the physical bondage has been destroyed there still remains the bondage of superstition, of ignorance, and of religious, class, and racial prejudice. The act of this Jew in kissing my hand was a revelation to me, not only of his own state of mind, but of the conditions by which he was surrounded.

I think this one incident, more than anything else I saw or heard while I was in Galicia, gave me an insight into the life of the people. It seemed to me I could understand, for example, from this alone, why the Jews have made little more progress in Galicia than they have in the neighbouring provinces of Roumania and Russia.

As for my guide, I might add that I never heard from him afterward. If he wrote to me the letter never reached me, and I do not know what finally became of the cousin whom he had lost.

Perhaps I ought, before I attempt to describe the condition of the poorer class of Jews in Cracow, to say something of another Ghetto which I saw while in Europe.

During my stay in Prague I took a walk one day through an ancient quarter of the city which had been formerly inhabited by Jews. The Ghetto of Prague is said to have been the largest and most famous in Europe. It was, in fact, a city in itself, for it contained not merely the oldest synagogue in Europe, with a famous old Jewish burial ground attached to it, but also a Rathhaus, or city hall, and a market in which, according to tradition, Jewish traders at one time sold Christian slaves. So thoroughly were the Jews at one time established in this quarter of the city that it went under the name of Judenstadt, or Jewtown. There they maintained, in a small way, a separate civil government of their own, just as they do, to a lesser extent, in Russia to-day. In his book on the Jews, already referred to, Mr. M. Fishberg, to whom I am indebted for many facts and statistics concerning the condition of the Jew, says of the Jews in Russia to-day:

They speak their own language, Yiddish, and many conduct their affairs, keep their ledgers, write contracts, wills, and many other documents in this dialect; the registration of births, marriages, and deaths is done by their rabbis, and the divorces granted by them are recognized by the state as valid; in the smaller towns they prefer to settle their differences before their own judiciary (Beth din), and not in the state courts; they collect the greater part of their own taxes for the Government in the name of the Jewish community; not only is each individual Jew required to do military duty, but the Jewish community as a whole is held responsible for delivering annually a certain number of recruits. This separateness goes as far as the calendar with many Jews, who date their letters and documents according to the Hebrew and not the Russian calendar. Up to about fifty years ago it was a disgrace for a Jew to be able to read Russian or German, or even to have in his possession a book in one of these vulgar languages; it was a sin next to apostasy. But during the last two generations a profound change has taken place.

At the time I was in Prague the ancient Ghetto was in process of demolition, and it illustrates the change which has come in recent years that most of the people living in the narrow streets and battered ancient buildings of the former Ghetto were not Jews but Christians.

After Prague, the city which has the oldest and most interesting Ghetto in Europe is Cracow, and the most interesting thing about it is the fact that it is still inhabited by Jews. They live there to-day very much, I suppose, as they did a hundred years ago, a race separate and apart, more removed, apparently, from the manners, customs, and comprehension of the rest of the world than any people this side of China.

I have known Jews nearly all my life. I have done business with them and have more than once talked to them in their synagogues, and have always found sympathy and support among them for the work I have had to do for my own people. I have frequently visited and studied, to some extent, the poorer classes in the Jewish quarter on the East Side in New York. In spite of this, however, when certain strange figures in long black coats, soft felt hats, with pale faces, lighted by dark glittering eyes and framed by glossy curls which hung down on either side in front of their ears, were pointed out to me in Vienna, I had not the slightest notion to what race or nationality of people they belonged. Later on, when I reached Cracow, these same slender figures and pale, delicate faces became very familiar to me, and I learned to recognize in them the higher type of Polish Jew.

The great majority of the Jews in Cracow still make their homes in a quarter of the city called the "Kazimierz," which gets its name from that of a Polish king who fell in love with a beautiful Jewess some four hundred years ago and, for her sake, made Poland a refuge for the members of her race, who, at that time, were hunted almost like wild beasts in other parts of Europe.

I visited the Kazimierz late one afternoon, when the narrow, dirty, and ill-smelling streets were swarming with their strange brood of slatternly, poverty-stricken, and unhealthy looking inhabitants.

I have been through the Jewish quarter in New York, with its confusion of pushcarts, its swarms of black-eyed children, and its strange old men with gray-brown beards wandering careworn and absorbed through the crowded streets, each anxiously intent on some thought or purpose of his own. The Jewish quarter on the East Side in New York is, however, a pale reflection of the Ghetto in Cracow. For one thing, the Jew in New York, though he retains many of the habits and customs of the country from which he came, seems, in most cases, to be making an earnest effort to make an American of himself; to learn the language, adopt the dress and, as far as possible, the manners of the new country of which he is soon to become, if he is not already, a citizen.

The masses of the Polish Jews, however, still cling tenaciously to the customs of their religion and of the Ghetto in which, for a thousand years or more, they have lived as exiles and, more or less, like prisoners. Instead of seeking to make themselves look like the rest of the people among whom they live, they seem to be making every effort to preserve and emphasize the characters in which they are different from the people about them.

Although I met in Cracow Jews in all the various stages of transition — as far as their dress is concerned — from the traditional Ghetto Jew to the modern literary, professional or business man, nevertheless the majority of the Jews still cling to the long black coat which they were compelled to wear in the Middle Ages. Certain ones have discarded this symbol of exclusiveness, but still wear the long beard, and the side curls in front of their ears, which seem to be especially dear to them, perhaps, because, for some reason I could not understand, they are forbidden to wear them in Russia.

Perhaps it was the effect of the costume, which gave them a strange and alien appearance, but it seemed to me, at first, as if every Jew in Cracow had exactly the same features, the same manner of walking, and the same expression of countenance. As I watched the different figures in the crowded streets more closely, however, I discovered that beneath the peculiar dress and manner many different types of human beings were concealed. There were the pale-browed students, who moved through the crowd with a hurried and abstracted air; there were slender and elegant aristocrats, who, while still wearing the uniform of their race, dressed with a scrupulous correctness and looked at you with an expression which seemed a curious mingling of the humility of the Jew and the scorn of the Pharisee.

There was the commonplace plodding Jew, following humbly in the common ruts of barter and trade and the daily and weekly routine which his religion prescribed. There was the outcast beggar, dirty and wretched, doddering aimlessly along the dirty street or sitting in some doorway, staring disconsolately into the street. There was, also, the dirty, gluttonous, ignorant, and brutal type, on whom neither suffering nor fanaticism seemed to have made any impression, and who, in his Jewish dress and manners, looked like a caricature of his more high-bred neighbour.

I visited the ancient synagogue while I was in Cracow, which they say was built for the Jews by that same Polish king, Kazimierz, who first invited them to take refuge in his country. I saw there the ancient Roll of the Laws and ancient Prayer Book which were brought from Spain when the Jews were expelled from that country.

Nearby the synagogue is the ancient Jewish market. A narrow street leads into an open square in the centre of which is a circular building. Before one of the entrances of this building a man, with the pale brow and delicate features which seem to be a mark of superiority among the people of the Ghetto, was publicly slaughtering geese. The square in which this building stood was surrounded on all sides by rows of little market booths, in front of which groups of men and women were dickering and trading for various small wares. A crowd of women stood about the building in the centre of the square and watched the pale-browed man, who did not seem to relish the job, as he rapidly and dexterously performed the ceremony of cutting the throats of the geese. These were handed to him by a good-natured looking woman, wearing an apron and high boots, red with blood. After the geese were killed they were hung over a pit to drain, while fresh victims were brought from the baskets and crates standing about in the open square. A foul smell from the open pit in which the geese were allowed to bleed filled the square. This did not add to the dignity of the proceedings, but it served to impress them upon my memory.

In one corner of the square I noticed a dull gray-coloured building from which troops of little Jewish children were issuing. It was one of those schools by means of which Jewish teachers, through all the persecutions and dispersions of nineteen centuries, have kept alive the memory of the Jewish history and the Jewish law and so kept the race together. I do not think I know of anything which so illustrates and emphasizes the power of education as the influences which these schools have had upon the Jewish people.

I was interested in all that I saw of the life of the Jew in Cracow, because it gave me some idea of the poverty, degradation, and squalor in which more than half of the Jewish race is living to-day in different parts of Europe. Of the twelve million Jews in the world, about nine millions live in Europe. Of this number more than six million live in Russia and nearly two million and a half in Austria, Roumania, and the other parts of southeastern Europe. I have given some idea of the poverty of the Jews in Galicia, where they are politically free. From all that I can learn the Jews in Russia and Roumania are very much worse off than they are in the Austrian province of Galicia. Most of us, who are acquainted with Jews only in America or in western Europe, have been led to believe, in spite of the evident poverty of many of the Jews who live on the East Side in New York and in the Whitechapel district of London, that, as a race, the Jews are extremely wealthy. I was surprised, therefore, to read recently the statement, made by Jews who have investigated the condition of their own people, to the effect that, while they are undeniably wealthier than their Christian neighbours in the countries in which, during the past hundred years, they have been granted their freedom, taking the Jews as a whole they are poorer than any other civilized nation in the world. In short, one writer has said: "If we were to capitalize their wealth and distribute it among the twelve millions of Jews they would dispute with any poor nation for the lowest place in the scale of wealth."*

*M. Fishberg, "The Jews: A Study of Race and Environment," p. 361.

The direction in which the Jews seem to be superior to all of the rest of the world is apparently not in wealth but in education. Even in Russia, where they do not have the same educational advantages that are given to the rest of the population, it is found that, while 79 per cent. of the total population can neither read nor write, the percentage of illiteracy among the Jews is 61 per cent. which is 18 per cent. less than that of the rest of the population.

In western Europe, where Jews have equal opportunities with their Gentile neighbours in the matter of education, they are far in advance of them in education. Statistics for Cracow show, for example, that while only a little more than 2 per cent. of the Jews who applied for marriage licenses were unable to read and write, between 15 and 20 per cent. of the Christians in the same category were illiterate. In Italy, where 42.6 per cent. of the men and 57 per cent. of the women of the Christian population over fifteen years of age are unable to read and write, only 3 per cent. of the men and 7.5 per cent. of the women among the Jews are illiterate.

In Austria over 25 per cent. of the students of the universities are Jews, although they represent only 5 per cent. of the population. In Hungary, where Jews represent 4.9 per cent.

of the population, they furnish 30.27 per cent. of the students in the universities and other schools of higher education. In Baden, Germany, Jews have proportionately three and a half times as many students as the Christians. Since 1851 the number of Jewish students in Austrian universities has increased more than sevenfold, while the number of Christian students has scarcely more than trebled in that time.

One reason for this is that the Jews have almost invariably made their homes in the cities, where the opportunities for education existed. They have, at the same time, been almost wholly engaged in business, which not only requires a certain amount of education, but is in itself, more than other occupations, a source of education.

The name rabbi, or teacher, has always been a title of respect and honour among the Jews from the earliest time. It was the name that his disciples bestowed upon Jesus.

If there were no other reasons why the story of the Jew should be studied, it would be interesting and inspiring as showing what education can do and has done for a people who, in the face of prejudice and persecution, have patiently struggled up to a position of power and preeminence in the life and civilization in which all races are now beginning to share.

CHAPTER XIV

A POLISH VILLAGE IN THE MOUNTAINS

IT WAS a Jewish trader who advised me to visit Jedlovka. He said that I would see the peasants living there now as they had lived for hundreds of years — in the simplest and most primitive fashion.

Jedlovka, I found, is a little straggling village in the foothills of the Carpathians — the mountains which divide Galicia from Hungary. In order to reach the village it was necessary to take the train at Cracow and ride for an hour or more in the direction of Lemberg, which is the Ruthenian, just as Cracow is the Polish, metropolis of Galicia.

At a place called Turnow we changed cars and continued our journey in a direction at right angles to that in which we previously travelled. It was another hour's ride by train to the foothills of the mountain. At Tuchow, at the point where the railway, running southward, plunges into the mountain, we disembarked again and continued our journey by wagon. The road led up out of the broad plain through which we had been travelling, into a narrow and sombre little valley. At the end of this valley there is a little wayside inn. Higher up, where the road, winding up out of the valley, leads out into a high, clear space at what seemed to be the top of the mountain, there is a church, and this tavern and the church, together with a few scattering log huts, were the village of Jedlovka and the end of our journey.

I had had a vague sort of notion that somewhere in this remote region I should meet peasants wearing sheepskin jackets, sandals, and leggings bound with thongs, driving their herds to pasture. I even had a wild hope that I should come upon some rustic festival, such as I had read about, where the young men and women would dance upon the greensward, to the music of shepherds' pipes. As a matter of fact, it chanced that our visit did fall upon a feast day, but there were no shepherds and no dances. What I saw was a crowd of women pouring out of the little church, high upon the hill, and crowds of drunken men carousing at the tavern below.

Before I proceed to tell what I learned of the peasant life in this mountain country, however, I want to refer to one feature of Polish life which was impressed upon me by what I saw on the way.

I have referred in the preceding chapter to the position which the Jew occupies in the economic organization of Polish life. He is the middleman and has the trade of the country very largely in his hands. I was particularly impressed with this fact by what I saw in the course of this journey. Although the Jews represent only about 13 per cent of the population of Galicia, I am certain that more than half of the people on the train on which we travelled were people of that race. There were Jews of all descriptions and in all stages of evolution, from the poor, patient pedler, wearing the garb of the Ghetto, to the wealthy banker or merchant fastidiously dressed in the latest European fashion. When we left the train at Tuchow it was a Jewish horse trader who drove us in his improvised coach the remainder of our journey into the mountains. A restaurant at which we stopped to get something to eat on our return was conducted by a Jew. Halfway to our destination we passed a tumbledown cottage, close to the roadside, with a few trinkets in the window and some skins hanging from the beam which ran along the front of the building. We stopped and spoke to an ancient man with a long white beard, who lives there. He, also, was a Jewish trader. As I recall, he was engaged in buying skins from the peasants, paying them in the junk which I noticed displayed in the window. When we reached the tavern at the end of our journey it turned out that the man who ran the tavern was a Jew. Apparently wherever in Poland money changes hands a Jew is always there to take charge of it. In fact, it seemed to me that the Jew in Poland was almost like the money he handled, a sort of medium of exchange.

It was a very curious conveyance in which we made the last stage of our journey into the mountains. Instead of the droske we had expected to meet at the station we found what, under ordinary circumstances, would have been a farmer's wagon, I suppose, although it was an altogether different sort of farmer's wagon from any I had ever seen in America. The frame of this vehicle was something like a great long basket, narrow at the bottom, where it sat upon the axles, and wider at the top. The rim of this basket was made of poles, about the size of a fence rail, and this rim was supported upon the frame, which rested on the wagon, by little poles or pickets fastened in the frame below and the rim above, like a fence paling. The frame was so formed that it might have served the purpose either of a hayrick or a carryall. In this case it had been converted into a sort of coach or omnibus, with hanging seats, supported with leather straps from the rim. Arranged in this way this farmer's wagon was a not inconvenient mode of travel, and, driving through the fresh green country, dotted with quaint, little moss-covered cottages which seemed as much a part of the landscape as if they had grown there, the journey was made very pleasantly.

The houses in this part of the country were, for the most part, smaller, more weather-worn and decrepit, than those I had seen in other parts of Galicia. In fact, in some cases the green-thatched roofs were so old, so overgrown with vegetation, and the little whitewashed frames of the buildings that supported them had so sunken into the soil, that some of them looked like gigantic toadstools. As the day we visited this part of the country was a holiday, we met along the way many of the peasants, dressed in the quaint and picturesque garb of the country, passing in groups of two or three along the road.

I had before this visited a number of the peasant houses and was familiar with the plan and arrangement of them. The interior of these houses is usually divided into two rooms, separated in most cases by an entrance or hallway. In one of these rooms the whole family, consisting of the parents and perhaps five or six children, live, eat, and sleep. In this room there is usually a very large brick or stone oven which, on the cold winter nights, I learned, frequently serves the purpose of a bed. In the other room are the cows, pigs, geese, chickens. If the farmer is well-to-do he will have a number of buildings arranged in a hollow square having a goose pond in the centre and, in that case, the servants will very likely sleep in the straw in the barns with the cattle. I can give a more vivid notion of some of these houses by quoting a few lines from the notes jotted down by Doctor Park at the time of our visit:

To-day, for the first time, we visited some of the peasant houses in a little village about three or four miles from Cracow. It was difficult at first to make friends with the people. After a time it transpired that they were afraid that, although we were evidently foreigners, we might be Government officials of some sort. This is, perhaps, not strange, since there are many races in this country and most of them are "foreigners" to each other. Our guide says the people fear the country will be some day handed over to Russia. We got on better when the people learned we were Americans.

Every window of the little cottages we passed was crowded with laughing, curious children, with pink faces and white teeth. We visited the home of a widow with ten "yokes" of land and two cows. The cows give fifteen litres of milk a day, which is about ten quarts. The woman carries this to the market in Cracow every day. In the narrow little kitchen the children were all lined up in a row against the wall as we entered. One of them darted forward suddenly to kiss my hand. Mother and children were barefoot. The cow is across the hall from the kitchen. These two rooms, the kitchen and the cow-stall, are all there is to the house. I discovered what the duck pond in front of the house is for. The woman was filling it with straw to make manure.

One of the leading men in the village has a brand-new house made of logs. The logs were neatly squared and the chinks between them carefully plastered and painted. The house had three rooms, besides a storeroom and cow-stall. I counted three barns in the court, besides three outdoor cellars, one for the milk and the others for the storing of vegetables. To my question as to what the farmer did in the winter our guide replied, "Nothing. When they want money they go to the hole where the potatoes and turnips are buried and carry a load to the town." The owner of this house was very proud of his new place and showed one room in which were several huge chests, decorated and stained in bright vermilion in the peculiar style of peasant art. These chests were filled with clothes — peasant costumes of very handsome material, very beautifully embroidered and decorated. The principal ornament of the costume shown us was a belt studded with brass nails with broad leather clasps, as large as a small platter, behind and in front. It must have occupied the hours of a good many long winter evenings to make the garments this man had stowed away in these chests. Although there was plenty of room in this house, it is evident that the family lives almost wholly in the one large living-room.

The houses I visited in the mountain were constructed on the same plan as those described, except sometimes there was only one room for the whole family, including the cow, the chickens, and the rest of the animals. It is very cold on the north side of the mountains in winter, and the peasants and cattle frequently live in the same room to keep warm.

In one of the little huts which I ventured to

enter I found two old women lying down, apparently asleep, on a heap of straw, while a cow standing nearby them was peacefully chewing her cud, and several chickens were busily scratching among the straw on the earth floor. As there was almost no ventilation the air in some of these houses was almost indescribable.

It was in this part of the country, in the vicinity of the village tavern, that I found people who were poor, even by the very moderate standard of comfort that prevails in rural Poland. We passed on the drive up the valley a number of little huddling straw-thatched huts. One of these, which did not seem to be inhabited, I determined to explore. The building was of the prevailing type, with the cowshed in one end and the living-room in the other, but the thatch was no longer green, and age had imparted to the whole of the outside of the building a very dismal, weather-worn appearance. The windows were evidently of skins, of the same brown colour as the building itself. The entrance was through what would evidently have been the cowshed, but this was empty. The door into the living-room was open, and, as I entered, I saw at first only a cow tied to a manger. At the other end of the room, hovering about a little stone hearth, on which a little fire of twigs burned, were an old man and woman. As is frequently the case in many parts of Poland, there was no chimney, and the rafters of the house were deeply incrusted with the smoke which had accumulated in the peak of the roof and filtered out through the thatch or through an opening at the end of the building. The old people seemed very poor and helpless and, as I was about to leave the room, they held out their hands and begged for alms. I should like to have stayed and talked with them, but unfortunately I had no one with me at the time who was able to speak the Polish language.

As I learned that a number of people had gone to America from this valley I suspected that these old people were some of those who had been left behind and perhaps forgotten by the younger generation who had gone across the seas. I made some attempt later to learn if my suspicions were well founded, but no one whom I afterward met seemed to know anything about the history of the old people.

The wealthiest landlord in the vicinity was, as I learned, a Polish priest, who owned four different farms, and most of the people in the neighbourhood seemed to be his tenants. He lived in a big, bare, rambling house, surrounded by great barns filled with cattle and produce of various kinds. I stopped to call at this house, thinking that I might learn something from him about the poor people I have referred to, but the good priest was not at home and the people whom I found at this house did not seem to be able to tell me anything.

The tavern, which was a long, low log structure, built on the same general plan as the houses in the village, was crowded with revellers and steaming with the fumes of beer. Men were standing about, swinging their arms and shouting at each other at the top of their lungs, and almost every one of them was drunk. Several of the men present, including the proprietor, had been, as I learned, in America. One of them, who could speak a few words of English, gave us an especially hearty welcome. Some of the money which pours into Poland from America had reached even this remote corner of the country, it seemed.

I asked the proprietor, who had lived in Newark, N. J., for a time and spoke a little English, whether he liked this part of the world better than America.

"It is easier to live here," he said. Then added, "when you have a little money."

"But when you haven't any money?" I suggested. He shrugged his shoulders. "Then go to America," he said.

He told me a good deal of land had been purchased in this part of the country with money earned in America. Land was worth from 500 to 1,000 guilder per "yoke," which is about $100 to $200 per acre, a very large sum in a country where wages are, perhaps, not more than 25 or 50 cents a day.

At nightfall we returned to Tuchow, which appeared to be a typical market town. The town is arranged, like many of our country villages in the South, around a large open square. In the centre of this square is a great covered well, from which the town draws its water. Four pumps, with long twisted iron handles, arranged in a circle about the well, serve to draw the water to the surface. Around the four corners of this square are the tradesmen's shops, most of them with low, thatched roofs projecting over the sidewalk to form a cover for the walk in front of the shops, and frequently supported, on the side toward the street, by curiously carved wooden posts. The little shops were not more than six or eight feet wide. There was usually one little room in front which was for the store, and another little room back in which the shopkeeper lived. As the ceilings were usually very low and the windows under the wide projecting roofs were very small, it made everything appear very snug and tight, somewhat as if every building were holding on to all that it contained with both arms.

It all looked very interesting but very quaint and old-fashioned. I noticed, however, that there were one or two new brick buildings in the town, and the evening we arrived every one was in great excitement over the installation in the public square of two new electric lights, the first, I suspect, that had been seen in that part of the country. It was evident that in spite of the apparent solidity and antiquity that things were changing here as elsewhere.

CHAPTER XV

A RUSSIAN BORDER VILLAGE

OF THE three former capitals of Poland the city of Cracow, the last of Polish territory to lose its independence, is now an Austrian fortress. One day, shortly after my arrival, I was driving in the suburbs of the city when my attention was directed to a number of low, grass-covered mounds scattered about at regular intervals in the level plain outside the city. To all appearances these mounds were nothing more than slight elevations of land sinking, in a direction away from the city, almost imperceptibly into the surrounding landscape. In all probability, if it had not been for a certain regularity in the positions which they occupied, I should not have noticed them. I had never seen a modern fortified city and I was therefore considerably surprised when I learned that these gentle elevations were fortifications and that beneath these grass-grown mounds enormous guns were concealed, powerful enough to keep a vast army at bay. These facts served to remind me that Cracow was a border city, guarding a frontier which divides, not merely two European countries, but two civilizations — I might almost say, two worlds. Cracow is, as a matter of fact, ten miles from the Russian frontier, and, although the people in Russian Poland are of the same race or nationality as those who live in the Austrian province of Galicia, speaking the same language and sharing the same traditions, the line which divides them marks the limits of free government in Europe.

Now, there were several things that made this frontier, where eastern and western Europe meet, peculiarly interesting to me. In the first place, I knew that thousands of people, most of them Poles and Jews, who were unwilling or unable to pay the high tax which Russia imposes upon its emigrants, were every year smuggled across that border in order to embark at some German or Austrian port for America. I knew at the same time that Jews and, to a lesser extent, perhaps, Poles, outside of Russia were making use of this same underground railway to send back, in return for the emigrants who came out, another kind of contraband — namely, books and bombs. In fact, I had heard that a few years ago, when Russian Poland was all aflame with civil war, it was from Cracow that the Jews, who were the leading spirits in that movement, directed the revolution.

Naturally all this served to increase my natural curiosity in this border country. So it was that one cool, clear day in September I rented a little droske for the day and started, in company with my companion, Doctor Park, for the Russian border.

We drove leisurely along a splendid military road, between broad fields, in which peasants were gathering, in the cool autumn sunlight, the last fruits of the summer's harvest. A country road in Galicia, as is true in almost any part of Europe, is a good deal more of a highway than a country road in most parts of America. One meets all sorts of travellers. We passed, for example, just beyond the limits of the city, a troop of soldiers, with the raw look of recruits — red-faced country boys they seemed, for the most, bulging out of their military suits and trudging along the dusty road with an awkward effort at the military precision and order of veterans. Now and then we passed a barefoot peasant woman, tramping briskly to or from the city, with a basket on her head or a milk can thrown over her shoulder.

Once we stopped to watch a group of women and girls threshing. One woman was pitching down sheaves of rye from the barn loft, another was feeding them to the machine, and all were in high glee at the wonderful way, as it seemed to them, in which this new invention separated the grain from the chaff. They were so proud of this little machine that, when we stopped and showed our interest in what they were doing, they insisted on showing us how it worked, and took pains to explain the advantages over the old-fashioned flail. There was a man sitting on a beam outside the barn smoking a pipe, but the women were doing the work.

On this same journey we stopped at a little straggling village and spent an hour or two visiting the homes of the people. We saw the house of the richest peasant in the village, who owned and farmed something like a hundred acres of land, as I remember; and then we visited the home of the poorest man in the community, who lived in a little thatch-roofed cottage of two rooms; one of these was just large enough to hold a cow, but there was no cow there. The other room, although it was neat and clean, was not much larger than the cow-stall, and in this room this poor old man and his daughter lived. Incidentally, in the course of our tramp about the village, Doctor Park managed to pick up something of the family histories of the people and not a little of the current gossip in the community, and all this aided me in getting an insight, such as I had not been able to get elsewhere, into the daily life and human interests of this little rural community.

At one point along the road we stopped for a few minutes at a wayside tavern. It was a log structure, with one great, long, low, desolate room, in one corner of which was a bar at which a sour-faced woman presided. Two or three men were lounging about on the benches in different parts of the room, but here again the woman was doing the work.

Every mile or two it seemed to me we met a wagon piled high with great bulging bags as large as bed ticks. In each case these wagons were driven by a little shrewd-faced Jew. These wagons, as I learned, had come that morning from Russia and the loads they carried were goose feathers.

A little farther on we came up with a foot passenger who was making toward the border with great strides. He turned out to be a Jew, a tall, erect figure, with the customary round, flat hat and the long black coat which distinguish the Polish Jew. Our driver informed us, however, that he was a Russian Jew, and pointed out the absence of the side curls as indicating that fact. Although this man had the outward appearance, the manner, and the dress of the Jews whom I had seen in Cracow, there was something in the vigorous and erect carriage that impressed me to such an extent that I suggested that we stop and talk with him. As we were already near the border, and he was evidently from Russia, I suggested that Doctor Park show him our passports and ask him if they would let us into Russia.

He stopped abruptly as we spoke to him, and turned his black, piercing eyes upon us. Without saying a word he took the passports, glanced them through rapidly, tapped them with the back of his hand, and handed them back to us.

"That is no passport," he said, and then he added, "it should have the visé of your consul."

Having said this much he turned abruptly, without waiting for further conversation, and strode on. We soon came up with and passed him, but he did not look up. A little later we halted at the border. I looked around to see what had become of our wandering Jew, but he had disappeared. Perhaps he had stopped at the inn, and perhaps he had his own way of crossing the border.

I was reminded of this strange figure a few months later when I noticed in one of the London papers a telegram from Vienna to the effect that some thirty persons had been arrested at Cracow who were suspected of being the ringleaders "in what is believed to be a widespread revolutionary organization of Russian refugees." The report added that "a whole wagon-load of Mannliches rifles, Browning pistols, and dynamite grenades, together with a large number of compromising documents and plans of military works, were siezed as a result of searches by the police in the houses of the arrested men."

I had frequently seen reports like this in the newspapers before this time, but they had a new significance for me now that I had visited the border country where this commerce with what has been called the "Underground" or "Revolutionary" Russia was part of the daily experience of the people. It all recalled to my mind the stories I had heard, when I was a boy, from my mother's lips of the American Underground Railway and the adventures of the runaway slaves in their efforts to cross the border between the free and slave states. It reminded me, also, of the wilder and more desperate struggles, of which we used to hear whispers in slavery time, when the slaves sought to gain their freedom by means of insurrection. That was a time when, in the Southern States, no matter how good the relations between the individual master and his slaves, each race lived in constant fear of the other. It is in this condition, so far as I can learn, that a great part of the people in Russia are living to-day, for it is fatally true that no community can live without fear in which one portion of the people seeks to govern the other portion through terror.

The Austrian and Russian border at Barany, the village at which we had now arrived, is not imposing. A wire fence, and a gate such as is sometimes used to guard a railway crossing, are all that separate one country from the other. On one side of this gate I noticed a little sentinel's box, marked in broad stripes, with the Austrian colours, and at the other end of the gate there was a similar little box marked in broad stripes, with the Russian colours. On the Austrian side there was a large building for the use of the customs officials. On the Russian side there was a similar building with the addition of a large compound. In this compound there were about twenty Russian soldiers, standing idly about, with their horses saddled and bridled. The reason for the presence of the soldiers on the Russian side of the border was due to the fact that it is the business of the customs officers not merely to collect the tolls on the commerce that crosses the border at this point, but to prevent any one entering or leaving the country. As Russia imposes an almost prohibitive tax on emigration, most of the Russian emigrants are smuggled across the border.

At the same time it is necessary to closely guard the frontier in order to prevent, as I have said, the importation of books and bombs, the two elements in western civilization of which Russia seems to stand most in fear.

Leaving our droske on the Austrian side of the boundary, Doctor Park and myself applied at the gate between the two countries. A big, good-natured Russian official grinned, but shook his head and indicated that we could not be allowed to cross over. Our driver spoke to him in Polish, but he did not understand, or pretended he did not. Then we found a man who could speak Russian as well as German, and through him we explained that we merely wanted to visit the town and be able to say that we had at least touched Russian soil. On this the man permitted us to go up to the customs office and make our request there. At the customs office we tried to look as harmless as possible, and, with the aid of the interpreter we had brought with us, I explained what we wanted.

At the customs office every one was polite, good-humoured, and apparently quite as much interested in us as we were in them. I was told, however, that I should have to wait until a certain higher and more important personage arrived. In the course of half an hour the more important personage appeared. He looked us over carefully, listened to the explanations of his subordinates, and then, smiling good-naturedly, gave us permission to look about the village. With this gracious permission we started out.

The first thing I noticed was that the smooth, hard road upon which we had travelled from Cracow to the frontier broke off abruptly on the Russian side of the border. The road through the village was full of ruts and mudholes and the mournful and mud-bedraggled teams which were standing near the gate, waiting to cross the border, showed only too plainly the difficulties of travel in the country through which they had passed. Now I had learned in Europe that roads are a pretty good index of the character of the governments that maintain them, so that it was not difficult to see at the outset that the Russians were very poor housekeepers, so to speak, at least as compared with their Austrian neighbours. This was evidently not due to a lack of men and officials to do the work. Counting the civil officials and the soldiers, I suppose there must have been somewhere between twenty and thirty persons, and perhaps more, stationed at this little border village, to collect the toll on the petty traffic that crossed at this point. They were, however, but part of the vast army of officials and soldiers which the Russian Empire maintains along its western border from the Baltic to the Black Sea, to keep the watch between the east and the west; to halt, inspect, and tax, not merely the ordinary traffic, but the interchange of sentiments and ideas.

I could not help thinking how much more profitable it would be if these soldiers, clerks, and officials, and the vast army of frontiersmen to which they belonged, could be employed, for example, in building roads rather than maintaining fences; in making commerce easier, opening the way to civilization, rather than shutting it out.

Indeed it was no longer strange that, with all the vast resources which Russia possesses, the masses of the people have made so little progress when I considered how large a portion of the population had no other task than that of holding the people down, hindering rather than inspiring and directing the efforts of the masses to rise.

I had not gone far on our stroll about the village before I discovered that the Pole who so kindly volunteered to help us was a man of more than ordinary intelligence. He had seen something of the world, and I found his rather gossipy comments on the character of the different individuals we met, and upon the habits of the people generally in the village, not only entertaining but instructive. He had, for example, a very frank contempt for what he called the stupidity of the officials on both sides of the border, and it was clear he was no lover of the soldiers and the Government. At one time, as we started down a side street, he said: "There's a gendarme down there. He is just like one of those stupid, faithful watch-dogs that bristle up and bark at every person that passes. You will see presently. He will come puffing up the street to halt you and turn you back."

"What shall we do when we meet him?" I asked.

"Oh, there's nothing to do but go back if he says so, but you will, perhaps, be interested to observe the way he behaves."

Presently we noticed a soldier clambering hastily over an adjoining fence, and in a few minutes he had come up with us, his face all screwed up in an expression of alarmed surprise.

"This is the gendarme I was telling you about," said our guide quietly, and continued speaking about the man just as if he were not present.

As we were not able to talk with this soldier

ourselves, and as he did not look very promising in any case, we strolled leisurely back while our guide entered into a long explanation of who and what we were. I imagine that he must have put a good deal of varnish on his story, for I noticed that, as the soldier glanced at us from time to time, his eyes began getting bigger and bigger, and his mouth opened wider and wider, until he stared at us in a stupid, awe-struck way. Finally the interpreter announced that the gendarme had come to the conclusion that we might go down the road as far as we wanted to, only he would be obliged to accompany us to see that we did not break the peace in any way.

Under the direction of our self-appointed guide we visited a dusty, musty little bar-room, which seemed to be the centre of such life as existed in the village. We found a few young country boys lolling about on benches, and the usual shrewish, sharp-faced, overworked woman, who grumblingly left her housework to inquire what we wanted.

The contents of the bar itself consisted of rows of little bottles of different coloured liquors, interspersed with packages of cigarettes, all of them made and sold under the supervision of the Government. I purchased one of these little bottles of vodka, as it is called, because I wanted to see what it was the Government gave the peasants to drink. It was a white, colourless liquid, which looked like raw alcohol and was, in fact, as I afterward learned, largely, if not wholly, what the chemists call "methylated spirits," or wood alcohol.

We visited one of the little peasant houses in the neighbourhood of the customs office. It was a little, low log hut with a duck pond in front of the doorway and a cow-pen at right angles to the house. There were two rooms, a bedroom and a kitchen. In the kitchen, which had an earthen floor, three or four or five members of the family were sitting on stools, gathered about a large bowl, into which each was dipping his or her spoon. The bedroom was a neat little room, containing a high bed, a highly decorated chest of drawers, and was filled with curious bits of the rustic art, including among other things several religious pictures and images.

Although everything in this house was very simple and primitive, there was about it an air of self-respecting thrift and neatness that showed that the family which lived here was relatively prosperous and well-to-do.

Quite as interesting to me as the houses we visited were the stories that our guide told us about the people that lived in them. I recall among others the story of the young widow who served in the customs office as a clerk and lived in a single room in one corner of the peasant's cottage to which I have just referred. She was a woman, he told me, of the higher classes, as her enterprising manner and intelligent face seemed to indicate; one of the lesser nobility, who had married a Russian official condemned for some fault or other to serve at this obscure post. He had died here, leaving a child with the rickets, and no means.

Another time our guide pointed out to us a more imposing building than the others we had seen, though it was built in the same rustic style as the smaller peasants' cottages around it. This house, it seems, had at one time belonged to one of the nobility, but it was now owned by a peasant. This peasant, as I understood, had at one time been a serf and served as a hostler in a wealthy family. From this family he had inherited, as a reward for his long and faithful service, a considerable sum of money, with which he had purchased this place and set himself up, in a small way, as a landlord.

I gained, I think, a more intimate view of the peasant life in Poland than I did in any other part of Europe that I visited. For that reason, and because I hoped also that these seeming trivial matters would, perhaps, prove as interesting and suggestive to others as they were to me, I have set down in some detail in this and the preceding chapters the impressions which I gathered there.

In the little village of Barany, in Russian Poland, I had reached the point farthest removed, if not in distance at least in its institutions and civilization, from America; but, as I stood on a little elevation of land at the edge of the village and looked across the rolling landscape, I felt that I was merely at the entrance of a world in which, under many outward changes and differences of circumstance, there was much the same life that I had known and lived among the Negro farmers in Alabama. I believed, also, that I would find in that life of the Russian peasants much that would be instructive and helpful to the masses of my own people.

I touched, before I completed my European experiences, not only the Austrian, but the Russian and German Polish provinces, but I should have liked to have gone farther, to Warsaw and Posen, and looked deeper into the life and learned more of the remarkable struggle which the Polish people, especially in these two latter provinces, are making to preserve the Polish nationality and improve the conditions of the Polish people.

In this connection, and in concluding what I

have to say about my observations in Poland, I want to note one singular, and it seems to me suggestive, fact: Of the three sections of the Polish race, German, Russian, and Austrian, there are two in which, according to the information I was able to obtain, the people are oppressed, and one in which they seem to be, if anything, the oppressors. In Russian Poland and in German Poland the Polish are making a desperate struggle to maintain their national existence, but in these two countries the Poles are prosperous. Russian Poland has become in recent years one of the largest manufacturing centres in Europe, and the masses of the Polish people have become prosperous citizens and labourers. In German Poland the Polish peasants have, within the past forty years, become a thrifty farming class. The large estates which were formerly in the hands of the Polish nobility have been, to a very large extent, divided up and sold among a rapidly rising class of small landowners. In other words, what was originally a political movement in these two countries to revive and reestablish the kingdom of Poland has become a determined effort to lift the level of existence among the masses of the Polish people.

In Austrian Poland, on the contrary, where the Austrian Government, in order, perhaps, to hold the political aspirations of the Ruthenians in check, has given them a free hand in the government of the province, they have vastly greater freedom and they have made less progress.

I am stating this fact baldly, as it was given to me, and without any attempt at an explanation. Many different factors have no doubt combined to produce this seeming paradox. I will merely add this further observation: Where the Poles are advancing, progress has begun at the bottom, among the peasants; where they have remained stationary the Polish nobility still rules and the masses of the people have not yet been forced to any great extent into the struggle for national existence. The nobles are content with opportunity to play at politics, in something like the old traditional way, and have not learned the necessity of developing the resources that exist in the masses of the people. On the other hand, oppression has not yet aroused the peasants as it has, particularly in Germany, to a united effort to help themselves.

I mention this fact not merely because it is interesting, but because I am convinced that any one who studies the movements and progress of the Negroes in America will find much that is interesting by way of comparison in the present situation of the Polish people and that of the American Negroes. My own observation has convinced me, for example, that in those states where the leaders of the Negro have been encouraged to turn their attention to politics the masses of the people have not made the same progress that they have in those states where the leaders, because of racial prejudice or for other reasons, have been compelled to seek their own salvation in educating and building up, in moral and material directions, the more lowly members of their own people.

I do not wish to make comparisons, but I think I can safely say, by way of illustration, that in no other part of the United States have the masses of the Negroes been more completely deprived of political privileges than in the state of Mississippi, and yet there is, at the same time, scarcely any part of the country in which the masses of the people have built more schools and churches, or where they have gained a more solid foothold on the soil and in the industries of the state.

In calling attention to this fact I do not intend to offer an excuse for depriving any members of my race of any of the privileges to which the law entitles them. I merely wish to emphasize the fact that there is hope for them in other and more fundamental directions than ordinary party politics. More especially I wish to emphasize one fact — namely, that for the Negroes, as for other peoples who are struggling to get on their feet, success comes to those who learn to take advantage of their disadvantages and make their difficulties their opportunities. This is what the Poles in Germany, to a greater extent than any of the other oppressed nationalities in Europe, seem to have done.

CHAPTER XVI

THE WOMEN WHO WORK IN EUROPE

SEVERAL times during my stay in London I observed, standing on a corner in one of the most crowded parts of the city, a young woman selling papers. There are a good many women, young and old, who sell papers in London, but any one could see at a glance that this girl was different. There was something in her voice and manner which impressed me, because it seemed to be at once timid, ingratiating, and a little insolent, if that is not too strong a word. This young woman was, as I soon learned, a Suffragette, and she was selling newspapers — "Votes for Women."

This was my first meeting with the women insurgents of England. A day or two later, however, I happened to fall in with a number of these Suffragette newspaper-sellers. One of them, in a lively and amusing fashion, was relating the story of the morning's happenings. I could hardly help hearing what she said, and soon became very much interested in the conversation. In fact, I soon found myself so entertained by the bright and witty accounts these young women gave of their adventures that it was not long before I began to enter with them into the spirit of their crusade and to realize for the first time in my life what a glorious and exciting thing it was to be a Suffragette, and, I might add, what a lot of fun these young women were having out of it.

It had not occurred to me, when I set out from America to make the acquaintance of the man farthest down, that I should find myself in any way concerned with the woman problem. I had not been in London more than a few days, however, before I discovered that the woman who is at the bottom in London life is just as interesting as the man in the same level of life, and perhaps a more deserving object of study and observation.

In a certain way all that I saw of the condition of woman at the bottom connected itself in my mind with the agitation that is going on with regard to woman at the top.

Except in England, the women's movement has not, so far as I was able to learn, penetrated to any extent into the lower strata of life, and that strikes me as one of the interesting facts about the movement. It shows to what extent the interests, hopes, and ambitions of modern life have, or rather have not, entered into and become a force in the lives of the people at the bottom.

Thus it came about that my interest in all that I saw of workingwomen in Europe was tinged with the thought of what was going to happen when the present agitation for the emancipation and the wider freedom of women generally should reach and influence the women farthest down.

In my journey through Europe I was interested, in each of the different countries I visited, in certain definite and characteristic things. In London, for example, it was some of the destructive effects of a highly organized and complicated city life, and the methods which the Government and organized philanthropy have employed to correct them, that attracted my attention. Elsewhere it was chiefly the condition of the agricultural populations that interested me. In all my observation and study, however, I found that the facts which I have learned about the condition of women tended to set themselves off and assume a special importance in my mind. It is for that reason that I propose to give, as well as I am able, a connected account of them at this point.

What impressed me particularly in London were the extent and effects of the drinking habit among women of the lower classes. Until I went to London I do not believe that I had more than once or twice in my life seen women standing side by side with the men in order to drink at a public bar. One of the first things I noticed in London was the number of drunken, loafing women that one passed in the streets of the poorer quarters. More than once I ran across these drunken and besotted creatures, with red, blotched faces, which told of years of steady excess — ragged, dirty, and disorderly in their clothing — leaning tipsily against the outside of a gin-parlour or sleeping peacefully on the pavement of an alleyway.

In certain parts of London the bar-room seems to be the general meeting place of men and women alike. There, in the evening, neighbours gather and gossip while they drink their black, bitter beer. It is against the law for parents to take their children into the bar-rooms, but I have frequently observed women standing about the door of the tap-room with their babies in their arms, leisurely chatting while they sipped their beer. In such cases they frequently give the lees of their glass to the children to drink.

In America we usually think of a bar-room as a sort of men's club, and, if women go into such a place at all, they are let in surreptitiously at the "family entrance." Among the poorer classes in England the bar-room is quite as much the woman's club as it is the man's. The light, the warmth, and the free and friendly gossip of these places make them attractive, too, and I can understand that the people in these densely populated quarters of the city, many of them living in one or two crowded little rooms, should be drawn to these places by the desire for a little human comfort and social intercourse.

In this respect the bar-rooms in the poorer parts of London are like the beer halls that one meets on the Continent. There is, however, this difference — that the effect of drink upon the people of England seems to be more destructive than it is in the case of the people on the Continent. It is not that the English people as a whole consume more intoxicating drink than the people elsewhere, because the statistics show that Denmark leads the rest of Europe in the amount of spirits, just as Belgium leads in the amount of beer, consumed per capita of the population. One trouble seems to be that, under the English industrial system, the people take greater chances, they are subject to greater stress and strain, and this leads to irregularities and to excessive drinking.

While I was in Vienna I went out one Sunday evening to the Prater, the great public park, which seems to be a sort of combination of Central Park, New York, and Coney Island. In this park one may see all types of Austrian life, from the highest to the lowest. Sunday seems, however, to be the day of the common people, and the night I visited the place there were, in addition to the ordinary labouring people of the city, hundreds, perhaps thousands, of peasant people from the country there. They were mostly young men and women who had evidently come into the city for the Sunday holiday. Beside the sober, modern dress of the city crowds these peasant women, with their high boots, the bright-coloured kerchiefs over their heads, and their wide, flaring, voluminous skirts (something like those of a female circus-rider, only a little longer and not so gauzy), made a strange and picturesque appearance.

Meanwhile there was a great flare of music of a certain sort; and a multitude of catchpenny shows, mountebanks, music halls, theatres, merry-go-rounds, and dancing pavilions gave the place the appearance of a stupendous county fair. I do not think that I ever saw anywhere, except at a picnic or a barbecue among the Negroes of the Southern States, people who gave themselves up so frankly and with such entire zest to this simple, physical sort of enjoyment. Everywhere there were eating, drinking, and dancing, but nevertheless I saw no disorder; very few people seemed to be the worse for drinking, and in no instance did I see people who showed, in the disorder of their dress or in the blotched appearance of their faces, the effects of continued excesses, such as one sees in so many parts of London. Individuals were, for the most part, neatly and cleanly dressed; each class of people seemed to have its own place of amusement and its own code of manners, and every one seemed to keep easily and naturally within the restraints which custom prescribed.

I do not mean to say that I approve of this way of spending the Sabbath. I simply desire to point out the fact, which others have noticed, that the effect of the drinking habit seems to be quite different in England from what it is in countries on the Continent.

I had an opportunity to observe the evil effects of the drinking habit upon the Englishwomen of the lower classes when I visited some of the police courts in the poorer parts of London. When I remarked to a newspaper acquaintance in London that I wanted to see as much as I could, while I was in the city, of the life of the poorer people, he advised me to visit the Worship Street and Thames police stations. The Worship Street station is situated in one of the most crowded parts of London, in close proximity to Bethnal Green and Spitalfields, which have for many years been the homes of the poorer working classes, and especially of those poor people known as houseworkers and casuals, who live in garrets and make paper boxes, artificial flowers, etc., or pick up such odd jobs as they can find. The Thames station is situated a little way from London Dock and not far from the notorious Ratcliffe Highway, which until a few years ago was the roughest and most dangerous part of London.

Perhaps I ought to say, at the outset, that two things in regard to the London police courts especially impressed me: first, the order and dignity with which the court is conducted; second, the care with which the judge inquires into all the facts of every case he tries, the anxiety which he shows to secure the rights of the defendant, and the leniency with which those found guilty are treated. In many cases, particularly those in which men or women were charged with drunkenness, the prisoners were allowed to go with little more than a mild and fatherly reprimand.

After listening for several hours to the various cases that came up for hearing, I could well understand that the police have sometimes complained that their efforts to put down crime were not supported by the magistrates, who, they say, always take the side of the culprits.

In this connection I might mention a statement which I ran across recently of a man who had served at one time as a magistrate in both the Worship Street and Thames police courts. He said that there was a great deal of drunkenness among certain of the factory girls of East London, although they were seldom arrested and brought into court for that offence.

He added: "It must not be forgotten that the number of convictions for drunkenness is not by any means a proper measure of insobriety. If a policeman sees a drunken man conducting himself quietly or sleeping in a doorway, he passes on and takes no notice. Those who are convicted belong, as a rule, to the disorderly classes, who, the moment liquor rises to their heads, manifest their natural propensities by obstreperous and riotous conduct. For one drunkard of this order there must be fifty who behave quietly and always manage to reach their homes, however zigzag may be their journey thither."

That statement was made a number of years ago, but I am convinced that it holds good now, because I noticed that most of the persons arrested and brought into court, especially women, were bloodstained and badly battered.

In the majority of these cases, as I have said, the persons were allowed to go with a reprimand or a small fine. The only case in which, it seemed to me, the judge showed a disposition to be severe was in that of a poor woman who was accused of begging. She was a pale, emaciated, and entirely wretched appearing little woman, and the charge against her was that of going through the streets, leading one of her children by the hand, and asking for alms because she and her children were starving. I learned from talking with the officer who investigated the case that the statement she made was very likely true. He had known her for some time, and she was in a very sad condition. But then, it seems, the law required that in such circumstances she should have gone to the workhouse.

I think that there were as many as fifteen or twenty women brought into court on each of the mornings I visited the court. Most of them were arrested for quarrelling and fighting, and nearly all of them showed in their bloated faces and in their disorderly appearance that steady and besotted drunkenness was at the bottom of their trouble.

I have found since I returned from Europe that the extent of drunkenness among Englishwomen has frequently been a matter of observation and comment. Richard Grant White, in his volume "England Within and Without," says:

> I was struck with horror at the besotted condition of so many of the women — women who were bearing children every year, and suckling them, and who seemed to me little better than foul human stills through which the accursed liquor with which they were soaked filtered drop by drop into the little drunkards at their breasts. To these children drunkenness comes unconsciously, like their mother tongue. They cannot remember a time when it was new to them. They come out of the cloudland of infancy with the impression that drunkenness is one of the normal conditions of man, like hunger and sleep.

This was written thirty years ago. It is said that conditions have greatly improved in recent years in respect to the amount of drunkenness among the poor of London. Nevertheless, I notice in the last volume of the "Annual Charities Register" for London the statement that inebriety seems to be increasing among women, and that it prevails to such an alarming extent among women in all ranks of society that "national action is becoming essential for the nation's very existence."

The statistics of London crime show that, while only about half as many women as men are arrested on the charges of "simple drunkenness" and "drunkenness with aggravations," more than three times as many women as men are arrested on the charge of "habitual" drunkenness. Another thing that impressed me was that the American police courts deal much more severely with women. This is certainly true in the Southern States, where almost all the women brought before the police courts are Negroes.

The class of people to whom I have referred represent, as a matter of course, the lowest and most degraded among the working classes. Nevertheless, they represent a very large element in the population, and the very existence of this hopeless class, which constitutes the dregs of life in the large cities, is an indication of the hardship and bitterness of the struggle for existence in the classes above them.

I have attempted in what I have already said to indicate the situation of the women at the bottom in the complex life of the largest and, if I may say so, the most civilized city in the world, where women are just now clamouring for all the rights and privileges of men. But there are parts of Europe where, as far as I have been able to learn, women have as yet never heard that they had any rights or interests in life separate and distinct from those of their husbands and children. I have already referred to the increasing number of barefoot women I met as I journeyed southward from Berlin. At first these were for the most part women who worked in the fields. But by the time I reached

Vienna I found that it was no uncommon thing to meet barefoot women in the most crowded and fashionable parts of the city.

Experience in travelling had taught me that the wearing of shoes is a pretty accurate indication of civilization. The fact that in a large part of southern Europe women who come from the country districts have not yet reached the point where they feel comfortable in shoes is an indication of the backwardness of the people.

What interested and surprised me more than the increasing absence of shoes among the countrywomen was the increasing number of women whom I saw engaged in rough and unskilled labour of every kind. I had never seen Negro women doing the sort of work I saw the women of southern Europe doing. When I reached Prague, for example, I noticed a load of coal going through the streets. A man was driving it, but women were standing up behind with shovels. I learned then that it was the custom to employ women to load and unload the coal and carry it into the houses. The driving and the shovelling were done by the man, but the dirtiest and the hardest part of the work was performed by the women.

In Vienna I saw hundreds of women at work as helpers in the construction of buildings; they mixed the mortar, loaded it in tubs, placed it on their heads, and carried it up two or three stories to men at work on the walls. The women who engage in this sort of labour wear little round mats on their heads, which support the burdens which they carry. Some of these women are still young, simply grown girls, fresh from the country, but the majority of them looked like old women.

Not infrequently I ran across women hauling carts through the streets. Sometimes there would be a dog harnessed to the cart beside them. That, for example, is the way in which the countrywomen sometimes bring their garden truck to market. More often, however, they will be seen bringing their garden products to market in big baskets on their heads or swung over their shoulders. I remember, while I was in Budapest, that, in returning to my hotel rather late one night, I passed through an open square near the market, where there were hundreds of these market women asleep on the sidewalks or in the street. Some of them had thrown down a truss of straw on the pavement under their wagons and gone to sleep there. Others, who had brought their produce into town from the country on their backs, had in many cases merely put their baskets on the sidewalk, lain down, thrown a portion of their skirts up over their heads, and gone to sleep. At this hour the city was still wide awake. From a nearby beer hall there came the sounds of music and occasional shouts of laughter. Meanwhile people were passing and repassing in the street and on the sidewalk, but they paid no more attention to these sleeping women than they would if they had been horses or cows.

In other parts of Austria-Hungary I ran across women engaged in various sorts of rough and unskilled labour. While I was in Cracow, in Austrian Poland, I saw women at work in the stone quarries. The men were blasting out the rock, but the women were assisting them in removing the earth and in loading the wagons. At the same time I saw women working in brick-yards. The men made the brick, the women acted as helpers. While I was in Cracow one of the most interesting places I visited in which women are employed was a cement factory. The man in charge was kind enough to permit me to go through the works, and explained the process of crushing and burning the stone used in the manufacture of cement. A large part of the rough work in this cement factory is done by girls. The work of loading the kilns is performed by them. Very stolid, heavy, and dirty-looking creatures they were. They had none of the freshness and health that I noticed so frequently among the girls at work in the fields.

While I was studying the different kinds of work which women are doing in Austria-Hungary I was reminded of the complaint that I had heard sometimes from women in America, that they were denied their rights in respect to labour, that men in America wanted to keep women in the house, tied down to household duties.

In southern Europe, at any rate, there does not seem to be any disposition to keep women tied up in the houses. Apparently they are permitted to do any kind of labour that men are permitted to do; and they do, in fact, perform a great many kinds of labour that we in America think fit only for men. I noticed, moreover, as a rule, that it was only the rough, unskilled labour which was allotted to them. If women worked in the stone quarries, men did the part of the work that required skill. Men used the tools, did the work of blasting the rock. If women worked on the buildings, they did only the roughest and cheapest kinds of work. I did not see any women laying brick, nor did I see anywhere women carpenters or stone-masons.

In America Negro women and children are employed very largely at harvest time in the cotton-fields, but I never saw in America, as

I have seen in Austria, women employed as section hands on a railway, or digging sewers, hauling coal, carrying the hod, or doing the rough work in brickyards, kilns, and cement factories.

In the Southern States of America the lowest form of unskilled labour is that of the men who are employed on what is known as public works — that is to say, the digging of sewers, building of railways, and so forth. I was greatly surprised, while I was in Vienna, to see women engaged side by side with men in digging a sewer. This was such a novel sight to me that I stopped to watch these women handle the pick and shovel. They were, for the most part, young women, of that heavy, stolid type I have referred to. I watched them for some time, and I could not see but that they did their work as rapidly and as easily as the men beside them. After this I came to the conclusion that there was not anything a man could do which a woman could not do also.

In Poland the women apparently do most of the work on the farms. Many of the men have gone to Vienna to seek their fortune. Many, also, have gone to the cities, and still others are in the army, because on the Continent every able-bodied man must serve in the army. The result is that more and more of the work that was formerly performed by men is now done by women.

One of the most interesting sights I met in Europe was the market in Cracow. This market is a large open square in the very centre of the ancient city. In this square is situated the ancient Cloth Hall, a magnificent old building, which dates back to the Middle Ages, when it was used as a place for the exhibition of merchandise, principally textiles of various kinds. On the four sides of this square are some of the principal buildings of the city, including the City Hall and the Church of the Virgin Mary, from the tall tower of which the hours are sounded by the melodious notes of a bugle.

On market days this whole square is crowded with hundreds, perhaps thousands, of market women, who come in from the country in the early morning with their produce, remain until it is sold, and then return to their homes.

In this market one may see offered for sale anything and everything that the peasant people produce in their homes or on the farms. Among other things for sale I noted the following: geese, chickens, bread, cheese, potatoes, salads, fruits of various sorts, mushrooms, baskets, toys, milk, and butter.

What interested me as much as anything was to observe that nearly everything that was sold in this market was carried into the city on the backs of the women. Practically, I think, one may say that the whole city of Cracow, with a population of 90,000 persons, is fed on the provisions that the peasant women carry into the city, some of them travelling as far as ten or fifteen miles daily.

One day, while driving in the market of Cracow, our carriage came up with a vigorous young peasant woman who was tramping, barefoot, briskly along the highway with a bundle swung on her shoulder. In this bundle, I noticed, she carried a milk-can. We stopped, and the driver spoke to her in Polish and then translated to my companion, Doctor Park, in German. At first the woman seemed apprehensive and afraid. As soon as we told her we were from America, however, her face lighted up and she seemed very glad to answer all my questions.

I learned that she was a widow, the owner of a little farm with two cows. She lived something like fourteen kilometres (about ten miles) from the city, and every day she came into town to dispose of the milk she had from her two cows. She did not walk all the way, but rode half the distance in the train, and walked the other half. She owned a horse, she said, but the horse was at work on the farm, and she could not afford to use him to drive to town. In order to take care of and milk her cows and reach the city early enough to deliver her milk she had to get up very early in the morning, so that she generally got back home about ten or eleven o'clock. Then, in the afternoon, she took care of the house and worked in the garden. This is a pretty good example, I suspect, of the way some of these peasant women work.

All day long one sees these women, with their bright-coloured peasant costumes, coming and going through the streets of Cracow with their baskets on their backs. Many of them are barefoot, but most of them wear very high leather boots, which differ from those I have seen worn by peasant women in other parts of Austria and Hungary in the fact that they have very small heels.

I had an opportunity to see a great many types of women in the course of my journey across Europe, but I saw none who looked so handsome, fresh, and vigorous as these Polish peasant women.

It is said of the Polish women, as it is said of the women of the Slavic races generally, that they are still living in the mental and physical slavery of former ages. Probably very few of them have ever heard of women's rights. But, if that is true, it simply shows how very little connection such abstract words have with the condition, welfare, and happiness of the people who enjoy the freedom and independence of country life. At any rate, I venture to say that there are very few women, even in the higher ranks of labouring women in England, whose condition in life compares with that of these vigorous, wholesome, and healthy peasant women.

How can work in the stifling atmosphere of a factory or in some crowded city garret compare with the life which these women lead, working in the fields and living in the free and open country?

The emigration to America has left an enormous surplus of women in Europe. In England, for instance, the women stand in the proportion of sixteen to fifteen to the men. In some parts of Italy there are cities, it is said, where all the able-bodied men have left the country and gone to America. The changes brought by emigration have not, on the whole, it seems to me, affected the life of women favourably. But the same thing is true with regard to the changes brought about by the growth of cities and the use of machinery. Men have profited by the use of machinery more than women. The machines have taken away from the women the occupations they had in the homes, and this has driven them to take up other forms of labour, of more or less temporary character, in which they are overworked and underpaid.

Everywhere we find the women in Europe either doing the obsolete things or performing some form of unskilled labour. For example, there are still one hundred thousand people, mostly women, in East London, it is said, who are engaged in home industries — in other words, sweating their lives away in crowded garrets trying to compete with machinery and organization in the making of clothes or artificial flowers, and in other kinds of work of this same general description.

The movement for women's suffrage in England, which began in the upper classes among the women of the West End, has got down, to some extent, to the lower levels among the women who work with the hands. Women's suffrage meetings have been held, I have learned, in Bethnal Green and Whitechapel. But I do not believe that voting alone will improve the condition of workingwomen.

There must be a new distribution of the occupations. Too many women in Europe are performing a kind of labour for which they are not naturally fitted and for which they have had no special training. There are too many women in the ranks of unskilled labour. My own conviction is that what the workingwomen of Europe need most is a kind of education that will lift a larger number of them into the ranks of skilled labour — that will teach them to do something, and to do that something well.

The Negro women in America have a great advantage in this respect. They are everywhere admitted to the same schools to which the men are admitted. All the Negro colleges are crowded with women. They are admitted to the industrial schools and to training in the different trades on the same terms as men. One of the chief practical results of the agitation for the suffrage in Europe will be, I imagine, to turn the attention of the women in the upper classes to the needs of the women in the lower classes. In Europe there is much work for women among their own sex, for, as I have said elsewhere, in Europe the man farthest down is woman.

CHAPTER XVII

THE ORGANIZATION OF COUNTRY LIFE IN DENMARK

IN EUROPE the man whose situation most nearly corresponds to that of the Negro in the Southern States is the peasant. I had seen pictures of peasants before I went to Europe, but I confess that I was very hazy as to what a peasant was. I knew that he was a small farmer, like the majority of the Negro farmers in the Southern States, and that, like the Negro farmer again, he had in most cases descended from a class that had at one time been held in some sort of subjection to the large landowners, the difference being that, whereas the peasant had been a serf, the Negro farmer had been a slave.

In regard to the present position of the peasant in the life about him, in regard to his manner of living, his opportunities and ambitions, I had but the vaguest sort of an idea. The pictures which I had seen were not reassuring in this regard. The picture which made the deepest impression upon my mind was that of a heavy, stupid, half-human looking creature, standing in the midst of a desolate field. The mud and the clay were clinging to him and he was leaning on a great, heavy, wrought-iron hoe, such as were formerly used by the Negro slaves. This picture represented about my idea of a peasant.

In the course of my journey through Italy and through Austria-Hungary I saw a number of individuals who reminded me of this and other pictures of peasants that I can recall. I saw, as I have already said, peasant women sleeping, like tired animals, in the city streets; I saw others living in a single room with their cattle; at one time I entered a little cottage and saw the whole family eating out of a single bowl. In Sicily I found peasants living in a condition of dirt, poverty, and squalor almost beyond description. But everywhere I found among these people, even the lowest, individuals who, when I had an opportunity to talk with them, invariably displayed an amount of shrewd, practical wisdom, kindly good nature, and common sense that reminded me of some of the old Negro farmers with whom I am acquainted at home. It is very curious what a difference it makes in the impression that a man makes upon you if you stop and shake hands with him, instead of merely squinting at him critically in order to take a cold sociological inventory of his character and condition.

Some of the pleasantest recollections I have of Europe are the talks I had, through an interpreter, of course, with some of these same ignorant but hard-working, sometimes barefoot, but always kindly peasants. The result was that long before I had completed my journey I had ceased to take some of the pictures of peasants I had seen literally. I discovered that the artist whose pictures had made so deep an impression upon me had sought to compress into the figure of a single individual the misery and wretchedness of a whole class; that he had tried, also, to bring to the surface and make visible in his picture all the hardships and the degradation which the casual observer does not see, perhaps does not want to see.

It was not until I reached Denmark, however, that I began to feel that I had really begun to know the European peasant, because it was not until I reached that country that I saw what the possibilities of the peasant were. Before this I had seen a man who was struggling up under the weight of ignorance and the remains of an ancient oppression. In Denmark, however, this man has come to his own. Peasants already own a majority of the land. Three fourths of the farms are in their hands and the number of small farms is steadily increasing. In Denmark the peasant, as a certain gentleman whom I met there observed, is not only free, but he rules. The peasant is the leader in everything that relates to the progress of agriculture. The products of the coöperative dairies, the coöperative egg-collecting and pork-packing societies, organized and controlled by the peasants, bring in the markets of the world higher prices than similar products from any other country in Europe.

The peasants are now the controlling influence in the Danish Parliament. When I was there half the members of the ministry in power were peasants, and half the members of the cabinet were either peasants or peasants' sons.

Let me add that there is a very close connection between the price of the peasants' butter and the influence which the peasants exercise in politics. For a good many years, up to about 1901, I believe, the most influential party in Denmark was that represented by the large landowners. Forty years ago the peasants had all the political rights they now possess, but they did not count for much in political matters. At that time there were two kinds of butter in Denmark: there was the butter made in the creameries of the large landowners, called gentlemen's estates, and there was the butter from the small farmers. In other words, there was "gentleman's butter" and "peasant's butter."

The peasant butter, however, was only worth in the market about one half as much as that from the gentleman's estate. When the price of peasant butter began to rise, however, the political situation began to change. Year by year the number of coöperative dairies increased and, year by year, the number of peasant farmers in parliament multiplied. In other words, the Danish peasant has become a power in Danish politics because he first became a leader in the industrial development of the country.

Denmark is not only very small, about one third the size of Alabama, but it is not even especially fertile. It is an extremely level country, without hills, valleys, or running streams worth speaking of. I was told that the highest point in Denmark, which is called "Heaven's Hill," is only about 550 feet above sea level — that is to say about half as high as the tower of the Metropolitan Building in New York. As a result of this a large part of the country is windswept and, in northern Jutland, where the Danish peninsula thrusts a thin streak of land up into the storm-tossed waters of the North Sea, there were, forty years ago, 3,300 square miles of heather where not even a tree would grow. Since that time, by an elaborate process of physical and chemical manipulation of the soil, all but a thousand square miles have been reclaimed. The result is that where once only lonely shepherds wandered, "knitting stockings," as Jacob Riis says, "to pay the taxes," there are now flourishing little cities.

Another disadvantage which Denmark suffers has its origin in the fact that more than one third of the country consists of islands, of which there are no less than forty-four. In going from Copenhagen to Hamburg the train on which I travelled, in crossing from one island to another and from there to the peninsula, was twice compelled to make the passage by means of a ferry, and at one of these passages we were on the boat for about an hour and a half.

Riding or driving through Denmark to-day is like riding through Illinois or any other of the farming regions of the Middle Western States, with the exception that the fields are smaller and the number of men, cattle, and homesteads is much larger than one will see in any part of the United States. I have heard travellers through Denmark express regret because with the progress of the country, the quaint peasant costumes and the other characteristics of the primitive life of the peasant communities, which one may still see in other parts of Europe, have disappeared. One of my fellow-travellers tried to make me believe that the peasants in Europe were very much happier in the quiet, simple life of these small and isolated farming communities, each with its own picturesque costumes, its interesting local traditions, and its curious superstitions.

This seems to be the view of a good many tourists. After what I have seen in Europe I have come to the conclusion, however, that the people and the places that are the most interesting to look at are not always the happiest and most contented. On the contrary, I have found that the places in which the life of the peasants is most interesting to tourists are usually the places that the peasants are leaving in the largest numbers. Emigration to America is making a large part of Europe commonplace, but it is making a better place to live in.

The reorganization of agricultural life in Denmark has come about in other ways than by emigration, but it has left very little of the picturesque peasant life, and most of what remains is now kept in museums. I noticed in going through the country, however, two types of farm buildings which seem to have survived from an earlier time. One of these consisted of a long, low building, one end of which was a barn and the other a dwelling. The other type of building was of much the same shape, except that it formed one side of a court, the other two sides of which were enclosed by barns and stables.

Upon inquiry I learned that the first type of dwelling belonged to a man who was called a *husmaend*, or houseman; in other words, a small farmer whose property consisted of his house, with a very small strip of land around it. The other type of dwelling belonged to a man who was called a *gaardmaend*, or yardman, because he owned enough land to have a *gaarde*, or yard. In Denmark farmers are still generally divided into *huse* and *gaarde;* all farmers owning less than twenty-four acres are called "housemen," and all having more than that are called "yardmen," no matter how their buildings are constructed.

As a matter of fact, it is not so long since conditions in Denmark were just about as primitive as they are now in some other parts of Europe. Jacob Riis, whom I learned, while I was in Denmark, is just as widely known and admired in Denmark as he is in the United States, says that he can remember when conditions were quite different among the homes of the people. "For example," he said, "I recall the time when in every peasant's family it was the custom for all to sit down and eat out of the same bowl in the centre of the table and then, after the meal was finished, each would wipe the spoon with which he had dipped into the common bowl, and without any further ceremony tuck it away on a little shelf over his head.

"To-day," he added, "Danish farmers wash their pigs. The udders of the cows are washed with a disinfecting fluid before milking. When a man goes to milk he puts on a clean white suit."

Not only is this true, but the Danish farmer grooms his cows, and blankets them when it is cold. He does this not only because it is good for the cow, but because it makes a saving in the feed. Although Denmark has more cattle in proportion to the number of inhabitants than any other part of Europe, I noticed very few pastures. On the contrary, as I passed through the country I observed long rows of tethered cattle, feeding from the green crops. As rapidly as the cows have consumed all the green fodder, usually four or five times a day, a man comes along and moves the stakes forward so that the cattle advance in orderly way, mowing down the crops in sections. Water is brought to the cows in a cart and they are milked three times a day. All of this requires a large increase of labour as well as constant study, care, and attention. In other words, the Danish peasant has become a scientific farmer.

One difference between the farmer in Denmark and in other countries is that, whereas the ordinary farmer raises his crops and ships them to the market to be sold, the Danish farmer sells nothing but the manufactured product, and as far as possible he sells it direct to the consumer. For example, until about 1880 Denmark was still a grain exporting country; in recent years, however, it has become a grain importing country. Grain and fodder of various kinds to the value of something like twenty-five millions of dollars are now annually purchased by Danish farmers in Russia and neighbouring countries. The agricultural products thus imported are fed to the cattle, swine, and chickens and thus converted into butter, pork, and eggs. The butter is manufactured in a coöperative dairy; the pork is slaughtered in a coöperative pork-packing house; the eggs are collected and packed by a coöperative egg-collecting association. Then they are either sold direct, or are turned over to a central coöperative selling association, which disposes of the most of them in England. The annual exports to England amount to nearly $90,000,000 a year, of which $51,000,000 is for butter, nearly $30,000,000 for bacon, and the remainder for eggs.

As a gentleman whom I met in Denmark put

it: "If Denmark, like ancient Gaul, were divided into three parts, one of these would be butter, another pork, and the third eggs." It is from these things that the country, in the main, gets its living. There are in Denmark, as elsewhere, railways, newspapers, telephones, merchants, preachers, teachers, and all the other accessories of a high civilization, but they are all supported from the sale of butter, pork, and eggs, to which ought to be added cattle, for Denmark still exports a considerable amount of beef and live cattle. The export of live cattle has, however, fallen from about $21,000,000 a year in 1880 to about $7,000,000, but in the same period the excess of butter, bacon, and eggs has risen from something like $7,000,000 to over $70,000,000. Meanwhile the raw production of the Danish farms has increased 50 per cent. and more, the difference being that, instead of producing grains for the manufacture of flour and meal, the Danish farmers have turned their attention to producing root crops to feed their cattle. This means that the peasant in Denmark is not merely a scientific farmer, as I have already suggested, but he is at the same time, in a small way, a business man.

The success of the peasant farmer in Denmark is, as I have already suggested, due to a very large extent to the coöperative societies which manufacture and sell his farm products. Through the medium of these the Danish peasant has become a business man — I might almost say, a capitalist. I do not know how much money is invested in these different coöperative dairies, egg-collecting and pork-packing concerns, but all Denmark is dotted with them, and the total amount of money invested in them must be considerable. There are, for example, 1,157 coöperative dairies, with a membership of 157,000. The number of coöperative pork-packing societies is 34, with a membership of 95,000.

As soon as I found to what extent the peasants were manufacturing and selling their own products, I naturally wanted to know how they had succeeded in getting the capital to carry on these large enterprises, because in the part of the country from which I hail the average farmer not only has no money to put into any sort of business outside his farm, but has to borrow money, frequently at a high rate of interest, to carry on his farming operations. I found that when the farmers in Denmark began establishing coöperative dairies some of the well-to-do farmers came together and signed a contract to send all their milk which they were not able to use at home to the community dairy. Then they borrowed money on their land to raise the money to begin operations. In borrowing this money they bound themselves "jointly and severally," as the legal phrase is, to secure the payments of the money borrowed — that is, each man became individually responsible for the whole loan. This gave the bank which made the loan a much better security than if each individual had secured a loan on his own responsibility, and in this way it was possible to provide the capital needed at a very moderate rate of interest.

When the farmer brought his milk to the common dairy he was paid a price for it a little less than the average market price. This added something to the working capital. At the end of the year a portion of the earnings of the dairy were set aside to pay interest charges, another portion was used to pay off the loan, and the remainder was divided in profits among the members of the association, each receiving an amount proportionate to the milk he had contributed. In this way the farmer in the course of some years found himself with a sum of money, equal to his individual share, invested in a paying enterprise that was every year increasing in value. In the meanwhile he had received more for his milk than if he had sold it in the ordinary way. At the same time, out of the annual profits he received from his share in the dairy, he had, perhaps, been able to put some money in the savings bank. The savings banks have always been popular and have played a much more important part in the life of the people than they have elsewhere. At the present time the average amount of deposits in proportion to the number of inhabitants is larger than is true of any other country in the world. For example, the average amount of deposits in the Danish savings banks is $77.88; in England $20.62; in the United States $31.22. At the same time the number of depositors in Danish savings banks is considerably larger than in other countries. For example, there are fifty-one depositors for every hundred persons in Denmark. In England the corresponding number is twenty-seven.

The most remarkable thing about the Danish savings banks, however, is that 78 per cent.—nearly four fifths—of them are located in the rural districts. That is one reason that Danish farmers have not found it difficult to secure the capital they needed to organize and carry on their coöperative enterprises. With the money which they had saved and put in the savings bank from the earnings in the coöperative dairies they were able to borrow money with which to start their coöperative slaughter-houses and egg-collecting societies.

But these are only a few of the different types

of coöperative organizations. A Danish peasant may be a member of a society for the purchase of tools, implements, and other necessaries, of which there are fifteen in Denmark, with a membership numbering between sixty and seventy thousand. He may belong to a society for exporting cattle, for collecting and exporting eggs, for horse breeding, for cattle, sheep, and pig breeding. Finally he may belong to what are known as "control" societies, organized for the purpose of keeping account, by means of careful registration, of the milk yield of each cow belonging to a member of the society, and of the butter-fat in the milk, and the relation between the milk yield and the fodder consumed. The value of these societies is found in the fact that the annual yield per cow in the case of members of the control society was 67,760 pounds, while in the case of cows owned outside of the society the amount was 58,520 pounds.

Through the medium of these different societies, some of which are purely commercial, while others exist for the purpose of improving the methods and technique of agriculture, the farming industry has become thoroughly organized. First of all, there has been a great saving in cost of handling and selling farm products. Not many years ago the Danish farmer used to send his butter to England by way of Hamburg, and there were at that time, I have been told, no less than six middlemen who came between the farmer and his customer. Now the co-operative manufacturing and selling societies sell a large part of their products direct to the coöperative purchasing societies in England. In this way the farmer and his customer, the producer and distributer, are brought together again, not exactly in the way in which they still come together in some of the old-fashioned market places in Europe, but still in a way to benefit both classes. For one thing, as a result of this organization of the farming industry, farming methods and the whole technical side of the industry have been greatly benefited. A striking evidence of this fact is found in the following statistics showing the rapid increase in the annual yield of milk per cow in the period from 1898 to 1908:

Year	Annual yield per cow in pounds
1898	4,480
1901	4,884
1904	5,335
1907	5,689
1908	5,874

I might add, as showing the extent to which Danish agriculture has been organized in the way I have described, that now Denmark produces about 253,000,000 pounds of butter every year. Of this amount 220,000,000 pounds come from the coöperative dairies.

Behind all other organizations which have served to increase efficiency of the farming population are the schools, particularly the rural high schools and the agricultural schools. It is generally agreed in Denmark that the co-operative organizations which have done so much for the farming population of that country could not exist if the rural high schools had not prepared the way for them.

I have described at some length, in another place, my impressions of the Danish schools, and shall not attempt to repeat here what I have said elsewhere.* I would like to emphasize, however, certain peculiarities about these schools that have particularly impressed me. In the first place, the schools that I visited, and, as I understand, practically all the schools that have been erected for the benefit of the rural population, are located either in the neighbourhood of the small towns or in the open country. In other words, they are close to the land and the people they are designed to help. In the second place, and this is just as true of the rural high schools, where almost no

*"What I Learned About Education in Denmark," chapter XI. "My Larger Education," Doubleday, Page & Company, 1911.

technical training is attempted, as it is of the agricultural schools, the courses have been especially worked out, after years of experiment and study, to fit the needs of the people for whom they are intended. There is no attempt to import into these schools the learning or style or methods of the city high schools or colleges. There is in fact, so far as I know, no school in existence that corresponds to or of which the Danish rural high school is in any way a copy.

In the third place, all these schools are for older pupils. The ages of the students range from sixteen to twenty-four years, and, in addition to the regular courses, conferences and short courses for the older people have been established, as is the case with many of the Negro industrial schools in the South. In fact, everything possible is done to wed the work in the school to the life and work on the land.

Finally, and this seems to me quite as important as anything else, these schools, like the coöperative societies to which I have referred, have grown up as the result of private initiative. The high schools had their origin in a popular movement begun more than fifty years ago by Nicola Frederik Severin Grundvig, a great religious reformer, who is sometimes referred to as the Luther of Denmark.

Denmark was at this time almost in despair.

England in the course of the war with Napoleon had destroyed the Danish fleet, and later, in 1864, Germany had taken from Denmark two of her best provinces and one third of her territory. Grundvig believed that the work of reconstructing and regenerating Denmark must begin at the bottom. He preached the doctrine that what Denmark had lost without she must regain within, and, with this motto, he set to work to develop the neglected resources of the country — namely, those which were in the people themselves.

The work begun by Grundvig has been taken up and carried on in the same spirit by those who have followed him. The results of this movement show themselves in every department of life in Denmark — in the rapid increase of Danish exports and in the healthy democratic spirit of the whole Danish population. The Danish people are probably the best educated and best informed people in Europe. This is not simply my impression; it is that of more experienced travellers than myself.

On my way from Copenhagen to London I fell in with an English gentleman who was just returning from five weeks of study and observation of farming conditions in Denmark. From him I was able to obtain a great many interesting details which confirmed my own impressions.

He told me, I remember, that he had noticed in the cottage of a peasant, a man who did not farm more than four or five acres of land, copies of at least four periodicals to which he was a regular subscriber.

"More than that," he continued, "the farmers' journals which I saw in the peasants' houses I visited seemed to me remarkably technical and literary." This remark struck me, because it had never occurred to me that any of the agricultural papers I had seen in America could be described as "technical and literary." If they were I am afraid the farmers, at least the farmers in my part of the country, would not read them.

As illustrating the general intelligence of the farming population, this same gentleman told me that he had at one time called upon a creamery manager in a remote district whose salary, in addition to his house, which was provided him, was about twenty-four shillings, or six dollars, a week. In his house he found a recent copy of the *Studio*, a well-known English art publication. On his book shelves, in addition to the ordinary publications of a dairy expert, he had caught sight of volumes in English, French, German, and Swedish.

I was impressed with the fact that almost every one I met in Denmark seemed to be able to speak at least three languages — namely, German, English, and Danish. I had been greatly surprised on the Sunday night of my arrival to meet an audience of fully 3,000 persons and find that at least the majority of those present were able to understand my speech. In fact I had not spoken ten minutes when I found myself talking as naturally and as easily to this Danish audience as if I was addressing a similar number of people in America. The people even flattered me by laughing at my jokes, and in the right places. I am convinced that any one who can understand an American joke can understand almost anything in the English language.

There is a saying to the effect that if you see a large building in Germany you may know that it is a military barracks, in England it is a factory, in Denmark a school. I never saw such healthy, happy, robust school children as I did in Denmark, and, with all respect to Danish agriculture, I am convinced that the best crop that Denmark raises is its children.

While other countries have sought to increase the national wealth and welfare by developing the material resources, Denmark, having neither coal, iron, oil, nor any other mineral, nothing but the land, has increased not only the national wealth but the national comfort and happiness by improving her people. While other nations have begun the work of education and, I was going to say, civilization, at the top, Denmark has begun at the bottom. In doing this Denmark has demonstrated that it pays to educate the man farthest down.

CHAPTER XVIII

RECONSTRUCTING THE LIFE OF THE LABOURER IN LONDON

AT THE end of my long journey across Europe I returned to London. I had seen, during my visit to Denmark, some results of the reorganization of country life. In this chapter I want to tell something of what I saw and learned in London of the efforts to reconstruct the life of the Underman in the more complex conditions of a great city.

In the course of my travels through various parts of the United States, in the effort to arouse public interest in the work we are trying to do for the Negro at Tuskegee, I have frequently met persons who have inquired of me, with some anxiety, as to what, in my opinion, could be done for the city Negroes, especially that class which is entering in considerable numbers every year into the life of the larger cities in the Northern and Southern States. The people who asked this question assumed, apparently because the great majority of the Negro population lives on the plantations and in the small towns of the South, that the work of a school like the Tuskegee Institute, which is located in the centre of a large Negro farming population, must be confined to the rural Negro and the South.

In reply to these inquiries I have sometimes tried to point out that a good many of the problems of the city have their sources in the country and that, perhaps, the best way to better the situation of the city Negro is to improve the condition of the masses of the race in the country. To do this, I explained, would be to attack the evil at its root, since if country life were made more attractive, the flow of population to the city would largely cease.

What is true in this respect of the masses of the Negroes in America is equally true, as I discovered, of similar classes in Europe. Any one who will take the trouble to look into the cause of European emigration will certainly be struck with the fact that the conditions of agriculture in Europe have had a marked effect on the growth and character of American cities.

This fact suggests the close connection between country conditions and the city problem, but there is still another side to the matter. The thing that was mainly impressed upon me by my observation of the lower strata of London life and the efforts that have been made to improve it was this: That it is a great deal simpler and, in the long run, a great deal cheaper to build up and develop a people who have grown up in the wholesome air of the open country than it is to regenerate a people who have lived all or most of their lives in the fetid atmosphere of a city slum. In other words, it is easier to deal with people who are physically and morally sound than with people who, by reason of their unhealthy and immoral surroundings, have become demoralized and degenerate. The first is a problem of education; the second, one of reconstruction and regeneration.

I think the thing that helped me most to realize the extent and the difficulty of this work of regeneration in London was the knowledge that I gained while there of the multitude of institutions and agencies, of various kinds, which are engaged in this work.

I had been impressed, during my visits to Whitechapel and other portions of the East End of London, with the number of shelters, homes, refuges, and missions of all kinds which I saw advertised as I passed along Whitechapel Road. When I inquired of Rev. John Harris, organizing secretary of the Anti-Slavery Society, who had at one time himself been engaged in mission work in that part of the city, whether it were possible to obtain a complete list of all the different types of charities and institutions of social betterment in London, he placed in my hands a volume of nearly seven hundred pages devoted entirely to the classification and description of the various charities, most of which were located in London.

This book, which was called the "Annual Charities Register and Digest," I have read and studied with the greatest interest. I confess that I was amazed as well at the number and variety of the different charities as at the amount of time, energy, and money necessary to keep up and maintain them.

In another volume, "London Statistics," published by the London County Council, I found the facts about London charities concisely summarized. From these books I learned that there are something like 2,035 charitable institutions of various kinds in London alone. Perhaps I can best give some idea of the character of these institutions, a number of which date back to the eighteenth century and perhaps to still earlier periods, by giving some details from these two volumes.

There are in London, for example, 112 institutions for the blind, and 143 institutions which give medical aid in one form or another, for which the total amount of money expended is about five million seven hundred thousand dollars annually. There are 214 institutions for the care of convalescents, for which the annual expenditure amounts to nearly a million and three quarters; 220 homes for children and training homes for servants, which are maintained at an annual expense of over four million dollars annually; 257 institutions for "general and specific relief," which are supported at an annual cost of nearly six millions.

There are, besides these, 159 institutions for "penitents," which receive an income of a million per year; 156 institutions for social and physical improvement, which include a multitude of the most varied sorts, as, for example, educational, temperance, and Christian associations, social settlements, boys' brigades, societies for the improvement of dwellings, for the improvement of national health, for suppression of the white slave traffic, etc. These 156 institutions are maintained at an expense of something over three million and a half dollars per year.

Finally, there are 47 so-called "spiritual" institutions which are engaged in propagating in various ways and in various forms a knowledge of the Bible and a belief in the Christian religion. Although the spiritual associations represent less than one seventeenth of the total number of charitable organizations, nearly one fourth of the total amount of the charities is expended in maintaining them.

According to the best estimate that can be made, the amount of money thus expended is not less than fifty millions annually. This does not include, either, the sums collected and expended by the different churches — the Congregational, Catholic, and Established churches. In two dioceses of the Church of England — namely, those of London and Southwark — the sums raised in this way amounted to more than six hundred thousand dollars.

My attention was especially attracted by the number of shelters and refuges where homeless men, women, and children are given temporary aid of one kind and another. In addition to eight shelters maintained by the Salvation Army in different parts of the city, where homeless men and women are able to obtain a bed and something to eat, there is the asylum for the houseless poor, which claims to have given nights' lodging during the winter months to 80,000; the Free Shelter, in Ratcliffe Street East, which has given nights' lodging to 125,000; the Ham Yard Soup Kitchen and Hospice, which in 1908-1909 cared for 343 for an average of sixteen nights; the Providence Right Refuge and Home, with reports of nearly 2,100 lodgings, suppers, and breakfasts every week.

In addition to these there is a considerable number of refuges and shelters for various classes of persons — for sailors, soldiers, Jews, Asiatics, and Africans; for ballet girls; "ladies who, on account of their conversion to the Catholic faith, are obliged to leave their homes or situations"; for "respectable female servants"; homeless boys and girls, governesses; "Protestant servants while they are seeking employment in the families of the nobility," and for "young women employed in hotels and West End clubs."

These are but a few of the many different homes, lodging houses, and shelters with which the city is provided. In most cases it is stated in connection with these institutions that vagrants are rigidly excluded, and the purpose of most of them seems to be to keep respectable but unfortunate people from going to the public workhouses.

In addition to the fifty millions and more spent in charity, nearly twenty millions more is expended by the different boroughs of London for relief to the poor in institutions and in homes. Altogether, it costs something like seventy million dollars annually to provide for the poor and unfortunate of the city.

In the Southern States, where nine of the ten million Negroes in the United States make their homes, practically nothing is spent in charity upon the Negro. In two or three states reformatories have been established, so that Negro children arrested for petty crimes may not be sent to the chain gangs and confined with older and more hardened criminals employed in the mines and elsewhere. At the last session of the state legislature of Alabama a bill was passed providing that the state should take over and support a reformatory for coloured children which had been established and supported by the Negro women of the state. In several of the larger Southern cities Young Men's Christian Associations have been started which are supported by charity, and in certain instances hospitals have been established.

The only purpose for which the Negro has asked or received philanthropic aid has been for the support of education. The people of the United States have been generous in their contributions to Negro education. In spite of this fact the income of all the Negro colleges, industrial schools, and other institutions of so-called higher education in the South is not one fiftieth part of what is expended every year in London in charity and relief, not for the purpose of education, but merely to rescue from worse disaster the stranded, the outcasts, and those who are already lost.*

*The annual income of twenty Negro colleges in the United States was, in 1908, $804,663.

I find, as most people do, I have no doubt, that it is very hard to realize the significance of a fact that is stated in mere abstract figures. It is only after I have translated these abstractions into terms of my own experience that I am able to grasp them. That must be my excuse here for what may seem a rather far-fetched comparison.

The Negro population of the Southern States is at present about nine million. In other words, the number of Negroes in the South is just about one fourth larger than the population of Greater London, which is something over seven million. Four fifths of this Southern Negro population still live on the plantations and in the small towns.

From time to time thoughtful and interested persons — some of them, by the way, Englishmen — have visited the Southern States, talked with the white people and looked at the Negroes. Then they have gone back and written despondently, sometimes pessimistically, about the Negro problem. I wish some of these writers might study the situation of the races in the South long enough to determine what it would be possible to do there, not with seventy nor even fifty, but with one million dollars a year, provided that money were used, not for the purpose of feeding, sheltering, or protecting the

Negro population, for which it is not needed, but in educating them; in building up the public schools in the country districts; in providing a system of high schools, industrial and agricultural schools, such as exists, for example, in Denmark; in extending the demonstration farming to all the people on the land, and in encouraging the small colleges to adapt their teaching to the actual needs of the people so that in the course of time Negro education in the South could be gradually organized and coördinated into a single coherent system.

Perhaps I can illustrate in a broad way the difference in the situation of the poor man in the complex life of a great city like London and that of a similar class in the simpler conditions of a comparatively rural community, by a further comparison. The state of Alabama is nearly as large as England and Wales combined. It had, in 1900, a little more than one third the present population of what is known as "Administrative London," which means a city of 4,720,729. Of this population there were, on an average, 139,916 paupers. In Alabama, with a population in 1900 of 1,828,696, there were, in 1905, 771 paupers in almshouses, of whom 414 were white and 357 Negroes. In other words, while in London there were nearly three paupers for every one thousand of the population, in

Alabama there were a little more than four paupers for every ten thousand of the population. This does not include the persons confined in asylums or those who are assisted in their homes. In Alabama the number of paupers cared for in this way is very small. As compared with the 2,000 charitable institutions in London, there were twenty such institutions in Alabama in 1904. Three of these, a hospital, an old folks' home and orphan asylum, and a school for the deaf and blind were for Negroes.

I have quoted these figures to show the contrast between conditions in a large city and a comparatively rural community. But Alabama contains three cities of considerable size, which may account for a fairly large number of its paupers, so that I suspect that if the comparison were strictly carried out it would be found that pauperism is a good deal more of a city disease than it seems.

The institutions in London to which I have referred, whether managed by private philanthropy or by the public, are mainly maintained for the sake of those who have already fallen in the struggle for existence. They are for the sick and wounded, so to speak. In recent years a movement has been steadily gaining ground which seeks to get at the source of this city disease, and by improving the conditions of city life do away to some extent with the causes of it.

The work of reorganizing the life of the poorer classes in London seems to have made a beginning some fifty or sixty years ago. The condition of the working population at that time has been described in the following words by Mr. Sidney Webb, who has made a profound study of the condition of the labouring classes in London:

> Two thirds of the whole child population was growing up not only practically without schooling or religious influences of any kind, but also indescribably brutal and immoral; living amid the filth of vilely overcrowded courts, unprovided with water supply or sanitary conveniences, existing always at the lowest level of physical health, and constantly decimated by disease; incessantly under temptation by the flaring gin palaces which alone relieve the monotony of the mean streets to which they were doomed; graduating almost inevitably into vice and crime amid the now incredible street life of an unpoliced metropolis.*

The first thing attempted was to provide public education for those who were not able to attend private schools, and, as one writer says, "rescue the children of the abyss." It was in this rescue work that England's public schools had their origin. These schools, begun in this way, steadily gained and broadened until now London has an elaborate system of continuation, trade and technical schools,

*London Education, Nineteenth Century, October 1903, p. 563.

culminating in the reorganized University of London. This system is by no means perfected; it still is in process, but it gives the outlines of a broad and generous educational plan, equal in conception and organization at least to the needs of the largest city in the world.

London already has, for example, 327 night schools, with 127,130 pupils, in which young men and women who have left the day schools may continue their studies at night or perfect themselves in some branch of their trade.

Cooking, household management, laundry work, and iron work are taught in more than half the elementary schools of London. The London County Council supports fourteen schools which give instruction in the arts and crafts, and in the trades. In addition, the Government lends its aid to something like sixty-one other institutions, with an attendance of over 6,000, in which technical and trade education of some kind is given. A number of these schools, like the Shoreditch Technical Institute and the Brixton School of Building, are devoted to a single trade or group of allied trades. In the Shoreditch Institute boys are fitted for the furniture trade. Half their time is given to academic studies and half to work in the trade. At the Brixton School instruction is given in bricklaying and masonry, plumbing, painting, architecture, building, and surveying. In other schools pupils are given instruction in photo-engraving and lithographing, in fine needlework and engraving, bookbinding, and in many other crafts requiring a high grade of intelligence and skill.

With the growth of these schools the idea has been gaining ground that it is not sufficient to rescue those who, through misfortune or disease, are unable to support themselves; that on the contrary, instead of waiting until an individual has actually fallen a victim to what I have called the "city disease," measures of prevention be taken against pauperism as against other diseases.

Along with this changed point of view has come the insight that the efficiency of the nation as a whole depends upon its ability to make the most of the capacities of the whole population. "Indeed," as Mr. Webb, the writer I have already quoted, says, "we now see with painful clearness that we have in the long run, for the maintenance of our preëminent industrial position in the world, nothing to depend on except the brains of our people. Public education has insensibly, therefore, come to be regarded, not as a matter of philanthropy, undertaken for the sake of the children benefited, but, as a matter of national concern, undertaken in the interest of the community as a whole."

After the schools, the next direction in which an attempt was made to improve the condition of the poor in London was in the matter of housing. The Board of Works first and the London County Council afterward began some forty years ago buying vast areas in the crowded parts of London, clearing them of the disreputable buildings, and then offering them for sale again to persons who would agree to erect on them sanitary dwellings for the working classes. The Metropolitan Board of Works, for example, purchased forty-two acres in different parts of the city for clearance. After the buildings had been torn down and the sites resold, it was estimated that the net cost would be about £1,320,619 or about $6,603,395. There lived on this area 22,872 persons, so that the net cost of cleaning up this area and moving the population into better quarters was something like $281 for each individual inhabitant.

Then the London County Council took up the work and it decided to begin building its own houses. Finally, a law was passed that the buildings so created should rent for more than the rents prevailing in the district and should pay the cost of maintenance, 3 per cent. on the capital invested.

On these terms the Metropolitan Board of Works and the London County Council have cleared in various parts of Central London an area of nearly eighty-six acres, containing a population of 41,584, at a cost which averages about $250 per person. On the property thus acquired the London County Council had in 1907 erected 8,223 tenements with 22,331 rooms. At this time, 1907, there were projected dwellings containing a total of 28,000 rooms, which, with those already erected, make a total of over 50,000 rooms. These tenements rent on an average of about 70 cents a week per room, so that the city of Greater London has an annual income of nearly $760,000 from its rents alone, on which the city earned in 1901, after all charges were paid, a profit of $10,000.

At first the County Council merely sought to replace the buildings which it removed, and the new buildings occupied the site of the older ones. On or near Boundary Street, in the neighbourhood of Bethnal Green, twenty-two acres were cleared of slums and covered with model dwellings, provided with wash houses, club rooms and every moden appliance for health and comfort. The sad thing about it was that after the buildings were completed and occupied it was found that only eleven of the former inhabitants remained. They had poured down into slums in the older part of the city and increased the population in those already over-crowded regions.

Meanwhile, in other parts of the country private enterprise and private philanthropy had gone in advance of the London County Council. Outside of Birmingham and Liverpool garden cities had been erected in which every family was provided with an acre of land, on some of which men employed in the factories, when they were not at work, increased their earnings in some instances as much as £50, or $250, a year.

Then the County Council began to acquire tramways radiating out in every direction into the suburbs. At the present time the city owns something over a hundred miles of tramway within the city, and of the 300 miles or more in Greater London the majority is either owned by London or the suburban boroughs.

At the ends of these lines the London County Council, and more frequently private individuals, have erected model dwellings on a large scale and are thus gradually moving the city population into the country.

In the meantime much has been done in recent years to increase the number of playgrounds and breathing spaces, to supply bathrooms, wash houses and other conveniences which make it possible to keep the city and people in a healthful and sanitary condition. In many of the principal streets in London I noticed signs directing the people to public baths which were located somewhere underneath the street. The different boroughs contributed in 1907 $738,545 in taxes to support these public baths and bath houses, and at the same time the people of London paid over $400,000 for bath tickets and $85,000 for laundry tickets in order to make use of these public conveniences.

Inner London, not including suburbs, has now an area of 6,588 acres in parks large and small, upon which the city has expended a capital of $9,125,910 and upon which it expends annually the sum of $548,065 or thereabout.

Now, the thing that strikes me about all this is that these vast sums of money which London has spent in clearing up its slums, in providing decent houses, wider streets, breathing spaces, bath houses, swimming pools, and washrooms have been spent mainly on sunshine, air, and water, things which any one may have without cost in the country.

I visited some of these wash houses and saw hundreds of women who had come in from the surrounding neighbourhood to do their week's washing. They were paying by the hour for the use of the municipal washtubs and water, but I am sure they were not any better provided for in this respect than the coloured women of the South who go down on sunshiny days to the brook to do their washing, boiling their clothes in a big iron kettle. I saw the boys in some of the swimming pools, but I did not see any of them that seemed happier than the boy who goes off to the brook with his hook and line and by the way takes a plunge in an old-fashioned swimming hole.

Thus it is that London seems to have found that the best if not the only way to solve the city problem is by transporting its population to the country, settling them in colonies in the suburbs, where they may obtain, at an enormous expense, what four fifths of the Negro population in this country already have and what they can be taught to value and keep if some of the money that is now expended or which will be expended on the city slums were spent in giving the people on the farm some of the advantages which the city offers, the principal one of which is a chance for an education.

CHAPTER XIX

JOHN BURNS AND THE MAN FARTHEST DOWN IN LONDON

I HAD heard a good deal, from time to time, about John Burns before I went to Europe, and when I reached London I took advantage of the first opportunity that offered to make my acquaintance with him a personal one. This meeting was a special good fortune to me at the time because, as I already knew, there is, in all probability, no one in England who better understands the hopes, ambitions, and the prospects of the labouring classes than the Rt. Hon. John Burns, President of the Local Government Board, himself the first labouring man to become a member of the British Cabinet.

John Burns was born in poverty and went to work at the age of ten. He had known what it is to wander the streets of London for weeks and months looking for work. He had an experience of that kind once after he had lost his job because he made a Socialistic speech. Having learned by experience the life of that industrial outcast, the casual labourer, he organized in 1889 the great dock labourers' strike, which brought together into the labour unions 100,000 starving and disorganized labourers who had previously been shut out from the protection of organized labour. Besides that, he has been an agitator; was for years a marked man, and at one time gained for himself the name of the "man with the red flag." He has been several times arrested for making speeches, and has once been imprisoned for three months on the charge of rioting.

Meanwhile he had become the idol of the working masses and even won the admiration and respect of the leaders of public opinion. He was elected in 1889 to the first London County Council, where he worked side by side with such distinguished men as Frederic Harrison and Lord Rosebery. He was chosen a member of parliament in 1890, where he became distinguished for the store of practical information which he accumulated during his eighteen years of practical experience in the London County Council.

When he was twenty-one years of age Mr. Burns went as an engineer to Africa, where he spent a year among the swamps of the Lower Niger, occasionally fighting alligators and devoting his leisure to the study of political economy. When he returned he spent the money he had saved in Africa in six months of travel and study in Europe.

Speaking of what he learned in Africa, Mr. Burns once said: "You talk of savagery and misery in heathen lands, but from my own experience I can tell you that there is more of all these, and more degradation of women, in the slums of London than you will see on the West Coast of Africa."

He has had a wider experience than most men with mobs, for he has not only led them, but in 1900 he defended himself with a cricket bat for two days in his home on Lavender Hill, Battersea, against a mob said to number 10,000 which hurled stones through the windows and tried to batter down the door of his house because he had denounced the Boer War in parliament.

In 1906, after he had been successful in writing something like one hundred labour laws into the acts of parliament, he accepted the position of President of Local Government and then became, as I have said, the first labouring man to accept a place in the British Cabinet.

In reply to the criticisms which were offered when he accepted this high and responsible position in the government, Mr. Burns said: "I had to choose whether, for the next ten years, I should indulge, perhaps, in the futility of faction, possibly in the impotence of intrigue, or whether I should accept an office which in our day and generation I can make useful of good works." I have noted this statement because this is a choice which most reformers and agitators have to make sooner or later.

He recognized, as he said, that "the day of the agitator was declining and that of the administrator had begun," and he did not shrink from accepting a position where he became responsible for administering laws he had helped to make. In his present position as the head of the Local Government Board Mr. Burns is probably doing more than any other man to improve the situation of the poor man in London and in the other large cities of England.

It is a rare thing for a man who began life in poverty to find himself in middle life in a position of such power and usefulness as the head of one great branch of the British Government occupies. It is still more remarkable, however, that a man who began life as an agitator, the representative of the unemployed, the most helpless and unfortunate class in the community, should find himself, a comparatively few years later, charged with the task of carrying into effect the reforms which he had preached from the prisoner's dock in a police court. It is all the more fortunate for England that the Government has found a man with these qualifications, who has at the same time the training and qualities of a statesman, to carry the reforms into effect. As Mr. Burns himself once said: "Depend upon it, there are no such places for making a public man as Pentonville Prison and the London County Council."

To me, however, the most surprising thing about it all is that a man with his history and qualifications should have found his way, by the ordinary methods of politics, into a position he is so well fitted to fill. It suggests to me that, in spite of all the misery that one still may see in London, in England, at least, there is hope for the man farthest down.

It is not my purpose in this chapter to write a biography of John Burns, but rather to describe what I saw, under his direction, of what has already been done in London in the work of "reconstruction," to which I have already referred. It seemed to me, however, that it was not out of place to say something, by way of introduction, in regard to the man who is, perhaps, as much if not more than any one else responsible for the work now going on, and whose life is connected in a peculiar way with that part of the city I had opportunity to visit and with the improvements that have been made there.

John Burns was born and still lives in Battersea, a quarter of the city inhabited, for the most part, by artisans, mechanics, and labourers of various kinds, with a sprinkling of gypsy pedlers and the very poor. Battersea is directly across the river from, and in plain sight of, the Parliament Buildings, and there is a story to the effect that, as he was coming home one winter night, helping his mother carry home the washing by which she supported herself and family, they two stopped within the shadow of those buildings to rest. Turning to his mother the boy said: "Mother, if ever I have health and strength no mother shall have to work as you do."

John Burns has health and strength, and is now making a brave effort to keep that promise to his mother. Aside from Colonel Roosevelt, I do not think I ever saw a man who seemed his equal in vigour of mind and body; who seemed able to compress so much into a short space of time; or one who goes at the task before him with a greater zest. In all England I do not believe there is a man who works harder, accomplishes more for the good of his country and the world, or one who is happier in the work he is doing.

I found him late in August, when every one else connected with the government had left London on their vacation, buried deep in the details and concerns of his office, but chock-full of energy and enthusiasm.

What John Burns is doing, and the spirit in which he is doing it, will, perhaps, appear in the course of my description of a trip which I took with him through his own district of Battersea and the region adjoining it in order to see what the London County Council is doing there to make the life of the poor man better. I am sorry that I will not be able to describe in detail all that I saw on that trip, because we covered in a short time so much ground, and saw so many different things, that it was not until I had returned to my hotel, and had an opportunity to study out the route of that journey, that I was able to get any definite idea of the direction in which we had gone or of the connection and general plan which underlay the whole scheme of the improvements we had seen.

I think it was about two o'clock in the afternoon when we left the offices of the Local Government Board. Mr. Burns insisted that, before we started, I should see something of the Parliament Buildings, and he promised to act as my guide. This hasty trip through the

Parliament Buildings served to show me that John Burns, although he had entered political life as a Socialist, has a profound reverence for all the historic traditions and a very intimate knowledge of English history. I shall not soon forget the eloquent and vivid manner in which he summoned up for me, as we passed through Westminster Hall, on the way to the House of Commons, some of the great historical scenes and events which had taken place in that ancient and splendid room. I was impressed not only by the familiarity which he showed with all the associations of the place, but I was thrilled by the enthusiasm with which he spoke of and described them. It struck me as very strange that the same John Burns once known as "the man with the red flag," who had been imprisoned for leading a mob of workmen against the police, should be quoting history with all the enthusiasm of a student and a scholar.

In the course of our journey we passed through a small strip of Chelsea. I remember that among the other places we passed he pointed out the home of Thomas Carlyle. I found that he was just as familiar with names and deeds of all the great literary persons who had lived in that quarter of London as he was with the political history.

When he afterward told me that he had had

very little education in school, because he had been compelled to go to work when he was ten years of age, I asked him how he had since found time, in the course of his busy life, to gain the wide knowledge of history and literature which he evidently possessed.

"You see," he replied, with a quiet smile, "I earned my living for a time as a candle maker and I have burned a good many candles at night ever since."

Mr. Burns had promised to show me, within the space of a few hours, examples of the sort of work which is now going on in every part of London. A few years ago, on the site of an ancient prison, the London County Council erected several blocks of workingmen's tenements. These were, I believe, the first, or nearly the first, of the tenements erected by the city in the work of clearing away unsanitary areas and providing decent homes for the working classes.

It was to these buildings, in which a population of about 4,000 persons live, that we went first. The buildings are handsome brick structures, well lighted, with wide, open, brick-paved courts between the rows of houses, so that each block looked like a gigantic letter H with the horizontal connecting line left out.

Of course, these buildings were, as some one

said, little-more than barracks compared with the houses that are now being erected for labouring people in some of the London suburbs, but they are clean and wholesome and, to any one familiar with the narrow, grimy streets in the East End of London, it was hard to believe that they stood in the midst of a region which a few years ago had been a typical London slum.

A little farther on we crossed the river and entered what Mr. Burns referred to as "my own district," Battersea, where he was born and where he has lived and worked all his life, except for one year spent as an engineer in Nigeria, Africa.

The great breathing place for the people of this region is Battersea Park, and as we sped along the edge of this beautiful green space, stopping to look for a moment at the refreshment booths on the cricket grounds, or to speak to a group of well-dressed boys going from school to the playgrounds, Mr. Burns interspersed his information about workmen's wages, the price of rents, and the general improvement of the labouring classes with comment on the historic associations of the places we passed. Where Battersea Park now stands there was formerly a foul and unwholesome swamp. Near here the Duke of Wellington had fought a duel with the Earl of Winchelsea, and a little farther up

Julius Cæsar, nearly two thousand years ago, forded the river with one of his legions.

It was a happy and novel experience to observe the pleasure which Mr. Burns took in pointing out the improvement in the people, in the dwellings, and in the life of the people generally, and to note, in turn, the familiar and cheerful way with which all sorts of people we met on the streets greeted him as we passed.

"Hello! Johnny Burns," a group of schoolboys would call as we went by. Once we passed by a group of some fifteen or twenty workingwomen sitting in one of the refreshment booths, drinking their afternoon tea and, apparently, holding a neighbourhood meeting of some kind or other. As they recognized the man who, as member of the London County Council, had been responsible for most of the improvements that had been made in the homes and surroundings in which they lived, they stood up and waved their handkerchiefs, and even attempted a faint and feminine "hurrah for Johnny Burns," the member from Battersea.

There are 150,000 people in Battersea, but Mr. Burns seemed to be acquainted with every one of them, and when he wanted to show me the inside of some of the new "County Council houses," as they are called, did not hesitate to knock at the nearest door, where we were gladly welcomed. The people seemed to be just as proud of their new houses, and of Mr. Burns, as he was of them.

The houses which we visited were, some of them, no more than three or four rooms, but each one of them was as neat and wholesome as if it had been a palace. They were very compactly built, but provided with every sort of modern convenience, including electric lights and baths.

There were houses of five and six rooms intended for clerks and small business men, which rented for a pound a week, and there were cheaper houses, for ordinary labouring people, which rented for two dollars per week. These houses are built directly under the direction of the London County Council, and are expected to pay 3 per cent. upon the investment, after completion.

The London County Council was not the first to make the experiment of building decent and substantial houses for the labouring classes. Some thirty years before, on what is known as the Shaftbury Park Estate, 1,200 houses, which provide homes for eleven thousand people, were erected and the investment had been made to pay.

I looked down the long lanes of little vine-covered buildings which make up this estate.

It seemed as if some great army had settled on the land and built permanent quarters.

These labour colonies were interesting, not merely for the improvement they had made in the lives of a large section of the people living in this part of the city, but as the forerunner of those garden cities which private enterprise has erected at places like Port Sunlight, near Liverpool; Bourneville, in the outskirts of Birmingham, and at Letchworth, thirty-four miles from London.

Not far from Battersea Park, and in a part of the city which was formerly inhabited almost wholly by the very poor, we visited the public baths and a public washhouse where, during the course of a year, 42,000 women come to wash their clothes, paying at the rate of three cents an hour for the use of the municipal tubs and hot water. Children pay a penny or two cents for the use of the public baths. The building is also provided with a gymnasium for the use of the children in winter, and contains a hall which is rented to workingmen's clubs at a nominal price.

What pleased me most was to see the orderly way in which the children had learned to conduct themselves in these places, which, as was evident, had become not merely places for recreation, but at the same time schools of good manners.

We passed on the streets groups of neatly dressed, well-bred looking boys, with their books slung over their arms, going home from school or making their way to the park. Mr. Burns was delighted at the sight of these clean-cut, manly looking fellows.

"Look at those boys, Mr. Washington," he would exclaim, as he pointed proudly to one or another of these groups. "Isn't that doing pretty well for the proletariat?"

Then he would leap out of the automobile, before the driver could stop, put his arm around the boy nearest him and, in a moment, come back triumphant with the confirmation of his statement that the boy's father was, as he had said, only a small clerk or a letter carrier, or, perhaps, the son of a common labourer, a navvy.

When I contrasted the appearance of these well-dressed and well-behaved boys with some of those I had seen elsewhere, with the children who attend the so-called "ragged" schools, for example, I understood and shared his enthusiasm.

From Battersea Park we went to Clapham Common and, as we were speeding along through what appeared to be a quarter of well-to-do artisans' homes, Mr. Burns nodded casually in the direction of a little vine-clad cottage and said:

"That is where I live."

Although Mr. Burns now occupies one of the highest positions in the British Government, in which he has a salary of $10,000 a year, he has not yet assumed the high hat and the long-tailed coat which are the recognized uniform in London of a gentleman. On the contrary, he wears the same blue reefer coat and soft felt hat, speaks the same language, lives in the same style, and is apparently in every respect the same man that he was when he was living on the $25 a week guaranteed him by the Battersea Labour League when he entered parliament. He is still a labouring man and proud of the class to which he belongs.

It was at Clapham Common, although Mr. Burns did not mention this fact, that he was arrested for the first time, away back in 1878, for making a public speech. It was somewhere in this region also, if I remember rightly, that Mr. Burns pointed out to us a private estate on which 3,000 houses of the cheaper class had been erected.

"And mind you, there is no public house," said Mr. Burns. Instead he showed us a brand-new temperance billiard hall which had been erected to compete with, and take the place of, the bar-rooms which have disappeared.

At Lower Tooting, an estate of some thirty-eight acres, the London County Council is building outright a city of something like 5,000 inhabitants, laying out the streets, building the houses, even putting a tidy little flower garden in each separate front door yard. It was as if the London County Council had gone to playing dolls, so completely planned and perfectly carried out in every detail is this little garden city.

Mr. Burns, who has all his life been an advocate of temperance, although he had once served as pot-boy in a public house, pointed out here, as he did elsewhere, that there was no public house.

In the building of this little paradise all the architectural and engineering problems had indeed been solved. There remained, however, the problem of human nature, and the question that I asked myself was: Will these people be able to live up to their surroundings?

It is fortunate, in this connection, that in Mr. Burns the inhabitants have a leader who dares to speak plainly to them of their faults as well as their virtues and who is able, at the same time, to inspire them with an ambition and enthusiasm for the better life which is opened to them. Engineering and architecture cannot do everything, but education, leadership of the right sort, may complete what these have begun.

At Warden Street and Lydden Road, on our

way back to the city, we stopped to look for a moment at what Mr. Burns said was the most wretched part of the population in that quarter of the city. The houses were two-story dwellings, with the sills flush with the pavement, in front of which groups of lounging idle men and women stood or squatted on the pavement. A portion of the street was given up to gypsy vans, and the whole population was made up, as I learned, of pedlers and pushcart venders, a class of people who, in the very centre of civilization, manage somehow to maintain a nomadic and half-barbarous existence, wandering from one place to another with the seasons, living from hand to mouth, working irregularly and not more than half the time.

A little farther on we passed by the Price candle factory, "where I began work at a dollar a week," said Mr. Burns in passing. A group of workmen were just coming from the factory as we passed, and the men recognized Mr. Burns and shouted to him as he passed.

Then we drove on back across the Chelsea Bridge and along the river to the Parliament Buildings again. "Now," said Mr. Burns at the end of our journey, "you have seen a sample of what London is doing for its labouring population. If you went further you would see more, but little that is new or different."

CHAPTER XX

THE FUTURE OF THE MAN FARTHEST DOWN

UPON my arrival in London I found myself, at the end of my journey, once more at my point of departure. A few days later, October 9th, to be precise, I sailed from Liverpool for New York. I had been less than seven weeks in Europe, but it seemed to me that I had been away for a year. My head was full of strange and confused impressions and I was reminded of the words of the traveller who, after he had crossed Europe from London to Naples, and had visited faithfully all the museums and neglected none of the regular "sights," wrote to friends he had visited in Europe a letter full of appreciation, concluding with the remark: "Well, I have seen a great deal and learned a great deal. and I *thank God it is all over.*"

It occurs to me that the readers who have followed me thus far in my narrative may find themselves at the conclusion of this book in somewhat the same situation as myself at the end of my journey. In that case it will, perhaps, not be out of place to take advantage of this concluding chapter to do for them as well as I am able what I tried to do for myself during my hours of leisure on the voyage home — namely, make a little clearer the relation of all that I had seen and learned to the problem of the Negro and The Man Farthest Down.

I have touched, in the course of these chapters, upon many phases of life. I have had something to say, for example, in regard to the poverty, education, Socialism, and the race problems of Europe, since all these different matters are connected in one way or another with the subject and purpose of my journey and this book.

In attempting to add the moral to my story, however, and state in general terms the upshot of it all, I find myself at a disadvantage. I can, perhaps, best explain what I mean by recalling the fact that I was born a slave and since I became free have been so busy with the task immediately in front of me that I have never had time to think out my experiences and formulate my ideas in general terms. In fact, almost all that I know about the problems of other races and other peoples I have learned in seeking a solution and a way out for my own people. For that reason I should have done better perhaps to leave to some one with more learning and more leisure than I happen to possess the task of writing about the Underman in Europe. In fact I would have done so if I had not believed that in making this journey I should gain some insight and, perhaps, be able to throw some new light upon the situation of my own people in America. Indeed, I confess that I should never have taken the time — brief as it was — to make this long journey if I had not believed it was going to have some direct relation to the work which I have been trying to do for the people of my race in America.

In this, let me add, I was not disappointed. As a matter of fact, if there was one thing more than another, in all my European experiences, which was impressed upon my mind, it was the fact that the position of the Negro in America, both in slavery and in freedom, has not been so exceptional as it has frequently seemed. While there are wide differences between the situation of the people in the lower levels of life in Europe and the Negro in America, there are still many points of resemblance, and the truth is that the man farthest down in Europe has much in common with the man at the bottom in America.

For example, the people at the bottom in Europe have been, in most cases, for the greater part of their history at least, like the Negroes in America, a subject people, not slaves, but bondmen or serfs, at any rate a disadvantaged people.

In most cases the different under-classes in Europe only gained their freedom in the course of the last century. Since that time they have been engaged in an almost ceaseless struggle to obtain for themselves the political privileges that formerly belonged to the upper classes alone.

Even in those places where the man at the bottom has gained political privileges resembling in most respects those of the classes at the top he finds, as the Negro in America has found, that he has only made a beginning, and the real work of emancipation remains to be done. The English labourer, for example, has had political freedom for a longer period of time than is true of any other representative of this class in Europe. Notwithstanding this fact, as things are, he can only in rare instances buy and own the land on which he lives. The labouring people of England live, for the most part, herded together with millions of others of their class in the slums of great cities, where air and water are luxuries. They are dependent upon some other nation for their food supplies, for butter, bread, and meat. And then, as a further consequence of the way they are compelled to live, the masses of the people find themselves part of an economic arrangement or system which is so vast and complicated that they can neither comprehend nor control it.

The result is that the English labourer, of whose independence the world has heard so much, is, in many respects, more dependent than any other labouring class in Europe. This is due not to the fact that the English labourer lacks political rights, but to the fact that he lacks economic opportunities — opportunities to buy land and opportunities to labour; to own his own home, to keep a garden and raise his own food.

The Socialists have discovered that the independence of the labouring classes has been undermined as a result of the growth of factories and city life, and believe they have found a remedy.

What the Socialists would actually do in England or elsewhere, provided they should manage to get into power, is difficult to say, because, as my experience in Europe has taught me, there are almost as many kinds of Socialists as there are kinds of people. The real old-fashioned Socialists, those who still look forward to some great social catastrophe which will put an end to the present régime, believe it will then be possible to use the political power of the masses to reorganize society in a way to give every individual an economic opportunity equal to that of every other.

Taking human beings as we find them, I have never been able to see how this was going to be brought about in precisely the way outlined in the Socialist programme. Some individuals will be good for one thing, some for another, and there will always be, I suppose, a certain number who will not be good for anything. As they have different capacities, so they will have different opportunities. Some will want to do one thing and some another, and some individuals and some people, like the Jews for example, will know how to make their disadvantages their opportunities and so get the best of the rest of the world, no matter how things are arranged.

I have referred to the Socialists and the revolution they propose not because I wish to oppose their doctrines, which I confess I do not wholly understand, but because it seemed to me that, as I went through Europe and studied conditions, I could see the evidences of a great, silent revolution already in full progress. And this revolution to which I refer is touching and changing the lives of those who are at the bottom, particularly those in the remote farming communities, from which the lowest class of labourers in the city is constantly recruited.

Let me illustrate what I mean: Under the

old system in Europe — the feudal system, or whatever else it may at various times have been called — civilization began at the top. There were a few people who were free. They had all the wealth, the power, and the learning in their hands, or at their command. When anything was done it was because they wished it or because they commanded it. In order to give them this freedom and secure to them this power it was necessary that vast numbers of other people should live in ignorance, without any knowledge of, or share in, any but the petty life of the estate or the community to which they belonged. They were not permitted to move from the spot in which they were born, without the permission of their masters. It was, in their case, almost a crime to think. It was the same system, in a very large degree, as that which existed in the Southern States before the war, with the exception that the serfs in Europe were white, while the slaves in the Southern States were black.

In Europe to-day the great problem to which statesmen are giving their thought and attention is not how to hold the masses of the people down but how to lift them up; to make them more efficient in their labour and give them a more intelligent share and interest in the life of the community and state of which they are a part. Everywhere in Europe the idea is gaining ground and influence that the work of civilization must begin at the bottom instead of at the top.

The great medium for bringing about these changes is the school. In every part of Europe which I visited I was impressed with the multitude of schools of various kinds which are springing up to meet the new demand. The movement began earlier and has gone farther in Denmark than it has elsewhere, and the remarkable development of Danish country life has been the result. What has been accomplished in Denmark, through the medium of the country high schools, and in Germany, through the universities and technical training schools, is being industriously imitated elsewhere.

In England I found that people were saying that the reason why German manufactures had been able to compete so successfully with the English products was because Germany had the advantage of better schools. In Germany I found that the German army, organized in the first instance for the national defence, is now looked upon as a great national school, in which the masses of the people get an education and discipline which, it is claimed, are gradually raising the industrial efficiency of the nation.

There, as elsewhere, education is seeking to reach and touch every class and every individual of every class in the community. The deaf, the blind, the defectives of every description are now beginning to receive industrial education fitting them for trades in which they will be more useful to the community and more independent than it was possible for them to be when no attempt was made to fit them for any place in the life of the community.

The effect of this movement, or revolution, as I have called it, is not to "tear down and level up" in order to bring about an artificial equality, but to give every individual a chance "to make good," to determine for himself his place and position in the community by the character and quality of the service he is able to perform.

One effect of this change in point of view which I have described is that to-day there is hardly any one thing in which the people of Europe are more concerned than in the progress and future of the man farthest down.

In all that I have written in the preceding chapters I have sought to emphasize, in the main, two things: first, that behind all the movements which have affected the masses of the people, Socialism or nationalism, emigration, the movements for the reorganization of city and country life, there has always been the Underman, groping his way upward, struggling to rise; second, that the effect of all that has been done to lift the man at the bottom, or to encourage him to lift himself, has been to raise the level of every man above him.

If it is true, as I have so often said, that one man cannot hold another down in the ditch without staying down in the ditch with him, it is just as true that, in helping the man who is down to rise, the man who is up is freeing himself from a burden that would else drag him down. It is because the world seems to realize this fact more and more that, beyond and above all local and temporary difficulties, the future of the man farthest down looks bright.

And now at the conclusion of my search for the man farthest down in Europe let me confess that I did not succeed in finding him. I did not succeed in reaching any place in Europe where conditions were so bad that I did not hear of other places, which friends advised me to visit, where conditions were a great deal worse. My own experience was, in fact, very much like that of a certain gentleman who came South some years ago to study the condition of the Negro people. He had heard that in many parts of the South the Negro was gradually sinking back into something like

African savagery, and he was particularly desirous of finding a well-defined example of this relapse into barbarism. He started out with high hopes and a very considerable fund of information as to what he might expect to find and as to the places where he might hope to find it. Everywhere he went in his search, however, he found that he had arrived a few years too late. He found at every place he visited people who were glad to tell him the worst there was to be known about the coloured people; some were even kind enough to show what they thought was about the worst there was to be found among the Negroes in their particular part of the country. Still he was disappointed because he never found anything that approached the conditions he was looking for, and usually he was compelled to be contented with the statement, made to him by each one of his guides in turn, which ran something like this: "Conditions were not near as bad as they had been. A few years ago, if he had happened to have come that way, he would have been able to see things, and so forth; but now conditions were improving. However, if he wanted to see actual barbarism he should visit" — and then they usually named some distant part of the country with which he had not yet become acquainted.

In this way this gentleman, who was hunting the worst that was to be seen among the Negroes, as I was hunting the worst that was to be seen among the people of Europe, travelled all over the Southern States, going from one dark corner to another, but never finding things as bad as they were advertised. Instead of that, backward as the people were in many of the remote parts of the country, he found, just as I did in Europe, that everywhere the people were making progress. In some places they were advancing more slowly than they were in others, but everywhere there was, on the whole, progress rather than decline. The result in his case was the same as it had been in mine, the farther he went and the more he saw of the worst there was to see, the more hopeful he became of the people as a whole.

I saw much that was primitive and much that was positively evil in the conditions in Europe, but nowhere did I find things as bad as they were described to me by persons who knew them as they were some years before. And I found almost no part of the country in which substantial progress had not been made; no place, in short, where the masses of the people were without hope.

It will, perhaps, seem curious to many persons

that, after I had gone to Europe for the express purpose of making the acquaintance of the people at the bottom, and of seeing, as far as I was able, the worst in European life, I should have returned with a hopeful rather than a pessimistic view of what I saw.

The fact is, however, that the farther I travelled in Europe, and the more I entered into the life of the people at the bottom, the more I found myself looking at things from the point of view of the people who are looking up, rather than from that of the people who are at the top looking down, and, strange as it may seem, it is still true that the world looks, on the whole, more interesting, more hopeful, and more filled with God's providence, when you are at the bottom looking up than when you are at the top looking down.

To the man in the tower the world below him is likely to look very small. Men look like ants and all the bustle and stir of their hurrying lives seems pitifully confused and aimless. But the man in the street who is looking and striving upward is in a different situation. However poor his present plight, the thing he aims at and is striving toward stands out clear and distinct above him, inspiring him with hope and ambition in his struggle upward. For the man who is down there is always something to hope for, always something to be gained. The man who is down, looking up, may catch a glimpse now and then of heaven, but the man who is so situated that he can only look down is pretty likely to see another and quite different place.